EDDY JOKOVICH +
DAVID LEWIS

DIVIDED OPINIONS

THE NEW POLITICS ANALYSIS OF THE 2019 YEAR
IN AUSTRALIAN POLITICS

Divided Opinions: The New Politics analysis of the 2019 year in Australian politics
ISBN: 978-0-6481644-5-6
ISBN (Amazon): 978-1-6611355-7-7

©2020 Eddy Jokovich & David Lewis
All rights reserved.
No part of this book may be reproduced in any form or by any electronic or mechanical means, including information storage and retrieval systems, without written permission from the authors, except for the use of brief quotations in book reviews and promotional material.

January 2020

 @NewPoliticsAU

Published by New Politics, an imprint of ARMEDIA Pty. Ltd.

New Politics
PO Box 1265, Darlinghurst NSW 1300
www.newpolitics.com.au

We're on Gadigal land.

Email: info@newpolitics.com.au

Production: ARMEDIA

 A catalogue record for this work is available from the National Library of Australia

Contents

About the authors 5
About the book 6
The media forgets how it destroyed Julia Gillard 8
Short changed by the banking Royal Commission 11
Unhappy holidays and apocalypse 2019 17
Scandal: Nothing to see here, please move on 37
Corruption, the cardinal and the fine art of lying 47
The evil crimes of George Pell 62
Scott Morrison and racism 69
NSW election wrap, Morrison's racism and the issues affecting the federal election 77
Budget 2019, the end of a zany Parliament and waiting for an election 93
Maths and media: where the election will be won and lost 109
Captain GetUp: The lost avenger? 115
On water matters set to sink Morrison 118
Sweet election victories from the 1990s 125
A most exciting 2019 election campaign continues 131
A Labor victory is in sight 147
A tale of two eggs: Gillard and Morrison 151
Who wins the 2019 election final countdown? 155
The 2019 federal election wrap-up, politics for sale, and the new Parliament 171
Surprise agendas, mandates and codes of conduct 192

Why democracy is broken 209

The divisive Scott Morrison 215

Unfunded empathy, choosing sides, diversionary nuclear
and s44 solutions 220

Going the nuclear option 236

Cracks appearing in the Morrison government 240

Indue and the small matter of political corruption 245

Economic disaster, compassionate conservatives, and do we
need to talk about Albo? 251

Mr Morrison goes to Washington, the mystery of QAnon and
celebrity politics 265

Another nail in the coffin for democracy 280

Forged democracy, Labor reviews itself, and climate change
politics fired up 288

The burning world of climate change denial 306

Pseudo-politics and the year in review 314

Looking at the future from the past 323

Music listing 328

About the authors

Eddy Jokovich is editor of *New Politics*, and co-presenter of the monthly New Politics Australia podcast. He has worked as a journalist, publisher, author, political analyst, campaigner, war correspondent, and lecturer in media studies at the University of Technology, Sydney and the University of Sydney; has a wide range of experience working in editorial and media production work and is Director of **ARMEDIA**, a publishing and communications company specialising in public interest media.

 @EddyJokovich

David Lewis is co-presenter of the monthly New Politics Australia podcast, historian, musicologist, musician and political scientist based in Sydney. His lecturing and research interests include roots music, popular music, Australian, UK and US politics and crime fiction. He has published in *Music Forum Australia*, *Eureka Street*, *Quadrant*, *Crikey* and has edited several books.

 @dlew919

New Politics Australia is a monthly podcast, providing analysis and opinions on Australia politics. It can be found at Apple and Google podcasts, Spotify and SoundCloud.

About the book

Divided Opinions is the story of the 2019 year in Australian federal politics, told through a collection of extended notes from the New Politics Australia podcast series, and a selection of political essays published online.

The reforms implemented in 2017 by the Turnbull government created an even higher concentration of media ownership in Australia and, because of this, it has become difficult to provide alternative perspectives within an increasingly hostile and manipulative conservative media landscape: these essays and notes aim to fill in the many gaps left behind by the mainstream media.

This book offers insights into the performances of the Liberal–National Party and the Labor Party throughout the year. It commences with the resignation of a senior Liberal minister early in 2019, which kick-started a series of further ministerial resignations over a period of several weeks; offers perspectives on the events that shaped and influenced the May election; provides an in-depth analysis of how the election was won for the Coalition—and lost for the Labor Party; and explores the issues that will reverberate throughout federal politics over the next parliamentary term, especially the government mismanagement of bushfires and climate change issues in the final months of 2019.

Australia is at a crossroads on many fronts: on the edge of an economic recession and long-term financial difficulties; facing an environmental apocalypse that not only affects the environment, economy and community, but the psyche of the nation; stranded

About the book

with a prime minister who is more concerned about personal niche issues, appearances and media management of problems as they arise, rather than action to resolve those problems; and a Labor Opposition unsure about what it needs to do to become more relatable to the electorate and make a return to office.

Contemporary politics is in a difficult space, governed by vested interests and divided by tribalism, not just in Australia, but in many advanced democracies throughout the world: 2019 proved to be an eventful year in Australian politics but how the political system removes itself from the quagmire of its own making and becomes more relevant to the community is unclear and will be one of the key factors to look for in future years.

January 2020

The media forgets how it destroyed Julia Gillard

23 January 2019

Eddy Jokovich

We should never underestimate the ability of the mainstream media to employ double standards, engage in collective amnesia, and paint a rosy picture of the conservative world, a world quite detached from reality.

Last Sunday, the Member of Higgins, Kelly O'Dwyer, announced her decision to not recontest this seat at the next federal election. The media quickly depicted her as a 'trailblazer for women' and someone who 'stood up to men in her party', without actually providing any evidence for how she trailblazed for the feminist movement, or which men in the Liberal Party she stood up to, or in which circumstances this occurred.

For sure, O'Dwyer achieved a great deal as the member for Higgins, a seat she claimed in a by-election in 2009, after the former Treasurer, Peter Costello, resigned. During her nine-year stint in Parliament, she became Minister for Women; Minister for Jobs and Industrial Relations; Minister for Revenue and Financial Services; Minister for Small Business; and Assistant Treasurer.

But instead of focusing on her time in Parliament, the media diverted their attention towards the vitriol against O'Dwyer published on social media, and were quick to point out that it was "a disgrace and as bad at the abuse Julia Gillard had to deal with".

O'Dwyer—or any other politician—shouldn't have to put up with public vilification and online abuse, and definitely not to the hyper-level that was thrown at Gillard.

Comparisons of abuse of politicians by the media is always fraught, but there is no equivalence between the media treatment of Kelly O'Dwyer and Julia Gillard, during her time in office.

At the time of her resignation, the media rolled the red carpet of empathy for O'Dwyer, outlining the "very personal reason" behind her decision to leave Parliament—a miscarriage and the desire of her family to have another child.

Without question, a miscarriage at anytime of a woman's life is distressing, and a desire to have another child is a question that many families around Australia would like to have positively answered. But I couldn't help thinking: how would the media have reacted if this was Julia Gillard?

While there have been very derisive and appalling comments on social media about O'Dwyer (some have actually come from Unions Australia News, fake Twitter and Facebook accounts created by the Young Liberals to discredit unions), there has been nothing at all that comes close to the treatment meted out to Julia Gillard.

"Ju-liar", "Ditch the Witch" and "Bob Brown's Bitch": these words are from the placards used in the anti-carbon tax rally in front of Parliament House in March 2011. Did Kelly O'Dwyer ever have to endure anything like this?

In September 2012, after Gillard's father died suddenly, 2GB broadcaster Alan Jones said "the old man recently died a few weeks ago of shame, to think that he had a daughter who told lies every time she stood for Parliament." He then went on to say Gillard should be "put into a chaff bag and thrown into the sea".

In June 2013, Liberal MP Steve Ciobo said many Labor members would welcome "the opportunity to slit Julia Gillard's throat". Liberal–National Party MP Mal Brough even went to the effort of creating a KFC poster, with the headline: "Julia Gillard Snack Pack: 2 Small Breasts, 2 Extra Large Thighs, 1 Red Box".

Extending the food theme, Mal Brough also held a fundraising event in March 2013, and included on the published menu: "Julia Gillard Kentucky Fried Quail: Small Breasts, Huge Thighs & A Big Red Box", as well as other references to her vagina and mussels.

Has anyone ever speculated on the sexuality of O'Dwyer's husband, Jon Mant? In June 2013 on Perth radio, shock-jock Howard Sattler asked Julia Gillard about her partner, Tim Mathieson: "Tim's gay? He must be gay, he's a hairdresser. You can confirm that he's not?".

This was quickly followed up with an appearance on ABC *Insiders* by News Corp journalist, Piers Akerman: "A lot of people in the Canberra gallery have been saying the same thing".

And before her first child arrived, did anyone claim O'Dwyer was unfit for leadership because she was "deliberately barren", as Liberal Senator Bill Heffernan claimed of Julia Gillard in 2007?

Did anyone ever throw a half-eaten Vegemite sandwich at O'Dwyer, like the one thrown at Gillard during her visit to Marsden State High School in Brisbane? Or did any television producer ever make an intrusive and derisory sit-com about her family, like the ABC-commissioned *At Home With Julia*?

Julia Gillard endured a great deal of public misogyny during her time as prime minister, encouraged and egged on by male-dominated media of all persuasions. It's sickening to recount how unhinged the behaviour of the media was at that time.

But it's the Labor women that bear the brunt of media derision and curiosity. Previously, we had Cheryl Kernot. In 2018, it was the Labor backbencher, Emma Husar.

Gillard was the true trailblazer for women in the Australian Parliament and while all of these attacks were taking place, Kelly O'Dwyer, as a parliamentarian, had a front-seat view of the events taking place in front of her, but never offered a public word of support to Gillard, or 'stood up to the men' in the Liberal Party, as claimed by Prime Minister Scott Morrison.

O'Dwyer is entitled to a retire from Parliament in peace and away from the media gaze (although I'm sure at some point, she'll be offered a healthy sinecure with her former employer, NAB). But never let it be said she had to endure the same public treatment as Julia Gillard and we (and O'Dwyer) should be thankful that it never came to this.

Conflating the two experiences is a false equivalence, and the media has shown how short its memory really is.

*

Short changed by the banking Royal Commission

6 February 2019

Eddy Jokovich

It's always amusing to see senior politicians caught in the headlights and that's exactly what we witnessed this week when the report from the Royal Commission into Misconduct in the Banking, Superannuation and Financial Services Industry was released.

The Treasurer, Josh Frydenberg, possesses a special kind of *chutzpah*, perhaps the type that helped to get him to where he is today, but that wasn't enough to disguise the weaving, mental gymnastics and deflection that he went through to try to abandon all responsibility and divert any negative fallout to the Labor Party.

While Frydenberg made himself look foolish, at least he had the tenacity to front up, even if he did show up with more front than his local Camberwell Place Shopping Centre.

As for the Prime Minister, Scott Morrison, who vehemently denied the need for a banking Royal Commission—on the day it was announced in November 2017, he said "the recklessness of the Leader of the Opposition and the shadow treasurer for over two years calling into question the integrity and the system security of our banking system and financial system"—he simply went missing, hiding in a military tank in far north Queensland.

The banking Royal Commission was a pertinent matter for many people and the ethics and actions of the financial services sector were seriously called into question. We discovered the big four banks—Commonwealth, ANZ, NAB and Westpac, along with financial giants AMP and Macquarie Bank—were engaged in highly unethical practices, as well as potentially criminal acts. Many thousands of its customers were severely affected by these questionable practices and, in many cases, advice was provided that was detrimental to the interests of the consumer.

The Royal Commission uncovered almost the full gamut of unethical and illegal acts by the banks: charging fees to clients who had died; charging fees to customers for services not rendered; bribery; forgery and falsifying paperwork; selling incorrect insurance products; loaning large sums of money to people on low incomes; and misleading the corporate regulator, the Australian Securities and Investments Commission.

For many thousands of people who had been seriously affected by corruption in the banking sector, the Royal Commission was an opportunity to uncover serious problems within the sector, as well as an opportunity to remedy those wrongful actions.

It would have been wise for the two politicians that accepted the report, Frydenberg and Morrison, to offer a simple apology to the public, to announce they seriously misread the mood of the public, to clearly work in the public interest to improve the services offered by the financial sector, and avoid the mistakes of the past.

But getting a public *mea culpa* from either of these two was more difficult than extracting a tooth embedded high up in the back of an elephant's jawbone. Both Morrison and Frydenberg are opportunists in the extreme—in the process of releasing the report, Frydenberg did his best to take credit for the Royal Commission, and tried to deflect all of the faults of the banking sector back to the Labor Party and Leader of the Opposition, Bill Shorten, even though Labor has been out of office for over five years and Shorten was the one who actively and consistently called for the investigation.

To find out where this all started, we need to go back to September 2013, when the incoming Liberal–National Party, under the leadership of Tony Abbott, was "determined to weaken protections" in the financial sector previously introduced by Labor. His infamous 'red-tape repeal day' in 2014 removed many of these regulations, but ended up being more like a 'brown-nose day' for corporate Australia.

This was further exacerbated by cuts to ASIC of $120 million in the 2014 Budget (a total of $200 million over the past five years) which severely curtailed ASIC's ability to regulate financial services and corporations. In response to these cutbacks, Abbott said "the onus was on the industry to self-regulate".

It's fair to say this didn't work out so well.

An ABC *Four Corners* report in 2014 exposed a wide range of malfeasance within the banking sector, including money laundering for drug syndicates, ignoring financing to terrorist groups, impropriety in foreign exchange trading, manipulating interest rates through bank bill swap rates, and fraudulently loaning millions of dollars to people who had no ability to pay the money back.

As result of the *Four Corners* report and the widespread outrage in the community, a Senate Economics References Committee assessed the performance of the Australian Securities and Investments Commission, and recommended a Royal Commission into the financial services sector.

The report from this Senate Committee was published in June 2014. Since this time, there have many demands to hold a banking Royal Commission: in a National Press Council speech before the 2016 election, Bill Shorten called for a commission and pledged to hold one if Labor won government.

Throughout 2016 and 2017, there were more calls to hold a commission, including from Liberal Party MP, Warren Entch, and National Party MPs, George Christensen, Llew O'Brien, Barry O'Sullivan and John Williams.

In the Senate, the government voted twenty-six times against holding a banking Royal Commission. The Treasurer at the time, Scott Morrison, called it "nothing more than a populist whinge" and advised Shorten to stop playing "reckless political games", adding Labor "just intended to bolster and prop up the stocks of a Leader of the opposition".

Attacking Labor MP Wayne Swan in Parliament in 2016, he said a Royal Commission would just be "crass populism".

The then Prime Minister, Malcolm Turnbull, and the Ministers responsible for financial matters—Morrison (Treasurer), Kelly O'Dwyer (Minister for Revenue and Financial Services, as well as former NAB executive), Mathias Cormann (Minister for Finance)—all ruled out the need for an investigation into the financial sector.

Even the night before the Royal Commission was announced, Turnbull said, almost proudly: "I can tell you we have, as a government, decided not to have a Royal Commission; we made the decision a long time ago".

But twelve hours is a long time in politics. Turnbull announced the Royal Commission the morning after the banks themselves requested it. The terms and conditions of the Royal Commission were curtailed but, nevertheless, the next fifteen months of inquiry managed to uncover enough evidence for the public to confirm what they already knew: banks are virtually a law unto themselves; are motivated solely by corporate greed; and will never ever act in the public interest unless they are regulated carefully and diligently.

Regulation and oversight of the financial sector was reduced under the watch of the Liberal–National government—not just since they were elected in 2013, but going back all the way to 1996. The Liberal–National Party has governed Australia for seventeen of the past twenty-three years, and the crisis in the banking sector has to be sheeted back to them and their constant calls for less regulation in the sector.

Last week, the commissioner of the inquiry, former High Court judge, Kenneth Hayne, released his findings to Treasurer Frydenberg. There are seventy-six recommendations, and a suggestion there are twenty acts of criminality that should be investigated further. These recommendations offer positive solutions for the financial sector, and will go a long way to restoring public confidence.

But it's an outcome that has been delivered far too late.

Frydenberg's immediate response to any criticism about denying the need for a Royal Commission was more well rehearsed than a Marcel Marceau performance: "Look, we can debate for hours what Labor failed when they were in office" [NB: years in office since 1996: LNP, seventeen years; ALP six] … "we did call the Royal Commission and today we've responded to it" [NB: technically yes, but they voted against it twenty-six times in the Senate, and brought it on only when the banks requested one].

Would he apologise for delaying the Royal Commission by almost two years? "We can debate for hours Labor's failures when they were last in opposition". Of course, this is standard political procedure—deny the obvious, deflect the blame to others, take no responsibility. But the report of the banking Royal Commission required a different response and Frydenberg's denials were too blatant for them to resonate with the public.

Fresh from his northern jaunt and donned in military fatigues, Morrison joined Frydenberg in his political spin cycle: "I called the Royal Commission. I introduced the banking executive accountability regime."

How does he reconcile this with his previous musings, when he claimed it would be "a lawyer's picnic" and "the government is not proposing a Royal Commission and we've opposed one consistently".

No mention of the $200 million they pulled out from ASIC funding? No mention of the correspondence between Scott Morrison and the Chairman of National Australia Bank, Ken Henry, which developed the terms of the Royal Commission, detailed who would be a suitable commissioner, and how the commission should proceed to minimise scrutiny on the banking sector?

Or was Morrison too busy counting the donations the Liberal Party receives from the big four banks, which tallied over $500,000 in 2016?

These are the days when the idiot is king but, even still, the performances offered by Morrison and Frydenberg won't wash with the public.

There has been great discussion about the 'trust deficit' now facing banks and what they can do to improve their trustworthiness to the Australian community.

The trust deficit is a problem for the banks, but there's an even bigger trust deficit for the two people who are now trying to claim all the credit for something they were determined would never happen and, based on all the evidence in front of us over the past four years, couldn't care less about.

Morrison and Frydenberg are even more untrustworthy than the banks they were enthusiastically defending and protecting from public scrutiny.

Fortunately, they won't be the people trusted to implement, as Frydenberg puts it, "the legislative framework to provide the regulators with the powers and resources to hold those who abuse out trust, to account." The Liberal–National government have always removed those powers and resources, so why should the public trust them now?

Parliament will only be sitting for eight days before the next election, due in May 2019: not enough time to enact a legislative framework—that's something that takes months. And only politicians with the *chutzpah* of Morrison and Frydenberg would claim they're doing everything possible, even if there's no chance of it ever happening under their watch.

Whatever the results are of Hayne's seventy-six recommendations, that is likely to be left to a different government to take care of.

*

Unhappy holidays and apocalypse 2019

11 February 2019

Eddy Jokovich + David Lewis / Podcast

In this episode, we looked at the big issues that kicked off the 2019 year in politics; discussed whether climate change and the environment would appear as the two big factors in the two main elections this year; inspected the Royal Commission into Misconduct in the Banking, Superannuation and Financial Services Industry and we asked the question: has the public been short-changed yet again? And in this episode, David Lewis appears as an international playboy and a man about town.

Eddy Jokovich: January is usually a quiet period for politics, but when there are elections to be won, there is always going to be a great deal of activity. It has been an action-packed start to 2019; we had three ministers resigning from the Liberal–National Party, preselection battles in the federal seat of Gilmore; franking credits floated around as a topic of discussion, as well as Captain Cook and the culture wars. And, importantly, there was a grand debate about the right to wear thongs and board shorts at Australia Day ceremonies. It has been quite an unusual summer.

David Lewis: We didn't get the break we so richly deserved as political analysts. The first issue to point out is we don't seem to have a quiet period in politics anymore, thanks to the 24-hour news cycle, but also the ubiquity of the internet, and it's a news cycle that doesn't even quieten down. Those old political tricks of releasing unpopular policy in the first week in January when everybody's on holidays doesn't work anymore: your smart phone beeps and the policy announcement is right in front of you. The 24-hour news cycle is an issue governments all over the world are struggling with.

EJ: We do have two elections coming up quite soon, and that explains why January wasn't so quiet: there is the New South Wales election on March 23 and the federal election, due before May 18. And it's unusual to have an election in Australia's largest state, and a federal election so close to each other.

DL: It's been an unusual summer in politics, and that follows a trend over the past five years. Ever since Tony Abbott became Leader of the Opposition in 2009, all the rules of politics have been suspended: I've said that before, but it's worth repeating. Politics as usual does not apply anymore and, as a result, we are looking for the new rules, and I'm not sure if there are any. We also have a federal government that is not terribly effective. There's also talk of another leadership spill—I don't know how serious that talk is—apparently the Peter Dutton forces are trying to mobilise again and partially, that would be to save his seat of Dickson, because he doesn't look likely to win this seat at the next election. And also, partly, it's because of the disappointing performance of the current Prime Minister. We've seen many resignations from the Liberal Party recently—Kelly O'Dwyer, Julia Banks, Michael Keenan, Nigel Scullion. Every lead-up to an election brings across Members of Parliament who decide it's time to leave politics: Nigel Scullion, for example, is sixty-two years old, and in his media release, he seemed genuine when he stated he wants to shoot feral pigs and catch yabbies, and enjoy his retirement. But it doesn't look good for the Liberal Party when other younger ministers whose careers haven't quite finished yet, are also jumping ship.

EJ: To paraphrase Oscar Wilde: to lose one minister in one week, that's a disaster. To lose two ministers in one week is quite careless. To lose three ministers is something else and this created a domino effect—because we did have the resignation of three ministers so quickly, there was speculation that there would be more to follow. Are we likely to see more ministers resigning over the next couple of weeks?

DL: There are whispers about particular ministers caught in inappropriate situations. But discussions about whether those ministers will resign have been sideswiped by even more misconduct from the member for Goldstein in Victoria, Tim Wilson, behaving abominably with the parliamentary inquiry into franking credits. He's used these inquiry sessions as a political sideshow, getting people attending these public inquiries to sign a pro-Liberal Party petition, or to sign up for Liberal Party membership, as well as the financial skullduggery involved with sponsorship and the promotion of these inquiries by a family relative, Geoff Wilson. These are very serious areas of misconduct and there have been sustained calls for Wilson's resignation from Parliament. Because of this, any other minister hoping to resign without too much disruption for the government—such as Julie Bishop or Christopher Pyne—would have been talked into holding off their announcements for as long as possible. For Tim Wilson and the Liberal Party, they're hoping these problems will just dissipate, whereas the Labor Party will be hoping he resigns in disgrace.

EJ: Tim Wilson has been running his franking credits roadshow all around Australia—holding public sessions in a wide range of city and regional areas—in which the Liberal Party hopes will create havoc for the Labor Party. The franking credits scheme is one of those barely understood and complex systems: it's a process where a tax refund is made to the company shareholder, even if they haven't actually paying the tax in the first place. It's quite an expensive scheme. It costs the federal government $5.2 billion per year—and that's an amount increasing dramatically each year—the equivalent of the salaries for 40,000 nurses and teachers. It compares to the $5.9 billion the government spends on public schools, and $8 billion they spend on early childhood education across Australia. That's $5.2 billion each and every year for this scheme: it's quite a substantial amount.

DL: It's one of those issues that would have been better managed twenty years ago, and this gets back to my previous point about the 24-hour news cycle, as well as social and alternative media. This has changed how politics is managed. If the franking credits issue occurred twenty years ago, the Murdoch media would have run messages about the 'terrible retiree tax,' putting just enough doubt in the minds of the electorate and that's where it would have remained. But social media sites such as Twitter and independent news sources have all pointed out this anomaly: it's a tax refund on tax that hasn't been paid. And the examples the Murdoch media has used, such as the infamous 'Joan' who was receiving $130,000 income per year through share dividends, and was going to lose $13,000 of that amount—compared to someone who's working three part-time jobs, or is receiving Newstart benefit, on a disability pension, or is in a low-paid job in a retail shop or in a factory, $130,000 per year is an executive wage, and it's hard to find sympathy. And then people on social media realised that not only is 'Joan' receiving $130,000, it's $130,000 tax free. I don't wish to disparage self-funded retirees; these are people who have saved and been financially clever enough to fund their own retirement and, sure, this should be encouraged where possible, but they shouldn't be the figures of great sympathy when compared to other sectors of society.

EJ: The main message conservative media put out into the public sphere is self-funded retirees have worked hard all of their lives, and that's totally understandable—some have worked extremely hard, some haven't, some have had good luck. But it's not a situation where the self-funded retirees receiving these franking credits tax refunds are the only hard-working people in society: everyone works hard, everyone contributes. The way the government has been pushing through this issue is very unfortunate—the franking credits tax refund is such an odd system the government is trying to defend, and Tim Wilson has been using the parliamentary inquiry process in an unethical way to defend this system.

DL: It shows the tin ear and the inept political maneuverings of the government, and shows how much they're out of touch: how

Wilson thought he'd ever get sympathy for such a scheme, once the full details came out, is hard to understand. By filling these parliamentary inquiries with Liberal Party supporters and then having the friendly mainstream media promoting these angry senior citizens whose lifestyle is at risk, should have backfired on Tim Wilson, but perhaps there's other factors at play here. Politics, of course, is the art of being able to sell ideas, and Wilson hasn't been able to do that. If anything, his inquiries have highlighted why the franking credits scheme is such a bad idea.

*

EJ: During the holiday period, we also had Australia Day on January 26. Australia Day has been held on that day for a long time and there was debate about whether it should be referred to as 'Invasion Day', or if it should be the commemoration of the landing of the first fleet at Jackson Cove in 1788. But one thing is for sure: many people are unsure about what Australia Day is actually about. We can put aside that debate for another time, but what Australia Day is great for is a good old-fashioned culture war day: in each year, the prime minister, especially if it's a Liberal Party prime minister, will bring up a new version of the culture wars, and this year, Scott Morrison decided it was going to be about Captain Cook, and whether Cook circumnavigated the country or not. And, of course, he didn't: the first people to officially circumnavigate Australia [New Holland] were Matthew Flinders and Bungaree in 1803. Scott Morrison suggested the 250-year commemoration in 2020 should be all about Cook's circumnavigation of the country, even though he never actually did that. But even though he did get his history totally wrong, Morrison is quite prepared to spend up to $60 million for this 2020 commemoration.

DL: Australia Day today is obviously a very problematic day in Australia. Even putting aside we're no longer an Anglo-specific society and haven't been officially since 1972—and we can't forget the first fleet in 1788 had so many nationalities: there were French; there were Russians; Maltese; Italians. Australia Day is a big problem for what it means to Indigenous people, and this is an argument the country has never properly had, or at least, it has never been properly played out fully in public. There are many Indigenous people and many non-Indigenous people who each and every year want the date changed to another day that might be more appropriate—that is an argument we do need to have. We can have both commemorations: a day of reflection and a day of celebration. But when the flag-waving patriotism comes out, which really just means that all the racists can come out and speak freely about who did what to whom and who really suffered, it is laughable and anti-historical. The other factor about Captain Cook is that he wasn't even the first Englishman to come to these shores, let alone the first European to visit the Australian continent: William Dampier had arrived in Australia [New Holland] ninety years before Cook.

EJ: Not content with misrepresenting history, Scott Morrison went one step further: he decided he was going to be the 'prime minister for standards' and wanted to introduce a dress code for Australia Day ceremonies. And that meant no thongs or board shorts for those people receiving their citizenship on Australian Day. I recall in the 1930s, the Italian dictator Benito Mussolini also wanted to introduce a dress code for the Italians: is this something of interest to the Australian public, or just silly prime ministerial thoughts? It's hard to know exactly what the 'prime minister for standards' actually means.

DL: There are some events, of course, where it is appropriate for formal attire, but there's also the Australian way: it's your own choice. Perhaps it's more of an attempt to convince people from other cultures away from traditional clothing, it's hard to know. But most people who accept Australian citizenship take it very seriously and see the citizenship ceremony as being a very important tradition to being a member of the Australian community, and most people dress up in at least smart-casual attire. It's usually too hot to wear a suit on Australia Day, and most people would be dressed to the standard Scott Morrison requires. I suspect Morrison was engaging in a little bit of dog-whistling, to subconsciously suggest: 'look at these loutish, awful foreign-looking people who can't even dress properly for a ceremony', and, of course, these are people who probably don't even exist. It was another form of inept race baiting.

EJ: Back in the 2015 Australia Day, the then Prime Minister Tony Abbott made a 'captain's call', and that's when he decided to award a knighthood to Prince Philip, Duke of Edinburgh. It's widely considered *that* day and *that* 'call' was the beginning of the end of Tony Abbott's prime ministership, and the day after Australia Day this year, Scott Morrison also made the 'captain's call' when he announced former ALP President, Warren Mundine, was going to be preselected as the Liberal candidate for the NSW seat of Gilmore. The problem was, the Liberal Party had preselected Grant Schultz six months before, but Morrison decided to parachute Mundine into the seat instead.

DL: It's certainly a mistake. Warren Mundine, who has been described as the only rat to run *onto* a sinking ship, was rejected as a candidate by the Labor Party. The reasons for this have never really come out but he had been President of the Labor Party some time ago and, generally, presidents of all political parties tend to have a fairly good chance of securing a seat and entering Parliament. After resigning from the Labor Party, he then joined the Liberal Democrats Party for a while—that strange and bizarre organisation for small-minded people with no imagination—and then finally secured what seems to be his lifelong dream: a preselection for a seat. I'm sure he would have preferred a safe seat, of course, all politicians would. But he's got the marginal seat of Gilmore instead.

EJ: It's not a good 'captain's call' at all by Scott Morrison. Warren Mundine doesn't live anyway near the seat of Gilmore—it's on the south coast of New South Wales and about 150 kilometres south of the North Shore of Sydney, the exclusive wealthy part of Sydney where Warren Mundine lives. If Scott Morrison really did want Mundine to enter Parliament, he should have given him a seat in North Sydney, and there's quite a few seats in the area he could have been parachuted into. The other problem in Gilmour is it's a very marginal seat, currently held by the Liberal Party [by the retiring Ann Sudmalis] by the wafer-thin margin of 0.7 per cent in two-party preferred voting. Why Morrison decided to place Mundine in an ultra-marginal seat, far away from where he actually lives, is a very strange decision. Politically, I can see the thinking behind that decision: Mundine is a member of the Bundjalung people and the seat of Gilmore does include a larger Indigenous population than the national average—the national average of Indigenous people is 3 per cent of the overall population, whereas in Gilmore, it's around 5 per cent. This might be factor when it comes to mathematics, but it could be cancelled out by Warren Mundine being quite a divisive character within the Indigenous community.

DL: The other factor to consider is the Liberal Party members in Gilmore, the ones who have spent the past twelve months preparing Grant Schultz for a good, hard political fight, a candidate they would have known and trusted for a long time; and then he's gone. And don't forget, this is the Liberal Party that intervened to save candidates such as Craig Kelly in the seat of Hughes, of all people. Grant Schultz, a popular and well-liked character in the Liberal Party is booted out for a man who doesn't even live in the area. Mundine now has a maximum of three months to find a house, move to the south coast of New South Wales, establish himself, get to know the community and then win the Liberal Party volunteers over, as well as the electors. It's a difficult ask of Warren Mundine.

EJ: Grant Schultz has also resigned from the Liberal Party, and he's decided to run in Gilmour as an independent candidate. There are also a few other prominent independents running against Liberal MPs in New South Wales and also in Victoria. The former Olympian, Zali Steggall, is running against Tony Abbott in the seat of Warringah. Julia Banks, the former Liberal Party MP who resigned after Malcolm Turnbull was ousted as prime minister, is running against Greg Hunt in the Victoria seat of Flinders. Oliver Yates, he's also a former member of the Liberal Party, is running up against Treasurer Josh Frydenberg in the seat of Kooyong. These independents are all ex-Liberals or light-Liberals challenging sitting Liberal MPs and, aside from Steggall, they haven't got much of a chance of winning.

DL: It's going to be interesting to see the outcome here. Nearly all of these independents differentiate from the Liberal MPs sitting in those seats on social issues, climate change policy or same-sex marriage. But all of them have stated they are economic conservatives who believe in lower tax rates, likely to keep the various tax advantages for the wealthy classes, such negative gearing and franking credits, and their presence is a reaction to the extremism of the right wing of the Liberal Party. Zali Steggall is in with an extremely good chance in Warringah. Famously, it was pointed out Tony Abbott's household was representative of Warringah in the same-sex marriage plebiscite, in that of the four family members living there, three voted in favour of same-sex marriage, while Tony Abbott voted against. In an unusual sight, Abbott was campaigning and lobbying for more permanent public toilets at Manly Beach, so it's clear he's not taking the seat for granted. However, it might not be enough: he may just scrape in, scraping back into office on preferences. There are twenty-three people vying to defeat Abbott in his seat, and most of them have virtually no chance, except for Steggall, a figure who is known nationally, who is qualified for public office, she's a barrister, has a grasp of legislation and how politics works, and shares the ambitions and ideas of the people Warringah and how public money should be managed.

EJ: Overall, it does get down to the quality of the candidates in all of those Liberal-held seats, but also the mathematical computations with preferences deals and the voting swings, and depends on how many other independents are running in each seat. As soon as Zali Steggall announced her intention to run in the seat of Warringah, other high-profile candidates dropped their candidacy, realising that too many high-profiles running in that seat would dilute the vote, and end up providing support to the Liberal member they all wanted to see the back of. Steggall does have a good chance in Warringah, but the chances of an independent winning the seat of Kooyong are not strong, although a recent opinion poll showed the Labor Party polling at 52 per cent in two-party preferred voting. But, polls are polls, and elections are elections, they're totally different beasts. It will be interesting to see how this independent movement plays out in the next federal election. In the current Parliament, there are six independents on the crossbench, and with Adam Bandt from the Greens, that makes seven. Whether or not there's an outright majority for either party at the next election, it's good for politics to have independent members in Parliament sitting on the crossbench.

DL: These independents are running in fairly safe Liberal seats and presenting to the electorate as ex-members of the Liberal Party, or aligned to the party. And this is where sitting members such as Josh Frydenberg and Tony Abbott may be in trouble. It's not really a stroke against the Liberal Party *per se*, it's a stroke against the candidate.

*

Climate change and the environment: how these issues will influence the next election

EJ: In 2007, former Prime Minister Kevin Rudd announced climate change was the greatest moral challenge of our generation, but it seems like it was too much of a challenge and it helped put an end to his prime ministership. In 2010, carbon pricing caused problems for Julia Gillard, and dithering over climate change and energy policy helped end Malcolm Turnbull's time as prime minister in 2018. We've seen ten years of policy paralysis on climate change and energy policy: so far in this summer, we've had fires in the south, floods in the north, fish kills in the Murray–Darling Basin: it has almost been like an apocalypse. Why is the political class, especially the conservatives, ignoring the public will on climate change?

DL: Essentially, it's because of politics. What's generally not recognised is that the first world leader to actually be concerned about climate change was that dangerous lefty, former British Conservative Prime Minister Margaret Thatcher, who was a scientist and read the numbers and understood the numbers in a way that many current political figures either can't or refuse to understand. Thatcher's solution to greenhouse emissions was nuclear power, which has its own problems—unless nuclear power becomes 100 per cent safe, I'm not sure if it's the best option.

EJ: We can also look back at the Republicans in the United States, where in the 1970s, they legislated the *Clean Energy Act* and implemented a range of environmental initiatives, and coming from a right-wing party in America, that's quite astonishing. It has been interesting to see how the issues of climate change and the environment have split according to party-political lines over the past decade. Those people in the community wanting action about climate change and protection of the environment: they're seen as left wing or progressive, and for those denying climate change is an issue and couldn't care less about the environment, they're right wing and conservative. But the big factor is, the environment doesn't discern between the left and right side of politics: climate change is affecting everyone; pollution is affecting everyone.

DL: We've just had the hottest month on record: not just the hottest January, but the hottest month ever. The month of February is not going to be pleasant in those parts of the country where February is the hotter month. Australian politics is well within the pockets of the mining lobby, and it was the mining lobby who essentially rolled Kevin Rudd as prime minister, with a $122 million advertising campaign against the mining and carbon taxes. And it's both major parties, even though Scott Morrison was the one who walked into Parliament with a lump of coal and was described by journalist Paul Bongiorno as "a clown". Obviously, for the Labor Party, with jobs and the unions being part of the issue, it's not an easy area to manage politically—there are thousands of jobs in the mining industry, and for the Liberal Party, it's making sure the mining business is looked after too.

EJ: Developing any policy is difficult work, whether it's financial policy, climate change policy, or environmental policy. The upshot is, political leaders need to bring the community along with them. One big factor about 2018 that appeared in the spate of federal by-elections and also in the 2018 Victoria state election was climate change. In exit polls, many people speaking to pollsters as they were walking out of election booths said the biggest issue for them was climate change and the environment. Obviously, that was a massive issue in the Wentworth by-election last year, which was won by the independent candidate, Kerryn Phelps; it was an issue in the Longman by-election in Queensland and it was a big issue in the Victoria state election as well. Each year is different politically and that all happened in 2018 but we've had many incidents relating to climate change issues in 2019. Since the beginning of this year; Queensland has had its floods, Tasmania has been on fire. Sydney is unusually hot, and we've had the fish kills in the Menindee Lakes, although that had more to do with Murray–Darling Basin Authority corruption and interference from Barnaby Joyce. But still, there are many climate change issues the public can see with their own eyes through the media and on the internet. These are climate change issues that are dovetailing into each other in the lead-up to the next federal election, and these factors could end up being quite significant to the electorate.

DL: The public is, on the whole, finally coming around to climate change, although the election outcome will probably show us whether the public is keen to just talk about the environment, but not happy to pay for climate change policies. The party mishandling the issue the most is the Greens, actually—they should be at the cutting edge of these issues, given their policy background but, instead, they're wrenched with internal division, certainly in New South Wales; they're splitting and members are leaving and it's not a pretty sight. Of course, this can happen to any political party, but it's just a matter of bad luck and bad timing that it's happening to the Greens, right at the moment where they could have been finally taking that dominance they have been craving for so many years.

EJ: The Greens should be in a more dominant political position—if climate change is a big issue for many people in the community, the Greens should be at the forefront of that. Of course, they are developing policy and strategies behind the scenes but it's that lack of media cut-through, and if there are so many external events, or if there's internal division within the party, it's difficult to get any political messaging out there. There have been rumours about the Liberal–National Party actually releasing a substantial climate policy soon—if they're politically sensible, that's what they should do but they do have a credibility problem on climate change. As you mentioned, Scott Morrison dragged a lump of coal into Parliament. If they did release a substantial climate change policy, would he be believed? The Liberal–National Party still has its woeful Direct Action policy in one form or another; it's a substantial sum of money paid to directly to polluters and it doesn't work. It's ineffective. But in the same way Direct Action is an insubstantial program, perhaps the Liberal–National Party will release yet another ineffective and poor climate change policy, just so they've got something to announce, and to let the electorate know they at least have a policy to match their opponents, similar to John Howard's unsuccessful strategy during the 2007 election campaign.

DL: The Liberal–National Party doesn't want to upset their big donors in the resources industries and they don't want to annoy some of their members, and they are losing members quite rapidly, thanks to the lack of policies in this area. The Greens were picking up a lot of ex-Liberal Party members, which is probably the reason behind the many divisions in the Greens. The Greens are going through a generational battle as well, the old-generation 'hippies' faction, versus the young inner-city 'nimbies', who don't want to vote Labor. There are a few other factions in there as well, but that's what's causing many of their tensions. The Liberal Party is in that awful position where they could release the best environmental policy that works, and pleases everybody, good for the environment and slows global warming; but nobody would believe them.

EJ: That process would be the case for their energy policy as well, as the areas of climate change and energy are intertwined. The only work carried out by the Liberal Party on energy policy is, pretty much, what Angus Taylor has been talking about over the past few months: pushing prices down. That's not much of an energy policy: renewables aren't mentioned; how prices will be 'pushed down' isn't outlined, and there are so many other factors not taken into account within their energy discussions. Taylor is a new minister and hasn't been around for very long within the energy portfolio. To be sure, a minister can argue that their energy policy is to 'get prices down' but that's the type of slogan seen at a Coles supermarket, and we should be expecting far more from our energy minister.

DL: Certainly, energy prices are at a special high point. I don't know how many people have died or been hospitalised over summer from the extreme heat because they couldn't afford to turn their air conditioning on, or couldn't afford to purchase an air conditioner for their home. For the government to focus on electricity prices, knowing that renewable energy is a much cheaper energy source, is cynical, as well as wrongheaded: it's playing to the worst instincts of their voters—of course, not all of their voters are horrible people with bad instincts. And to put so much emphasis on saving $100 on an energy bill, which is the amount the government is claiming: is that worth all the flooding in Townville, or Tasmania burning, or Sydney burning or losing all those rural properties because all the top soil has been eroded away, despite the best efforts of farmers?

EJ: It will be up to the electorate to decide whether the promise of saving $100 on an electricity bill is enough of a trade-off to not worry about action on climate change or the environment: I'd suggest it's possible to do both. It would be better if we didn't have such cynicism in politics, but that's the name of the game and we've got an election coming up: we're going to see many more cynical policy announcements and cynical political behaviour.

DL: These are the last-ditch attempts from the government trying to save itself, and nothing has worked so far. However, I'm not going to make any definite pronouncements of the Liberal–National government being thrown out at the next election, because it's so easy to get it wrong.

*

The Banking Royal Commission

EJ: There has been a great deal of heat over summer, but the greatest amount of heat is being generated by the Banking Royal Commission, with the final report recently delivered by former High Court Judge, Kenneth Hayne. It's a damning report on the conduct of the 'big four' banks: Commonwealth Bank, ANZ, NAB and Westpac and other institutions such as AMP and Macquarie Bank. The Treasurer, Josh Frydenberg, has claimed all of the credit for all of the good parts of the report and, predictably, blamed Labor for all of the negatives, even though it was the Liberal–National Party voting on twenty-six occasions in the

Senate against holding the Commission and consistently denied the need for the Commission for over four years. Is this politics as usual, or will the public see right through the spin generated by Josh Frydenberg and Scott Morrison?

DL: For a Royal Commission the Liberal Party didn't want and a Royal Commission that they limited the terms of so severely, what came out in the final report damaged the banks quite dramatically. The release of the report didn't damage the banks in the short term though: share prices went up probably because nobody from the banking sector has gone to jail yet and the banks seemed to have got away with it, yet again. Nevertheless, the public anger is palpable, as could be seen in that notorious video footage of Kenneth Payne refusing to shake the hand of Josh Frydenberg when he officially handed over his report. Much of that frustration from Payne was because there was so much more he could have investigated but wasn't able to, because of the restrictive terms of the Royal Commission, and because of its relatively small budget.

EJ: Kenneth Haynes could only achieve what the terms of the Royal Commission allowed him to, he is more of a 'black letter' type of lawyer and was on the High Court for eighteen years, retiring at the age of seventy a few years ago. The impetus for this Royal Commission started back in 2014, after an ABC *Four Corners* report exposed the sales-driven culture of the Commonwealth Bank. Many other scandals were uncovered, and there was a Senate Inquiry into these matters which ultimately recommended the creation of a Royal Commission. That was in June 2014, so it almost took four years for the Liberal–National government to do something about the issue. Here is what some government ministers have said consistently over the past four years:

> Malcolm Turnbull: We have, as a government, decided not to have a Royal Commission. We made that decision a long time ago. Not because we don't believe there's nothing going on in terms of problems of the banks...
> MT: ...No, we're not having a banking Royal Commission...

> Scott Morrison: This is nothing more than crash populism seeking to undermine confidence in the banking and financial system...
>
> SM: ...Bill Shorten might be interested in political point scoring about this issue. In fact, he's only been interested in political point scoring...
>
> SM: ...a lawyer's picnic for three years, costing 150 million is not going to get an answer for anyone...
>
> Mathias Cormann: Having more inquiries and just continuing to look at issues without actually having the capacity to take effective action is not the best way forward... [it's] not time for yet another inquiry that essentially would not be able to do anything about what it finds.

EJ: There we have it: responses from the prime minister at the time, Malcolm Turnbull; Treasurer at the time, Scott Morrison, and Finance Minister, Mathias Cormann. They all said, consistently for four years, there is absolutely no need for a Royal Commission, and former Prime Minister John Howard shouting from the sidelines, called it "rank socialism". Scott Morrison called it a "whinge-fest". They're all on the wrong side of history here, so many people in the Liberal Party simply misread the room and it took them a long time to come around to the public's point of view. This Royal Commission should have commenced two years ago; three years ago, or even more.

DL: It's incredible what the banks have been able to keep getting away with. An economy really is only as good as its banking and currency system, the banking system needs absolute integrity, even down to making sure every single cent in its system is accounted for.

EJ: The Royal Commission did uncover almost the full gamut of unethical and illegal acts by the banks: fees-for-no-service; charging people who had died; defrauding people. There was bribery, forgery and falsifying paperwork; deliberately selling incorrect insurance products; loaning large sums of money to customers who had no chance at all of repaying the money. The banks also misled the corporate regulator, ASIC and APRA. Generally, there is a mistrust of banks by the public; there's always that feeling of being ripped-off. But this behaviour uncovered by the Royal Commission is on another level. This is absolutely obscene and these are the types of behaviour the Liberal–National Party was determined would never be seen by the public or by anyone else, and that has to be a big mark against the Liberal Party. Over the past four years, they've been determined not to have this Royal Commission, although there have been some from within government speaking out about it: Liberal–National MP Warren Entch from far north Queensland; he said there should be a Royal Commission in 2016, as did several other National Party members. John Williams said there should be a Royal Commission, as did George Christensen. Others spoke out from the Coalition backbench. But most of the demands came from Leader of the Opposition, Bill Shorten, who first mentioned the Royal Commission at the National Press Club in 2016. There was the whistle blower, Jeff Morris, an internal Commonwealth Bank employee, and he's been calling for an investigation since 2008. So it has been a long time coming. The Liberal–National Party, not only did they completely misread the public mood, but they came across as people who wanted to offer a protection racket for the banks.

DL: That's exactly it. And to deflect from the bad news coming from the Royal Commission, there was another mishandled, poorly thought-through 'dropped ball' by the Prime Minister who was to trying start up a scare campaign about 'union thugs': this backfired. Union membership has grown in the past ten years, and it was quickly pointed out that the average unionist is a 45-year-old woman, working as a nurse—so Scott Morrison has managed to alienate quite a large proportion of the electorate and also get the public offside.

EJ: Deflection is a fine art within politics and, of course, that's what all politicians generally try to do: deflect all the bad news to their opponents, and then take credit for all the positive items. Here's a fine example of this—Josh Frydenberg in response to the Banking Royal Commission report:

> Georgie Gardner, Nine, *Today Show*: The Coalition,
> of course, fought tooth and nail against this Royal

Commission, blocking it twenty-six times. What was the rationale behind resisting it?

Josh Frydenberg: Well, Georgie, look, we can debate the failure of the Labor government when they were last in power and they had a number of financial scandals on their watch.

GG: All right, you did, of course, vote against it twenty-six times. So now you concede that the industry does in fact need an overhaul, and you say the recommendations will be implemented pretty much in full. I guess the question, though, why should we trust a government that had to be dragged into this investigation in the first place?

JF: Well, actually, Georgie, we will be making a number of significant...

Leigh Sales, ABC, *7.30*: Was the Coalition wrong to strenuously oppose a Royal Commission into the banks for as long as it did?

JF: Look we can debate for hours about what Labor have failed to do when they were...

LS: ...no, I'm asking about you...

JF: ...well, I'm looking to the future. And when we first came to government, one of the first...

EJ: It's a classic deflection, and it's pretty obvious. But it's a deflection that is too obvious. There are many people that have been burnt by the banking sector, and there's many people furious about the information that's been coming out from the Royal Commission. Josh Frydenberg didn't strike the right tone and just deflected all of the issues to the Labor Party immediately, even though they've been out of office since 2013. It would have been better if he was more contrite, offering a heartfelt apology to the public: to say the government is sorry; they should have acted sooner and then they could have moved on from that. That's what a mature grown-up government should do: take responsibility.

DL: Certainly, hindsight is 20:20 vision, but to blame Labor? You could almost hear the eyeballs all around Australia rolling so hard, it almost caused a wobble in the rotation of the Earth. Including the Prime Minister—and this is going to be a big call—

Josh Frydenberg seems the minister most out of his depth. To be sure, he was handed a hospital pass that he wasn't really expecting in terms of the Banking Royal Commission: it was commissioned before he became Treasurer. But his policy development work as Minister for Environment, hasn't been successful. The Monday before he became Deputy Leader of the Liberal Party and Treasurer in August 2018, he'd had a major policy—the National Energy Guarantee—that he'd been working on for months, comprehensively rejected by the Liberal party room. So, he has a lot to learn. He should have got up and said 'yes, we should have called the Royal Commission earlier. We were wrong. However, we have called it and look at these results', and then he could try to play out the recommendations for consideration, without committing to anything, because clearly, they have no intention of implementing many of the recommendations. But if Frydenberg acted with more humility, some reflection and some contriteness, he would have come as more genuine.

EJ: Frydenberg did come out and say the government will be offering a suite of legislative frameworks, resources and more powers to the regulators to act, as they have in the past. But this isn't going to happen. There's only ten more parliamentary sitting days before the next election. The Liberal Party are also the ones that cut out $200 million from ASIC and APRA over the past five years. And to say that they have been providing enough resources to the regulators in the past, when they haven't, and they'll provide the regulators with the powers and resources in the future, is simply not the case. Traditionally, the Liberal Party doesn't support regulation within the banking sector, just like their conservative counterparts in Britain and the United States. We have to remember since 1996, the Coalition has been the government for seventeen of those twenty-three years, with the Labor Party in office for just six of those years—many regulations have been repealed and thrown away. And certainly since 2013, if we can remember when Tony Abbott held his infamous 'red tape repeal day', which ended up being more like a 'brown-nose day' for corporate Australia, the Liberal Party is not the party of good regulation. Those types of checks and balances will probably be the responsibility of a different government.

DL: It was a Liberal government which established the Independent Commission Against Corruption in New South Wales, and its first major success was against the NSW Liberal Premier Nick Greiner, although that finding of corruption was later overturned in the Supreme Court. It was also a Liberal government in New South Wales who cut funding to ICAC while eight of its members of NSW Parliament were being investigated, and the Liberal Party has had the same approach to ASIC, the national corporate regulator. It's funny how the budgets were cut at a time when the organisation needed it the most. The philosophical argument over regulation will continue naturally: those who are bound by regulation will want less of it; those who end up being affected because of a lack of regulation will want to have more but a balance between those two positions has to be found. In general, regulations do work, when implemented and policed effectively. We're currently seeing the end days of the neoliberal experiment, the experiment which started with Thatcherism and Reaganomics in the 1980s, initiated in Australia by Hawke and Keating, and then fast-tracked by John Howard. Neoliberalism is in its final death throes, although it will take a good twenty years or more to really remove it completely, because there are still many people in parliaments and in positions of power all around the world who still believe in neoliberalism—because they and their corporate relationships benefit from it.

*

Music in this episode
Cosby Sweater, Hilltop Hoods
Dayan Cowboy, Boards of Canada
Sweet Refined Things, Jess Ribeiro

Scandal: Nothing to see here, please move on

24 February 2019

Eddy Jokovich

One of the greatest take-home surprises from a visit to Parliament House during the House of Representatives Question Time for many people is the sheer ferocity of it, the hurling of insults and, importantly, the lack of transparency and scrutiny. While I haven't been to Question Time in Canberra for some time, I was always struck by the amount of head-shaking as people vacated the public area, quite often in the disbelief Parliament actually operates in this way.

In New South Wales, schoolchildren from Year 5 make the journey to Canberra to see their Parliament in action and are quite shocked to learn about the typical behaviours on the floor of the House of Representatives. It's usually quite reprehensible and inhumane behaviour and if these schoolchildren were to replicate these acts on their return to school, they'd probably be handed long-term detentions or expulsion.

I'll admit it's not as severe as the Yugoslav Parliament in 1928, when the leader of the Croatian Peasant Party, Stjepan Radić, was assassinated on the floor of parliament, but it must come close in other ways.

Question Time, in theory, serves a defining purpose in democratic systems: it's an essential part of making governments accountable for their actions, and scrutinising their performances and policies.

In practice, it's a one-hour slug-fest session where the opposite occurs: questions of government are pushed aside, a highly partisan Speaker of the House heavily favours the government to ensure any scrutiny is deflected and bypassed; and a certain type of *rigor mortis* sets in for a bemused public.

Many democratic parliaments around the world hold some form of question time: in Canada, it's referred to as 'Question Period', the European Parliament holds 'Question Hour', New Zealand has 'Oral Questions'. The first recorded question to government in the British Westminster system occurred in 1721, but it didn't become a formal process until 1869. Question Time was also a feature of the Australian Parliament at the time of federation as an *ad hoc* arrangement and became a formal part of Parliament in 1962.

The public has lost trust in Australia's political system and sees Question Time as a futile waste of resources.

But it's a classic case of theory and practice colliding: Question Time should be an essential part of a parliamentary democracy but, in its current form, it's a total turn-off for the electorate—at least for those who are prepared to watch—and it's fuelling the public's distrust of Parliament, and heightening the disdain for partisan party-based politics.

The worst of Question Time was on display last week where, time and again, the government used the full arsenal of parliamentary weaponry against the Labor Opposition. So much that it seemed the entire frontbench was moving towards a collective hernia.

It was the last week of Parliament before the next federal election and, to me, it had the feel of 'last-shot-in-the-locker' for the government. And it really showed. On the four days of sittings this week, the government asked thirty-three questions to itself (the classic 'Dorothy Dix' questions), and all but four included clear and obvious references to border security and asylum seekers.

A question about the economy? Sure, but let me now show you how that relates to strong borders, asylum seekers and demonstrate how Labor is letting in rapists, murderers and paedophiles.

And the reasons for the government's focus on border security? Parliament had just passed the Migration Amendment (Urgent Medical Treatment) Bill, put forward by the crossbenchers, and agreed to by Labor. The Bill is nothing remarkable—it simply outlines the circumstances for providing desperately-needed medical services to refugees and asylum seekers on Manus Island and Nauru who require urgent medical care—but the government proceeded to misrepresent the legislation in every possible way.

The Prime Minister, Scott Morrison, led the attacks: "They may be a paedophile, they may be a rapist, they may be a murderer, and this Bill will mean that we would just have to take them. This is what will happen if Bill Shorten does not put national security ahead of his own political opportunism."

The Minister for Home Affairs, Peter Dutton, added: "Under the arrangements that Mr Shorten and The Greens passed, we have people that can come to our country from Manus or Nauru. People that have been charged with child sex offences. Child charged or allegations around serious offences including murder."

And if you missed the message, the Deputy Prime Minister, Michael McCormack, claimed the legislation will allow "spivs, and rapists and murderers" to be transferred to Australia for medical treatment, and Finance Minister, Mathias Cormann, claimed "rapists and paedophiles will still get a free pass into this country".

It was *ad infinitum*, but four days of constant harping and misrepresentation of border security? The Liberal–National Party perceive the issue to be their strongest point of attack against Labor, but it was evident after day four, the enthusiasm was starting to wane, and other events towards the end of the week became a distraction from their cause.

In a contest between border security and corruption, it's government corruption that's always going to pique the interest of the electorate, and so it proved to be towards the end of the parliamentary week.

First, some context. To say the government is on the nose would be an understatement. Since the last federal election in July 2016, it has been in electoral losing positions for 163 consecutive opinion polls.

It has been a seriously underperforming government. It has not been able to control the political agenda—or its own Members of Parliament—changed its leader again, when Scott Morrison replaced Malcolm Turnbull as prime minister in August 2018, and is lacking the ability to seriously prosecute any case for policy or legislative reform. And it also has the small matter of trying to function without having outright control of the Parliament.

For a government so bereft of policy initiatives, of course it was going to seize a small political opportunity on border security to provide a fillip for its MPs and offer some type of loose platform to launch a winning campaign strategy for the upcoming election.

But just as the media started pondering whether the tables had been finally turned on Labor and whether Morrison was going to lead the Coalition to an unlikely election victory—Napoleonic-style—along came the issues that have dogged this government since it first claimed office in September 2013: corruption.

Corruption is a practice that should be not tolerated by the public in any country in the world—nor should it be—and is rightly punished in democratic systems. It's the only real option available to the electorate, especially when they see a system that covers up and protects its own kind.

The final stages of the NSW Labor government during 2009–2011 were examples of self-interest, navel-gazing and extreme corruption in politics, and the electorate handed NSW Labor a severe punishment in 2011. At this election, NSW Labor was left with twenty of ninety seats in the Legislative Assembly, and 35.8 per cent of the two-party preferred vote. Subsequent to this election, Labor powerbrokers Eddie Obeid and Ian Macdonald were found guilty of attempting to steal up to $100 million of public assets through secretive water licence deals, and were sentenced to jail in 2016 and 2017, respectively. [Footnote: Ian Macdonald won an appeal in the NSW Court of Criminal Appeal and had his conviction quashed on 25 February 2019. He is likely to face a retrial.]

While the federal government has not engaged in the excesses of Obeid and Macdonald—as far as we know, although it's clear that something is not quite right with the landholdings of Barnaby Joyce in Narrabri—it has the same whiff of corruption and political favouritism as NSW Labor in the final stages of its government, has engaged in highly unethical practices and evaded the law.

Helloworld!

On Tuesday, there were revelations in the Senate Estimates Committee that Mathias Cormann had booked a family holiday to Singapore to the value of $2,780, but not paid for it. On face value, there's probably not that much to see here, but who gets to book an air flight, flies to the destination, and doesn't get charged for it? Not many people.

Cormann's problem was that he booked his holiday directly with Andrew Burnes, the CEO of Helloworld, the travel booking company that has received over $3 billion of federal contracts to provide all federal departmental travel, including politicians.

Andrew Burnes also happens to be the Treasurer of the federal Liberal Party, and it was Cormann's department that lobbied strongly to replace the multi-provider panel that previously provided federal departmental travel, with just one provider—Helloworld. This removed the competition and efficiencies that had previously existed with the multi-provider panel, and provided a major boost to the value of Helloworld, with its share price increasing after these contracts were awarded.

Helloworld is also a donor to the Liberal Party. The former Treasurer and now Australian Ambassador to the United States, Joe Hockey, also facilitated meetings between Helloworld and embassy staff to provide travel services between Australia and United States.

Hockey also owns shareholdings in Helloworld to the value of $1 million.

While it might not be up to the level of corruption shown by Obeid and Macdonald—as far as we know—the Helloworld saga drowned out the key messages on asylum seekers the government was pushing, and dovetailed into other actions that seem to be the key feature of this government: one rule for them, and totally different rules for everyone else.

How can it be that a senior minister of government can directly contact the CEO of an ASX-listed company, ask for services, and not be charged for it? What does the public think when the CEO of this ASX-listed company happens to be the Treasurer of the Liberal

Party, a recipient of large government contracts, a close friend of the Prime Minister, and donates to the Liberal Party? And what does the public think about the former Treasurer of Australia who smoothed the passage of the contracts for Helloworld and also owns $1 million worth of shares in that company?

If this isn't corruption, well, the laws need to be re-written, and the Australian Federal Police needs to start investigating properly.

And Helloworld isn't the worst of it.

There are other events where Liberal Party MPs simply don't understand the duties of public service and behave as if their only duty in Parliament is to self-enrich themselves and offer access to benefactors of the Liberal Party and corporate friends.

Cash oversteps the mark

Senator Michaelia Cash has doggedly searched for a nefarious link between GetUp! donations of $100,000 to Labor candidates, at the time when Opposition Leader Bill Shorten headed the Australian Workers' Union—in 2006.

The AWU has stated all monies have been documented and accounted for, the donations were approved by the AWU executive, and has consistently claimed the pursuit of any malfeasance is a politically-motivated witchhunt by Senator Cash, more than twelve years after the donations were made. It's a very obvious case of a minister unable to find any wrong doing, but then deciding on political options to destroy the reputation of an opponent.

In October 2017, raids on the offices of the AWU were performed by the Australian Federal Police. The media was also tipped off, ensuring maximum television coverage and maximum political damage to Shorten, the AWU, and the Labor Party.

But as with most politically-motivated actions, there was a high level of overkill, and the pursuit by Cash has backfired and produced ongoing political problems for the government.

We've since discovered Cash's advisor at the time, David de Garis, was the one who tipped off the media and admitted in the Federal Court his actions were primarily to damage Bill Shorten's reputation. He also revealed he shared this information with Michael Tetlow, the media advisor for former Minister for Justice, Michael Keenan. Keenan has denied all knowledge of this information, as has Cash.

Both Cash and Keenan have refused to provide statements to the AFP, and the fact that they haven't been forced to resign by Scott Morrison is a sign of how low parliamentary standards have fallen.

Why has the AFP not pursued Cash and Keenan in the same way they pursued documents from the offices of the AWU? Why has the Federal Court instructed de Garis to give evidence, and not Cash and Keenan?

The Deputy Commissioner of the AFP, Leanne Close, agrees "a *prima facie* case that a conviction could be recorded beyond reasonable doubt" if Cash and Keenan provided statements to the police. The AFP has asked Cash and Keenan to provide evidence twice. Why have they not pursued this matter further?

Unanswered questions

There are questions about other contracts and arrangements made by the government. It was revealed security contractor Paladin was awarded $423 million in a select tender to manage the Nauru immigration detention centre. Paladin also has strong connections to the Liberal Party, and it has been difficult to scrutinise how this money is to be spent and which services it is being spent on. Reports from asylum seekers on Nauru, as well as from refugees advocates, suggest very few services are being provided on security and it's difficult to ascertain how this $423 million is being used.

The money trail for Paladin's activities on Nauru, as well as Manus Island, are difficult to track and the avenues for corruption here with the involvement of the Papua New Guinea and Nauru governments go far and wide.

The Great Barrier Reef Foundation was granted $444 million in 2018, following a clandestine meeting between former Prime Minister, Malcolm Turnbull, then Environment Minister, Josh Frydenberg and executives from GBRF. The meeting was not requested by the GBRF, but we've since discovered there are several links back to the Liberal Party.

Last week, a Senate Environment & Communications References Committee inquiry report, *Great Barrier Reef 2050 Partnership Program*, found the granting of this money was a highly irresponsible and "off-the-cuff" decision, "hastily concocted by relevant ministers, without proper consideration of risks and potential effectiveness, no consultation with key stakeholders, and without having undertaken due diligence". The Committee also recommended the termination of the Foundation Partnership and all unspent funds returned to the Commonwealth.

Franking credits fiasco

Liberal Party backbencher, Tim Wilson, is the chair of the House of Representatives economics committee, and recently held a series of four roadshows in the eastern states to rail against Labor's policy to remove franking credits, in those instances where no tax has been paid.

Aside from the exorbitant cost of $160,000 to go through the unusual process of an inquiry into opposition policy—which, of course, was purely a campaign to misrepresent and smear the policy—Wilson failed to disclose his shareholdings in Wilson Asset Management, a company owned by a cousin, and a company that contributed to the cost of the inquiry website.

He also used official Commonwealth insignia on the inquiry website (against Commonwealth rules on the use of the insignia), and used one of the forums to fundraise for the Liberal Party, as well as distribute Liberal Party membership forms.

And the reprimand provided for a clear breaking of rules and convention?

The Speaker of the House, Tony Smith, criticised Wilson for breaking convention and acknowledged there was "potential for interference" but said there was a significant hurdle to establish any contempt of Parliament, and then let the matter slide.

Different rules for different people? Yes, that is most evident. And do conventions matter? To the Liberal Party, apparently not.

There are too many examples where the Liberal–National Party, desperate in its quest to win a mostly undeserved third term, has engaged in corrupt practices, stretched the rules to suit themselves, used the powers of Parliament to cover up their actions, or simply hope that time will make problems disappear.

Once such case is Assistant Treasurer, Stuart Robert, who incurred home internet costs of $37,975 over eighteen months. He simply paid the money back, rode out the storm for a month, and no further questions or investigations have been made. It's a pity the former Speaker of the House, Peter Slipper, wasn't allowed to pay back the $954 he allegedly used dishonestly in 2010, was forced to resign, and subsequently convicted.

Again, different rules for Liberal Party members. Slipper had his conviction overturned in 2015, but the damage had already been done.

No stone is left unturned in the quest to find an undeserved and unethical electoral advantage. And there is no end in sight.

Just yesterday, the Liberal Party preselected candidate in the South Australian seat of Mayo, Georgina Downer, provided a large $127,373 novelty cheque with a photograph of her face and the Liberal Party logo, to the Yankalilla Bowling Club. The problem for Downer is she is not the local member and, as the election hasn't been called, doesn't even have status as a candidate.

Members of Parliament are solely responsible for announcing funding allocations, and Centre Alliance MP Rebekha Sharkie is the one who assisted the bowling club secure the grant: Downer had nothing to do with it. Labor has referred the matter to the Auditor-General for further investigation to see if any Australian Electoral Commission rules have been broken.

Politics, of course, seeks advantages at all opportunities, but there are limits to how these advantages are obtained. If the electorate considers there is corruption involved in obtaining these advantages, or feels they've been taken for a ride, the candidate and their party, will lose the votes they so desperately seek.

Bill Shorten has already announced if Labor is to form government at the next election, the first agenda item for its proposed federal integrity commission will be exploring the links between Helloworld and the Liberal Party. It's sure to uncover a great deal more than is simmering at the surface.

Newspoll

Much has been reported about the recent Ipsos poll, which showed a narrowing of the polls, but the latest Newspoll is showing the Liberal–National Party is still further behind Labor on a two-party preferred basis, at 53/47 per cent. This the same result as the previous two Newpoll surveys.

Given the poor performance of the government during this term, and the reports of ongoing scandals within its ranks, it's not difficult to see why there is a shift away from the LNP. Certainly, the government would have hoped the noise generated by the Migration Amendment Bill in Parliament would have had some effect on opinion polls, but once the electorate follows the stench of corruption and sees where it's coming from, it's difficult to wave it away.

Corruption, the cardinal and the fine art of lying

12 March 2019

Eddy Jokovich + David Lewis / Podcast

In this episode, we looked at the continuing crisis of corruption in the government; Pell-mal and how the conservative media is supporting a distressed cardinal; and the art of lying in politics: had the government been spinning far too much for its own good? And in this episode, David Lewis appears as a *Cosmopolitan* centrefold and glamorous cat burglar.

Eddy Jokovich: Parliament is almost over for this term of office, which means there will be no more scrutiny on this government before the next election, expected to be called within the next three months. There has been a wave of retirements from the government: this time, we're saying goodbye to Julie Bishop, Christopher Pyne, Steve Ciobo, and there are rumours of more to follow. The 'sinking ship' analogy keeps cropping up, where the scandals keep coming for the government, and there's an eye-rolling moment that appears almost every single day. There are now so many scandals, it's hard to know where to begin: we've had scandals in 'Helloworld', Paladin, the Great Barrier Reef Foundation, Australian Federal Police and Michaelia Cash, and the stacking of government department boards. Is this normal behaviour for a government at this point of the electoral cycle?

David Lewis: Clearly not. For a government that is convinced it's going to win the next election, or at least it says it's convinced it's going to win, they're not doing very much about these issues. The Helloworld scandal—involving free personal travel tickets for ministers from a business that has government tenders and Liberal operatives with its ownership—which compromised our US Ambassador, Joe Hockey, whose it was said by Helloworld chief executive Andrew Burnes, to have 'owed him a favour'. But what type of diplomat owes favours, and grubby favours like that? The free trips provided to Mathias Cormann: it was just a bad idea. Even if it was a genuine error, in that Helloworld had 'forgotten' to charge him for the tickets, you can't get a plane ticket under normal circumstances without the money being cleared. This is smart business sense and smart security sense but, whatever the case was, this is still not a good look.

EJ: Andrew Burnes is the Treasurer of the federal Liberal Party, and it's not a case where this issue just stops at one specific free ticket to a minister—Joe Hockey also has $1 million worth of shares in the Helloworld company.

DL: It's incredible—Menzies, Deakin, Fraser and all of the leaders of the Liberal Party who have since passed on would be spinning in their graves at this level of corruption.

EJ: It's a difficult set of events to comprehend: Helloworld has received $3 billion in contracts from the federal government for air travel services to government MPs and affiliated people from government departments. Helloworld is now the sole provider for air travel management to government, and they replaced a multi-provider panel in 2014, soon after the Abbott government was elected. Generally, a multi-provider panel for government services means there's a number of different companies competing for government contracts and business but, for air travel service and accommodation, that was scrapped by the Liberal government, and replaced by Helloworld. If a multi-provider panel is replaced with just the one provider—as always happens in these cases—competition is reduced and prices go up. And, in this case, a monopoly has been created for friends of the Liberal Party, paid for by the government, and taxpayers' money.

DL: It's the usual scam: the government privatised the green slip system for cars in New South Wales; privatised electricity services. After privatisation, prices go down very quickly in the short-term, and then they shoot up after that: Woolworths and Coles engage in the same type of practice. It's fair to say Helloworld have received a massive windfall in the past, and will be looking at massive windfalls in the future.

EJ: The Helloworld issue took up media space for several days— once the information about these issues comes out, some in the electorate can barely believe it, and they think: 'how on earth could this actually happened?' And the corruption didn't stop there: there was the Paladin company, a company providing security services in Australian immigration detention centres in Nauru and Manus Island. Putting aside the ethical and moral issues related to immigration detention, let's look at Paladin. They were awarded a $423 million contract through a select, non-competitive tender, a situation where a government department can go directly to a particular company and instruct: 'this is what we want done, this is the amount of money, go ahead and do the job'. Select tendering is usually for smaller amounts of between $10,000 and $20,000 for specialised services that need to be completed quickly, but $423 million? This is a sizable amount, and the cash trail in the contract with Paladin is very difficult to follow. Locals are suggesting Paladin does very little on those islands, and it's hard for them to see where these funds have been spent.

DL: The money certainly hasn't been spent on wages: staff on Manus Island went on strike because they were being underpaid.

EJ: An anti-corruption commission set up in the future could look at some of those factors, such as the $423 million contract for Paladin. There's also another issue to be inspected—it was almost one year ago, but there's the $444 million funding provided to the Great Barrier Reef Foundation: in that case, there wasn't even a tender, and the Foundation didn't even ask for the money. There was also a recent Senate report which severely admonished the government for its poor behaviour, and they instructed the Great Barrier Reef Foundation to return any unspent money back to the Commonwealth Government. That report was prepared by a bipartisan committee and they were completely astonished the government could actually simply hand out such a large amount of money without any oversight. $10,000, $20,000, $30,000 or even $50,000: sometimes it is possible for government departments to just hand out those amounts of money to a suitable tenderer but, in this case, $444 million without scrutiny is astronomical.

DL: And it's not appropriate. It's not as though the Foundation is a group of scientists or biologists, or reef specialists: it's a small group of unknowns who happened to have links and relationships with the Liberal Party. I don't know what the Great Barrier Reef Foundation is supposed to achieve, or how it's meant to achieve it—it's very unclear.

EJ: There has also been the stacking of government boards quite recently. The Attorney–General, Christian Porter, has made thirty-four new appointments and they are all former Liberal Party MPs, Liberal Party members or affiliates of the Liberal Party. In some cases, it's people that have missed out on Liberal Party preselection in the upcoming federal election, such as Jane Bell; she wasn't preselected in the Victoria seat of Higgins, so she's been appointed to the Administrative Appeals Tribunal as a consolation prize. Governments need good quality personnel in these positions, good qualified people—and I'm sure in most cases they are—but all appointees are from the Liberal Party, and having the positions skewed to one side of politics is not good for the public service.

DL: Both sides of politics reward favours of friends, but there's a way of doing it, and governments should be sure their decision-making process is absolutely watertight. For example, the position of UK High Commissioner should not have been given to George Brandis, just because he's pouting that he missed out on a more senior position in government. He's not appropriate for the position; he hasn't impressed in the role. He hasn't performed as poorly as some people were expecting, but he's not an outstanding High Commissioner by any standard.

Christian Porter's own appointment as Attorney–General bemuses me. There is a hierarchy in the law that's probably not understood by those outside the law, where there's a set of unwritten rules about where you stand as a lawyer within the system, and judges can pretty much come from anywhere within that system. But if you are appointed to a judiciary position, you have to have a certain amount of experience, a certain amount of legal knowledge, life experience, and a certain amount of qualification. But you also have your place in the hierarchy. And for Christian Porter, a lawyer, to subvert these processes, just seems insane.

EJ: Appointments made in the final six months of a parliamentary term: that's what governments usually do in the lead-up to an election, where they are never too sure if they will win or lose the election. In these cases, they stack government boards with like-minded people from their own political party. But this extreme level of stacking of the boards suggests the Liberal–National Party itself doesn't think they've got much chance of winning the next election.

DL: This is the behaviour of a government that strongly suspects it is going to lose: ministers resigning, the stacking of government boards. However, we know that since the 2007 election, the political rules have changed and what seemed to be obvious before that time, is not so obvious today. There is every indication the government is facing a massive election loss, but that doesn't mean they necessarily will lose.

EJ: The evidence for an election loss is there though, and it has been there for some time. The Liberal–National government has actually lost 164 consecutive opinion polls since August 2016, and that's not a good sign for a government at the end of the term and needing to hold an election before May 2019. And more recently, the Newspoll is showing the government actually slipping behind even further. These figures are within the statistical margin of error, but for some time, Newspoll has been consistently showing a two-party-preferred vote of 53 per cent to 47 per cent to the Liberal–National Party, but the most recent Newspoll slipped away down to 46 per cent. Voting swings are never consistent on election day, but these figures suggest a win of ninety seats for Labor, and around fifty seats for Liberal–National. That's what you'd call a wipeout.

DL: Losses in 164 consecutive opinion polls: that is unprecedented, but Newspoll does tend to skew more conservatively, so there might be other factors at play here. One interesting factor is disenchanted Liberal voters aren't siphoning off to the Australian Conservatives or to One Nation, which is where you'd expect those disaffected Liberal voters to go to. But they're not going to the Greens either, so something else is going on here, which is hard to pick-up, and this might result in election-day voting that's a little bit different to the published opinion polls.

*

George Pell's final parting of the waves and how the conservative media has come to the rescue

EJ: The biggest news of the week wasn't even the most recent news. George Pell was found guilty of child sexual assault: the verdict was handed down in December 2018, but due to strict media suppression laws, it couldn't be reported until a second trial of child sexual abuse against George Pell was completed. That trial was dropped last week by the public prosecutor in Victoria, which meant the suppression order from the first case was lifted. The acts committed by Pell are atrocious: child sexual assault is a serious crime and usually results in a lifetime of psychological trauma for victims, including mental health problems, drug abuse and high suicide rates. These are not the "vanilla crimes" that Pell's barrister has suggested. What has been intriguing, however, has been the parting of the waves along political lines, the 'tin ears' from the many supporters of George Pell, including John Howard, Tony Abbott, Andrew Bolt, Gerard Henderson, Joe Hildebrand, Craig Kelly and Frank Brennan. The Archbishop of Sydney, Anthony Fisher, said we shouldn't be too quick to judge George Pell. Well, it's a little bit too late for that because he has already been tried by a jury in a Court of law and he has been found guilty.

DL: These are the same people, mostly, who complain about jails existing as four-star hotels; that we have a soft judiciary that lets criminals off, who are now saying the judiciary is too hard and jail is a terrible punishment. John Howard writing a reference after the decision had been made, that surprised me—he's normally not so tin-eared. Tony Abbott: his response didn't surprise me, neither did Andrew Bolt, or most of the others who supported Pell. The Archbishop of Adelaide, who claimed Catholic schools didn't need to apply for working with children checks—even though his predecessor had been concealing child sexual abuse—that schools should sort out those issues themselves, was perhaps the most tin-eared response, in a week filled with clangers.

EJ: It is understandable for people to show their support for a convicted criminal, irrespective of how heinous that crime might be. Those actions are a part of the Catholic and Christian ethos, to show support for those that have sinned and on some level, that's understood. But there's much more playing out here politically, and support for Pell has come from conservatives within the media. Not only have these interests come out to support Pell, they've gone one step further and claimed his innocence, and completely trashed an adjudication from a Court of law. But we can see the links here: George Pell was the guest of honour at the 75th anniversary of the Institute of Public Affairs in 2013: the master of ceremonies at that event was Andrew Bolt, and also in attendance were Rupert Murdoch, Gina Rinehart, Tony Abbott, Hugh Morgan: rich and powerful people. Whatever happened to the Christian ethic of 'the meek shall inherit the earth'? It's a big part of the New Testament.

DL: This is not widely known but Rupert Murdoch is a Catholic knight: he's not Catholic, and this is a very unusual. Papal knighthoods are usually provided for service to the church, and Murdoch donated $10 million to the Catholic church in the late 1990s. The conservative split in support for George Pell seems to be those who are associated with Rupert Murdoch and News Corp, in one way or another, and those who are not. The broadcaster Ray Hadley was highly critical of Tony Abbott, a regular guest on Hadley's talkback radio show, and of John Howard for coming out in support of George Pell—now a convicted pedophile. Ray Hadley: he's not a dangerous leftist, or even a moderate leftist; he's very much on the hard right of politics. So there's a split there that many people in the media haven't quite noticed yet: I haven't seen any non-News Corp-affiliated conservatives come out in favour of George Pell.

EJ: There is also the doctrine of the split between the church and the state—it goes all the way back to the Reformation, and it's a political practice that protects both the church and the state. It appeared in 1791 in the United States Constitution and this separation is a hallmark of most democracies. This separation is there for very good reasons, but the Western Australian Young Liberals, a highly conservative part of the main Liberal Party, have come out to say politics is 'quiet on religion' and that factor needs to change. It's a good idea to separate the church from the state—the main reason why we're having these political issues today with George Pell and the support from conservative leaders and the media is they're doing their best to dilute that link between the church and the state.

DL: This is not a good development. The Australian Constitution was written by people who had a Christian faith but understood Christian faith was a personal matter that shouldn't intrude on public life, except perhaps in the terms of shaping ethical approaches to policy. The Prime Minister in the early 1900s, Alfred Deakin was a spiritualist and not Christian at all: he thought humans had evolved past Christianity and into something higher. Bob Hawke declared Australia as a secular state in 1983. We have freedom of religion: citizens can have any spiritual belief they want to hold, provided it doesn't undermine the laws of Australia. Dietary restrictions or worshiping restrictions that don't impinge on the rights of others are more than welcome, and people can even have opinions on the righteousness or fallibility of other religions: this is how it should be in an open democracy. Political leaders should not be seeking to turn Australia towards being a more Christian country, or a more Muslim country, or Jewish, or Hindu, or any other religion, because that's not how a democracy functions. Democracy has room for everybody: yes, politicians can shape their political beliefs based on their spiritual beliefs to provide an ethical and moral structure, but they cannot make their religion superior to anybody else's.

EJ: George Pell has been convicted by a Court of law and, as is his legal right, he has appealed the decision, but this first has to be accepted by the Court of Appeal. There is some way to go in this case but, essentially, George Pell is currently a convicted criminal and convicted pedophile. This is a big moment for the Catholic church in Australia, and it follows the sexual scandals that have appeared in almost every country in the world, wherever the Catholic church has a presence. There have been major investigations in the United States and in Ireland; there's been sexual slavery of nuns in France; sexual abuse of young children in many parts of the world. Yet the conservative media—mainly the Murdoch media—wants the public to forget about these misdemeanours. It's almost a case of not forgiving the former Prime Minister, Julia Gillard, for her role in setting up the Royal Commission into institutional child sexual abuse in 2012: George Pell's conviction is a culmination and almost the end point of that Royal Commission.

DL: The hatred these conservative men, and some women, have for Julia Gillard is palpable. Gillard wasn't one of the greatest prime ministers this country has had: but she was reasonable, and if she had been allowed to do more during her tenure, she may well have become a great prime minister. She is an important prime minister, not just because she's a woman, although that is a big part of it, but she had a very successful legislative program, in terms of what she managed to achieve. And even if she had achieved nothing else, this Royal Commission was absolutely vital into opening up some of the dirty little secrets of Australian society.

*

The fine art of lying and truth in politics

EJ: Politics is based on the fine art of lying or evading the truth and there's a number of reasons for this: to keep opponents at bay, and to play games with the media. Being truthful invites too many problems and too many questions, and makes the life of a politician far too difficult. But there's an art to the lie in politics: it's usually well disguised and based on spurious evidence, or comes from a made-up 'fact' produced by a friendly think tank but, as bad as that process is, that has almost been superseded in politics. We've arrived at an age in politics where the outright lie has become the friend of the idiot king: Donald Trump in the US; Nigel Farage in the United Kingdom during the Brexit campaign; and, increasingly in Australian politics, barefaced lies have been coming from the mouth of Prime Minister Scott Morrison and Treasurer Josh Frydenberg. Trust in politics; trust in the banks; trust in the clergy has fallen. The public understands politicians stretch the truth, and that's part of the job, but have we almost reached the point where the scale of the lie and the egregious nature of the lie is no longer an issue?

DL: Certainly in the 2016 Brexit referendum, there were exaggerations coming from all sides. The European Union isn't an organisation that has never got anything wrong, but the 'remain' side campaigned as though the EU was perfect. There were outright lies in the 'leave' campaign, pushing the idea Britain would gain complete control back of its legislative processes and be able to trade with the rest of the world, even though Britain never lost control of its legislative process, and already trades with the rest of the world. Donald Trump in the US: the CNN network calculated that Trump has told over 4,000 outright lies since he became President—and how many of those were just to Melania! Every time Trump opens his mouth, a lie comes out. Of course, politicians might deliberately obfuscate and sometimes events can change so quickly that what seemed to be the truth at the time of the statement, actually turned out not to be the truth. In those situations, generally, politicians have to accept what they said was a lie and they have to work their way around it. It would be interesting to count the amount of lies Home Affairs Minister Peter Dutton has made regarding asylum seekers. Certainly, the idea asylum seekers who come to Australia will displace Australians from hospital waiting lists is a lie. He claimed there were no refugee children on the island of Nauru—except for those who were still there—so, there's another outright lie. Josh Frydenberg: we're still trying to work out whether he just doesn't understand economics or whether he tells bald-faced lies, but in his case, it might be more of the former.

EJ: More recently, Josh Frydenberg was admonished by the Treasury department for continuing to claim that under Labor's negative gearing policy—which restricts tax benefits to new housing only and increases the levels of capital gains tax—housing prices would fall and rents would go up. Treasury has announced this is not their advice at all, and although Frydenberg was presented with those facts and presented with the information from Treasury, he just kept on ignoring that advice and kept repeating his own factually incorrect information.

DL: Just because Treasury has provided information, it shouldn't be just accepted on face value but Treasury tends to be able to back up most of their claims with very well-researched facts, figures and analysis. We are in a very strange period of politics, where outright lies and obvious misinformation is reported as fact and we can see the shadowy figure of Rupert Murdoch as a part of this. News Corp newspapers report and repeat these lies, and in Australia where conservative interests own 90 per cent of the media, this material is repeated without much analysis and very little criticism.

EJ: There was one exchange which piqued my interest recently, and that was between Barrie Cassidy from ABC's *Insiders* program and the Minister for Energy, Angus Taylor.

> Barrie Cassidy: Emissions are up over the last five years, not down.
> Angus Taylor: Well, actually, the latest greenhouse gas report that came out last week says that emissions are down by over 1 per cent in the electricity sector, which—
> BC: No, no—
> AT: That's in my area—
> BC: They're up by 1 per cent on every—
> AT: No, no, no, no, no, no: you're wrong Barrie. And a report came out last week saying they are coming down and...
> BC: ...but this is the Energy Department report?...
> AT: No, this is the Greenhouse Gas Inventory Report, they are coming down and the department rightly believes

they're going to continue to go down and the result of this is we will reach not just our Kyoto targets—and we're still in the Kyoto period—we will reach our Paris targets.

BC: Are you talking about total emissions across the economy?

AT: Total emissions are coming down—

BC: They're up by 0.9 per cent over the year!

AT: ...in the last quarter, they've come down one and a half per cent—

BC: No, not a quarter: over the year, they're up by 0.9 per cent, and they have increased every year for the last five years!

AT: Well, they are coming down right now, Barrie. And if we go right back when we got in into government—

BC: That's not what they're saying at all.

AT: Well, I'm telling you what the figures were from the report that came out last week, and you should have a read of that report because 1.4 per cent down, three-and-a-half per cent down in the electricity sector—

BC: You're relying on one quarter, where for the last five years, the figures have shown an increase!

AT: ...hang on Barrie, let's go back and look at the extended period of time when we got in together...

EJ: In that exchange, Angus Taylor was referring to the quarterly update to the National Greenhouse Gas Inventory: I've looked through this document and I must say, it reads like a very politicised report, and provides very spurious evidence. The report comes from a government agency, of course, but as is the case with so many items prepared by this government, it's highly political and created to favour the government. Taylor claimed emissions had decreased across the board: this is not true at all. The report stated emission levels had decreased by 1.4 per cent relative to the previous quarter on a "seasonally-adjusted and weather-normalised basis"—who would ever be able to understand what that could mean? And, whatever that statistic does mean, it's only within the electricity sector over the past quarter. Taylor has engaged in that classic political process where a politician cherry-picks a small skerrick of information, but in his case, he then magnified that information to make it apply to absolutely everything. Angus Taylor got that material totally wrong, but he was persistent: he kept on repeating "emissions have gone down". That's one tactic Taylor has been using, but it's across the entire ministry: he keeps repeating the lie, and Scott Morrison is claiming it as well, as are Michael McCormack, Barnaby Joyce; even though the information is completely wrong.

DL: It's a strategy to destabilise the discussion and swing any negative into a positive for the government. There's that quote attributed to the Nazi Joseph Goebbels: "if you tell a lie big enough and keep repeating it, people will eventually come to believe it". And then there's George Costanza from *Seinfeld*: "it's not a lie if you truly believe it"; and it feels like Australia is being run by a bunch of George Costanzas who want to be like Joseph Goebbels.

EJ: The classic media strategy for a politician is to have the three talking points developed and sticking to them rigidly, and whenever the conversation strays away, a politician will drag themselves stubbornly back to those three points. And those are the three strategic points that magnify and amplify the political points the politician wants to emphasise. But the strategy now includes inserting the greatest lies as part of the mix, and that's a serious problem.

DL: These outright lies always come back to bite you: I'm not quite sure what the logic is. I realise that ultimately it's the strategy of trying to hold on to power at all costs but it comes a point where political leaders just have to either give up on this strategy and do the actual work of government until the election, instead of all this infantile obfuscation. Start telling the truth, and maybe the electorate will come around to their line of thinking.

EJ: There is that old adage about lies, damn lies, and then there are statistics. But we've been taken to another level of hysterical lies. We have government ministers such as Peter Dutton coming out to claim refugees are "stealing our hospital beds"—it's almost reached a level where Dutton will soon be accusing refugees and asylum seekers of stealing yogurt from people's kitchens and putting the empty container back into the fridge: it's like a pantomime act. Scott Morrison is claiming Australia will reach Paris climate agreement targets by 2030 "in a canter", another lie—factually incorrect. More recently, we've had the Deputy Prime Minister, Michael McCormack, claiming that if Labor's 45 per cent emissions reduction target is met by 2030, there won't be any more night-time cricket or Friday night football. This follows on from the claptrap talk from Barnaby Joyce about the cost of roasts skyrocketing to $100 and the city of Whyalla completely disappearing off the map because of Labor's carbon tax. It's absolutely incorrect, and it's obviously ridiculous. But, it seems to work politically, perhaps it works on a subconscious level.

DL: At a time when there are so many people using Twitter, Facebook, Reddit and other social media, it's easy to be called out. And it's not even the opposition leading this: many people in the electorate are coming out to debunk the myths. Information is no longer controlled, and pretty much anything a politician says can be checked in real time, debunked in real time, and used against them in real time.

EJ: For the political lie to work effectively, there has to be an element of believability to it, and there isn't much believability going on in this government. Perhaps their strategy is to go totally over the top and hope no one in the electorate will notice the lie and perhaps the political thinking is that the government hasn't got too much to lose under this type of strategy.

DL: It's the strategy of a continual random scattergun, in the hope that something will eventually stick, but I'm not sure if the government will be able to turn around their fortunes of being behind in 164 consecutive opinion polls. At this point, the Liberals would be trying to save as many seats and hold out vague hope for an election win. And there are problems for the state Liberals in New South Wales, where Premier Gladys Berejiklian will soon face the voters. And continuing from the federal sphere, we've had all kinds of lies thrown up in state politics.

EJ: There was the state leaders' debate last Friday night between Berejiklian and NSW Labor leader, Michael Daley. During that 30-minute leaders' debate, Gladys Berejiklian accused Michael

Daley of lying no less than sixteen times. In the post-debate assessment, analysts were suggesting Berejiklian repeated this too many times: the public understand politicians tell lies. It was an incredibly disruptive process and to continuously accuse your opponent of lying when in fact you're doing it yourself is counterproductive.

DL: Ask the people of the inner west suburbs of Haberfield or Erskineville, where the WestConnex tunnel is going through, what they think about the truth-telling capabilities of the current New South Wales Liberal Party. Sydney is not impressed with all the unfinished construction work that's going on everywhere, most of it running over time, and over budget. And then there was the attack by Gladys Berejiklian on a *Newcastle Herald* journalist, for simply asking a question about unfinished tram projects in the heart of Newcastle. That was a complete overreaction.

EJ: That's the behaviour of a government that's under severe pressure. They were probably expecting to romp home in the NSW election, but it hasn't turned out the way they were expecting. There are predictions of a hung parliament and or a slim majority for the Liberal Party, but we'll certainly find out on March 23.

*

Music in this episode
A Whisper, Coldplay
Would I Lie To You, Eurythmics

The evil crimes of George Pell

14 March 2019

Eddy Jokovich

George Pell has been sentenced to jail for a total of six years, after being found guilty of five charges—one offence of sexual penetration of a child under sixteen years and four offences of committing an indecent act on a child under sixteen years.

The sentencing remarks by Chief Judge Peter Kidd were lengthy and considered and, while Pell could have been incarcerated for up to ten years, Kidd decided to strike a balance, taking into account Pell's advanced age and medical condition.

Is six years long enough?

Pell will be eligible for parole after three years and eight months, and many are suggesting this is not sufficient, in account of the nature of the crimes, the position Pell had within the Catholic church, and his actions during the Melbourne Response, where he was more determined to protect the church from liability and limit damages payouts, than seek any meaningful retribution and rehabilitation for victims.

It's always difficult to find the right balance in sentencing: child sexual assault is a serious crime and usually results in a lifetime of psychological trauma for victims, future mental health problems, drug abuse, and high suicide rates.

Because of this, punishments need to be severe, but my solution is more extreme and has nothing to do with Pell. Sure, it's absolutely fantastic that he's been sentenced to jail for at least three years and eight months, and it was important that he be punished for his crimes, and as a deterrent to others. But what more could be done? We'll get to that soon.

My Catholic schooling

My own Catholic experience is instructive. I attended a Catholic boys school on the edge of the Perth CBD for nine years and, undoubtedly, these were the worst years of my life. The first few weeks were spent becoming accustomed to the aura of the new school but, after this, it was all downhill.

My first hideous experience occurred within a few weeks. I was in Grade 4 at the tender age of eight, when a relief teacher, Brother Greene, decided discipline was best administered not by just throwing a chair at me, but the table as well. Greene was dark-haired, tall, incredibly strict, and wore the traditional buttoned cassock, a black ankle-length garment, typically worn by the more conservative brothers. To an eight-year-old boy, he was an offensive and repugnant sight. My crime? Talking in class, but for someone ill-equipped to teaching young students, it was the only method of discipline Greene knew of.

There's a host of many other acts perpetrated by others in the religious cloth: a blackboard duster thrown point-blank which hit me just above the eye.

A leather strap with a solid lead implant, six times on each hand, which left my fingers swollen and bruised for a week, and impossible to close. Administered by Brother McMaster, he even had the gall to utter that old-fashioned cliché: "This is going to hurt me more than it hurts you". Somehow, I doubted that very much.

A cricket bat swung onto my backside, four times, with so much pain I had to sit on the edge of the chair for the rest of day and walk with a limp to get home.

And then there were the psycho-sadistic sexual punishments. As punishment for whatever the misdemeanour might be, bending over to receive a swinging leather strap on the buttocks, sometimes with pants dropped, and on one occasion, the underpants as well, to inflict the pain but extend the humiliation. And provide some sexual gratification for the teacher instigating the punishment.

A different Brother Green (that's "Greene" without the "e") smashed his left hand into my jaw at lunch, for dropping a football onto the grass ground seconds before the regulation play bell allowed. I was only eleven at the time, but it was the first time I'd ever seen stars from a hit, and my jaw, probably dislocated, hurt for about two weeks. Over forty years later, I still find it difficult to close my jaw without discomfort.

These are some of the worst of the experiences I can recall (there were many others), but for nine long years, psychological humiliation and physical punishment seemed like a regular event and, with no one to talk to about it for fear of further retribution, it's a lot for a young child to hold in and comprehend why it's happening.

Obviously, these are not normal behaviours for any person in a position of authority at any school. These people were brutal animals and while I can accept that not all were like this, many were. If any of these acts were carried out today at any school throughout Australia, a common assault charge would be lodged, with a likely suspension, sacking or even jail time. But the times were different then.

The 'calling'

As painful and psychologically damaging these incidents were, among the many others during my nine years at this Catholic school, the most distressing was during 'pastoral guidance' with the school priest, Father Paul Kyte.

Father Paul had an avuncular look to him and spoke in well-mannered and deep dulcet tones. Grey haired and bespectacled, he seemed innocuous, and the guidance session took place in his small office room, with two lounge chairs adjacent to each other. After buttering up the conversation with small talk and how my school subjects were going, he rested his hand on my knee, moved his hand towards my groin and asked: "have you had the calling?".

As a twelve-year old, I had no idea what to expect or what to do. I was petrified and can still smell the pungent priestly aftershave and cigarette breath of Father Paul, as he retracted his hand, levered on my knee to get up from his chair, and turned around to get two glasses of water. What was going to happen next?

While he had his back turned, I got up and left the room and, as it was class time, went to the toilet block and hid in a cubicle until the lunch bell. Was Father Paul going to come looking for me? Is he going to tell anyone? Will I get into even more trouble?

After the lunch bell, I left the cubicle, still unsure about what to do, but the daily angst about running into Father Paul receded by the day, and the only times I ever saw him again was from a distance behind a pew at the regular school mass. I never spoke to Father Paul ever again.

Years of psychological and physical trauma takes it toll and, for sure, I wasn't sexually abused like so many others at the hands of the Catholic church. But I came close.

What happened to other students in that room with Father Paul during the 'pastoral guidance' sessions? He was a priest at the school for many years. How many other students did he ask about 'having the calling'?

Why was old Brother Collopy so keen to assist the Grade 4 boys change into their swimmers during swimming carnivals? I still recollect the gleeful look on his face helping young kids get undressed and slowly pulling up their swimmers, just to extend his ogling time.

Why were so many priests and brothers keen to cram into the change rooms after a football game, win, lose or draw? It makes sense now: it was to check out the nude adolescent bodies, to catch glimpses of well-formed penises, to salve their lust of seeing hot water and steam run over the young skin of naked teenaged boys. In the pre-internet age, it was their version of free downloadable pornography.

One of those who was a frequent visitor during the after-game 'celebrations' was Brother Daniel McMahon. While I was researching a story about child sexual abuse many years ago, I uncovered some details about McMahon, and discovered he'd been accused of child sexual abuse, molestation and rape, yet over a 20-year teaching career, was moved from school to school, despite a number of reports made to those schools at the time.

He was finally moved as far away as possible, over to Tasmania, where he was hidden away in the seminary, and was even upgraded to priest status. Despite the many allegations, nothing was ever done about McMahon and he died in 2012.

Clearly, there was something very wrong in many Catholic schools and over a long period of time. These were God's people, but they were doing the work of the Devil.

Cover ups and obfuscation

It's one thing to accept there's something wrong, but for many years, the Catholic church engaged in cover up, moved priests and brothers to other locations when problems arose, and sought to deny any wrongdoing.

This was a process the Catholic churched engaged regularly, not just in Western Australia or Victoria, but worldwide. I often wondered why a brother would appear at the school for one or two terms, but then disappear and never to be heard of again. After the evidence presented during the Royal Commission into Institutional Responses to Child Sexual Abuse, we now know why. Offending priests and brothers were simply moved from parish to parish, or from school to school, where they could continue their abuse.

Whenever there's any reporting in the media about a Catholic priest or brother being sentenced for child sexual abuse—which has become more prevalent in recent years—my anxiety levels always increase.

I watched most of the live broadcasts from the Royal Commission: the pitiful figure of former priest Gerald Ridsdale who was found guilty of 217 offences against sixty-five victims—*sixty-five*—and didn't seem to understand his wrong doing; Pell's woefully inadequate and hostile evidence broadcast from Victoria in 2015; the ongoing coverage of Pell's trial; and, finally, the seventy minutes of Chief Judge Kidd's sentencing remarks.

It was painful, riveting, cathartic and, ultimately, satisfying. My overall reaction: these bastards are finally being caught. Not all, but the most important ones.

I've often compared my own son's development—he's sixteen now—with my horrible schooling experiences: I looked at the size of him at the same age when I had a chair and desk thrown me (eight); the beatings on the backside with a cricket bat (nine); bruised and battered hands (ten); a punch in the face (eleven); or a sexual advance (twelve). It's hard to imagine how any adult, no matter how psychotic, could do that to a child and consider it might be the right thing to do.

And with the continuous coverage over the past five years during the Royal Commission and Pell's trial, it's hard to imagine how anyone in the future will consider it could ever be the right thing to do.

The future of religion in Australia

So, my solution? Pell and his associates can be sent to ten years, twenty years, fifty years: in reality, it's of little consequence. They'll do their time in jail, a strong message has been sent to the community, and any other perpetrators that are caught for historical child sexual abuse now have a sentencing benchmark. That is, if they are caught before they die.

And it doesn't really matter how much the conservative media, especially Rupert Murdoch's empire, tries to downplay the gravity of Pell's crimes and claim his innocence in all different shades of vanilla. They're only doing this because he's a member of the Institute of Public Affairs and a key member of their culture wars battalion, but the public can see right through this.

No, it needs to far more reaching than this. The institution of the Catholic church, like so many other religious institutions, is corrupt and rotten to the core, and has been for thousands of years. It's hard to believe their sexual abuse of young children is a phenomenon of the late twentieth century only.

I'd suggest that having your way with young boys has been one of the implied perks of Catholic office for millennia, and the priesthood and brotherhood have been magnets for paedophiles for a long time.

There is no special place for them in the public realm, and these institutions need to be removed from their pedestal and treated like everyone else in the community.

For a start, all religious schools throughout Australia should be closed down, and converted to public schools or other worthwhile community enterprises. Australia is a secular state, and there is no room for religious instruction in public education. In most cases, these schools were built on land the churches were given after European settlement commenced in Australia, and it's only right that it be handed back, if not to the state, then to the traditional owners.

The option for religious instruction in NSW public schools (and in any other state or territory) should be removed. These are usually run by religious fanatics who see their main purpose as inculcating the minds of young students and to act as a recruitment drive.

Remove the sanctity of the confessional. This is one of the recommendations from the Royal Commission, and should be introduced immediately. Mandatory reporting of crimes and sexual abuse is obligatory for many people, so why should those in religion be treated any differently?

All religious institutions in Australia must pay taxes. A dollar is a dollar is a dollar, and all profits and surpluses earned by these institutions should be taxed, just like any other institution. And they must all become incorporated, so they cannot evade the law when claims of compensation are made against them, as was the case in 2007 when abuse survivor John Ellis made a claim against the Catholic church, only to find unincorporated entities could not be held responsible for the actions of individuals.

This would all be a great start.

It will never undo the crimes committed in the past, but it really is time for the Catholic church to serve its penance and contribute to the community in a far more meaningful and relevant way.

*

Scott Morrison and racism

18 March 2019

Eddy Jokovich

Fifty people. That's a large number of people, and it's still difficult to comprehend this is how many died in the Christchurch shootings last Friday. The Islamic community is still grieving from the gravity of the events, but it's best not to let up in the quest to apportion responsibility for one of worst peace-time gun massacres in history.

Who can we blame for the Christchurch killings?

The white nationalist who pulled the trigger, purportedly in revenge for attacks by Islamic fundamentalists in Western Europe? The relatively lax gun laws in New Zealand? Social media? Where can we look for solutions to ensure the chances of these events ever happening again are minimised?

Let's not prevaricate or look for euphemisms. While they weren't the ones pulling the triggers in New Zealand, we need to look at the senior political figures that have fanned the flames of discord and discontent for too long, aided by key figures within Australia's conservative media.

The two key figures in Australian politics that have done their best to inflame discontent are the current Prime Minister, Scott Morrison, and Minister for Home Affairs, Peter Dutton.

They've constantly fuelled anti-Muslim, anti-immigrant and anti-asylum seeker sentiment for well over a decade.

While there are many contributing political players we can also apportion blame to, such as Senators Pauline Hanson, Cory Bernardi, and Fraser Anning, these are just riff-raff anti-intellects always on the look out for self-serving opportunities, and are part of a freak political circus act. They're on the outer fringe, and will always remain there, no matter how many times fellow opportunists in the mainstream media promote them on breakfast television and try to validate their extremist views.

Morrison is the one who needs to be interrogated here for his actions and comments from the past, irrespective of how much the media is trying to deflect and provide cover for him. He entered Parliament in 2007 but his anti-Muslim and anti-refugee sentiment appeared a long way before this time.

Reaching for the worst in people

Irfan Yusuf was the Liberal Party candidate for the seat of Reid in the 2001 federal election and Morrison was the NSW campaign director. During the campaign, Morrison threatened Yusuf with disendorsement if he spoke publicly about the grief of an Afghan Australian who had lost two nieces when they drowned with the 353 other asylum seekers during the SIEV-X catastrophe.

Morrison allegedly said to Yusuf: "We both hate Pauline Hanson … the best way to destroy someone like Pauline Hanson is to express policies that make us look like her."

During the 2004 federal election, a conservative Liberal group affiliated with Morrison (by now, he was the NSW Liberal Party executive director) distributed thousands of fake leaflets to smear Labor candidate, Ed Husic. The leaflets replicated official Labor campaign material and election slogans, but inserted the words: "Ed Husic is a devout Muslim. Ed is working hard to get a better deal for Islam in Greenway". Husic, whose background is Bosnian Muslim, went on lose the election by 883 votes. The victor was Louise Markus who, like Morrison, is a member of the Pentecostal church.

In the preselection battle for the seat of Cook during 2007, Morrison was easily defeated in the Liberal Party ballot by Michael Towke. Dissatisfied with the result, Morrison highlighted Towke's Lebanese background as one of the reasons for disendorsement and, the Liberal Party overturned the result and installed Morrison as the candidate.

In late 2010, when he was shadow immigration minister, he urged the Liberal Party to capitalise on concerns in the electorate about Muslim immigration, as well as questioning the role of multiculturalism. Although the Prime Minister's office has issued a statement that this never occurred and is threatening legal action against anyone in the media making the claim, Morrison did acknowledge in 2012 there "are real tensions out there ... my comments were more about, 'Let's not just write people off because they have strong views about this. We've got to listen to what their concerns are'."

While there is some dispute about what Morrison actually said during that shadow ministry meeting, there is no doubt he has constantly brought up the issue of insecurity within the electorate about Muslim immigration, and his ongoing commentary ever since 2010 suggests he's taken up his own advice, wholeheartedly.

Whether it be in the portfolio of Immigration or Treasury, or in the position of prime minister, Morrison has taken every opportunity to denounce Muslims, asylum seekers and refugees.

After the 2010 Christmas Island SIEV-221 disaster, when forty-eight asylum seekers died after their boat collided with the rocks at Flying Fish Cove, he attacked the Labor government for paying for the costs of the funeral services and said it was not reasonable for a single cent to be spent on holding the funerals in Sydney, when the victims had died at Christmas Island.

As shadow immigration minister, Morrison released a media statement: "Typhoid cases on latest boats highlight the risk of Labor's border failures", where he made comments about asylum seekers sick with typhoid and other communicable diseases as a reason why the Australian population should be fearful about allowing them passage to the mainland.

Morrison's comments exaggerated the health risks out of all proportion and many health professionals at the time pointed out his factually incorrect information and reprimanded him for his base political opportunism.

In the lead up to the 2013 federal election, among other issues, Morrison claimed asylum seekers "may be carrying guns", and that he'd seen asylum seekers carrying "wads of cash ... large displays of jewellery and a lot of money floating around when these boats come in". He also called for 'behaviour protocols' and mandatory police notifications of asylum seekers that were released into the community.

Morrison sings the same song in government

After the Liberal–National Party won office in September 2013, the vilification didn't stop. Morrison instructed the Department of Immigration to stop using the term 'asylum seekers', and introduced the term 'illegal arrivals', even though this is not factually correct according to the UN Refugee Convention and Australia's *Migration Act 1958*.

The entire process of seeking asylum or refugee status in Australia was criminalised under Morrison's watch, a process progressed by his successor, Peter Dutton.

Even after he moved into the position of Treasurer, Morrison continued. In 2015, he lashed out at teachers at a Victorian primary school in Cranbourne, accusing them of allowing Muslim children to refrain from singing the national anthem. "This was just pathetic. Some do-gooders trying to make a point," Morrison said at the time, as well as announcing they had won his 'Muppet of the Year Award'.

Some context: it was the holy month of Muharrum, and Muslims are supposed to refrain from singing and music at this time. The children, unsure of whether it was acceptable to sing the national anthem, decided, with the support of the school, to refrain. It was not a sign of disrespect.

Among the febrile anti-Islamic atmosphere at the time in Bendigo, where right-wing extremists were targeting Muslim communities and lobbying councils against building a new mosque in the area, Morrison's comments were inflammatory and highly irresponsible.

Morrison was at it again in November 2018 in the week before the Victoria election. Hassan Khalif Shire Ali set fire to his car in central Melbourne and stabbed three people, resulting in the death of Sisto Malaspina, the owner of the Pellegrino's Espresso Bar.

Following the incident, Morrison commented that Muslims in Australia were partly responsible for failing to report extremism and admonished community leaders: "If you're an imam or a leader in one of those communities, you need to know who those people are in your community that might be doing that" and claiming, without proof, that "in many cases" imams and community leaders knew who was "infiltrating and radicalising members of their flock".

He went on to talk about the "vile presence" of Islam and talked about the "shady character who is at the periphery of the mosque, the one talking to young people".

He dismissed the "lame excuse" of Ali's mental health issues: "This bloke, radicalised here in Australia with extreme Islam, took a knife and cut down a fellow Australian in Bourke Street". As it turned out, Ali has not been radicalised and, indeed, was suffering from severe mental and substance abuse issues.

And, in his most recent effort, Morrison smeared the asylum seekers on Manus Island and Nauru, suggesting "child molesters, rapists and murderers" could come to Australia if the laws for evacuating sick asylum seekers from offshore detention are changed.

There's clear evidence throughout his political life Morrison has actively sought to demonise asylum seekers and refugees and the attack the Islamic community, wherever possible.

A failed rehabilitation

Since the New Zealand attacks, Morrison has tried to rehabilitate his political image, again with the support of a compliant and absent-minded media, as if all the things he has said about asylum seekers, refugees and the Islamic community never happened. He's announced $55 million in funding for security enhancements at places of worship, and pushed out a message decrying "us-and-them tribalism", even though he's been the most tribal of all politicians in federal Parliament.

His Liberal Party colleagues are also adding to the collective amnesia and stepping up to offer their support in this rehabilitation.

On Morrison's comments from 2011 to shadow cabinet, Minister for Health, Greg Hunt, is now disputing Morrison said them at all and now trying to argue the opposite in a fairy land speech: "I saw him [Morrison] in tears of sadness at the loss of beautiful young Muslim, and other, lives at the hands of the people-smugglers and he vowed then to protect them and that this tragedy would never happen on his watch. He cared then with every fibre of his being and that same compassion still drives him."

Compassion? Where was this compassion when he said asylum seekers were "diseased"? Or when he besmirched their reputation when he claimed they had "wads of cash" and "large displays of jewellery", implying they were rich criminals? Or when he complained about Labor covering the costs of funerals for victims that drowned at Christmas Island?

Or when he accused asylum seekers of carrying guns? Or denounced the recent Medevac legislation that was meant to create safe passage to Australia for seriously ill refugees on Manus Island and Nauru?

No, there hasn't been any compassion at all. Compassion might be something Morrison's family and close parliamentary colleagues might see but, as far as any public evidence is concerned, there is absolutely nothing. Morrison has demonised asylum seekers and sought to gain political benefit by attacking Muslims at every opportunity.

He was lost for meaningful words last Friday afternoon in response to the New Zealand attacks because he is so used to seeking the political message that will provide benefit to him.

He tried to weave security and safety into the message, trying to find words and an avenue to attack Labor on border security but it wasn't forthcoming. Morrison may have a loud mouth but he can't speak unless he's in attack mode. He is like the monkey in the two-part organ grinder act, seeking opportunity to appease the audience that will give his master the highest return, in this case, the Liberal Party.

While his counterpart in New Zealand, Prime Minister Jacinda Ardern spoke forcefully, truthfully and openly, Morrison floundered. Perhaps he was overawed. Perhaps. But it was more likely to be the realisation that the Australian export of terrorism who had just inflicted the biggest mass murder in New Zealand's history might have been influenced to act because of the history of Morrison's coded words and racist dog whistling. Just like a Manchurian candidate.

Criminologists and behavioural scientists suggest there are many factors that influence perpetrators of such violence and their decision to enact what initially commences as a fantasy, or in the case of the New Zealand killer, a manifesto.

In most cases, they are very average people that live out normal lives but are influenced by the magnification of key messages they either receive through mainstream media, or reach out for through social media outlets.

Like many people, they are susceptible to messages that appear from people in authority, such as politicians, media influencers, shock-jocks and right-wing polemicists. Messaging that appears from politicians has the imprimatur of the electorate who elected then in the first place and the belief that whatever these people are saying—such as US President Donald Trump; UKIP leader, Nigel Farage; Brazilian President, Jair Bolsonaro; or Scott Morrison—has a further authority provided by the media.

Every time Morrison publicly complained about asylum seekers being "diseased", or used the words "vile" and "shady" when referring to the Islamic community, someone else in the community added another thought about purchasing a bullet or a gun to take matters into their own hands, or enact their manifesto to inflict mass murder.

High office requires great responsibilities and, so far, Morrison has failed to show anything that might bring communities closer in Australia. To paraphrase his own language, historically, he's been quite happy to bring some people down, so that other people can rise; in this case, white extremists.

Morrison might not have realised it at the time, but his endless over-blown commentary about the Islamic community, asylum seekers and refugees over the past decade influenced an Australian radical who enacted his fantasy and gunned down fifty innocent people in New Zealand.

Freedom of speech does have its limits and consequences, and we saw the end results of Morrison's anti-Muslim rhetoric last week.

After the death of Princess Diana in 1997, the media moved into a rare contemplative mood and reflected that perhaps they had gone too far in pursuit of a story, and they should be more responsible and considerate of people's privacy. That lull in extreme *paparazzi* behaviour and invasive journalism lasted for several months, before they were at it again, and the public soon forgot about their disgust with the tabloid media and rekindled their voracious appetite for inane celebrity reporting.

Morrison will do the same, perhaps with the speed of politics in this era, wait a few weeks and fall over himself in the rush to get to the mosques he has mostly avoided during his time in politics.

And then it will be back to politics as usual, back to humiliating refugees and asylum seekers, and trying to capitalise on the "electorate's growing concerns about Muslim immigration, Muslims in Australia and the inability of Muslim migrants to integrate", just like he suggested to his colleagues in 2010.

*

NSW election wrap, Morrison's racism and the issues affecting the federal election

26 March 2019

Eddy Jokovich + David Lewis / Podcast

In this episode we analysed the New South Wales state election held on 23 March; racism and white extremism in the Australian community: how much responsibility should our Members of Parliament and the media have in this? And we assessed the next big event on the political calendar: the 2019 federal election. How will recent events affect the result? This episode was recorded against the backdrop of the killings in Christchurch, New Zealand, where an Australian terrorist gunned down fifty people at two mosques; and a damaging live interview on national television for Scott Morrison, explaining his actions from a 2010 shadow cabinet meeting, where he was accused of trying to exploit concerns in the electorate about Islam for political gain.

Eddy Jokovich: The counting is still going on in the New South Wales state election, but there has been enough counting for the Liberal–National Party to pick up enough seats to just hang on to government. On the night, they were hovering between minority and government in their own right but they've now claimed the seat of Dubbo and it looks like they've reached the magical number of forty-seven seats needed to form government. Labor only picked up one seat—they did have a 2.5 per cent swing towards them, but it wasn't anywhere near the 7 per cent swing they needed. And there will be soul searching about what they need to do to win back government in four years' time. Do they have the right leadership? And what can they do to convince the electorate in 2023, the date of the next New South Wales election? The LNP has won this election, but is it the strong election result the media is making it out to be? It actually lost seats: they've allowed the Shooters Fishers and Farmers Party to fill in the breach, and they've only just hung onto government. The final result will be a relief for the LNP but it's not a result they should be making such a big deal about.

David Lewis: It was a fairly muted victory and it did come from nowhere. I think many people were expecting them to lose, and it wasn't the lay down misère that all governments or parties hope for. But it looks like they will have a very slim majority in their own right, although a slightly hung parliament looks like it could be the other option. The result says a lot about the electorate in New South Wales, too.

EJ: Winning three elections in a row in modern politics: that is very difficult to do. That hasn't happened for a Coalition government since the 1971 election, that's when Robert Askin won his third election in a row, and he did actually go on to win a fourth in 1973. Winning government and winning elections is hard: the Coalition previously had two in a row [after 2011 and 2015] and now they've got three and that means they'll be in office for at least twelve years. It's very odd to see they've actually lost seats, they're barely clinging onto government—albeit, they did win the election—but it's being reported as though it's a landslide victory and I just can't see that.

DL: There are two ways of looking this: for a government that has not achieved very much in eight years, it has done surprisingly well. And for a government that has the shadow of the federal Liberal Party, which is seemingly not popular, it did very well. As every party tends to say during state elections, state elections and federal elections aren't related. It's true in one sense but in another sense, it's not true. I'm wondering if the Morrison Cabinet is now breathing somewhat of a sigh of relief, and now thinking they might be able to do much better in New South Wales in the upcoming federal election than expected.

EJ: It might be a false dawn for them though—during the entire New South Wales state election campaign, Scott Morrison was not seen anywhere near the state Liberal Party. When the Liberals had their campaign launch just last week, Morrison didn't actually speak at all. But when victory was assured on Saturday night and it was all over, bar the shouting, Scott Morrison spoke first at the victory podium, and it was almost like he was the leader of the New South Wales Liberal Party, and not Gladys Berejiklian.

DL: It was a risky move, for sure. He may see the state of New South Wales as a saving grace for him. The state Liberals did distance themselves from Morrison during the campaign, which was a smart move, given some of the results. In other results, former Labor leader and now One Nation member Mark Latham returned to politics and entered the Upper House, with the Shooters Fishers and Farmers Party knocking out the Nationals. It is a real case of the immortal words of Pete Townshend from The Who: "Meet the new boss, same as the old boss". In many ways, New South Wales has suddenly become a very interesting state, politically.

EJ: In the aftermath, the odd point being made in the media is that for the federal Labor Party, there are no seats in New South Wales to be gained at the next federal election, based on the New South Wales state election results. But that's basically using the same amount of votes, applying the template from the New South Wales election and placing it over the federal seats. There are differences and there are similarities between state elections and federal elections: they're never the same, and they're never held at exactly the same time, although this federal election will be held within two months of the state election that's just been held on Saturday night. Elections are never, ever the same. To say New South Wales is not an area where federal Labor can pick up seats, just based on the state election results, was a bit disingenuous from the media.

DL: The media have played a very odd role in the state election. Labor leader Michael Daley was slammed as a racist, yet Mark Latham wasn't. Minister for Home Affairs, Peter Dutton at the federal level hasn't been criticised, though he clearly is racist. MPs who have defended convicted pedophiles have been allowed to do so without criticism or question.

EJ: Let's see what Michael Daley did say last September and I have to point out, he wasn't actually the leader of the Labor Party when he made this statement.

> Michael Daley: There's a transformation happening in Sydney now, where our kids are moving out and foreigners are coming in and taking their jobs. Our young children will flee and being replaced by young children, young people, from typically, Asia, with Ph.Ds. I don't want to sound xenophobic, it's not a xenophobic thing, it's an economic question.

EJ: That was Michael Daley making the comment about Chinese Ph.Ds taking the jobs of Australians but I can't see what's wrong with having a highly educated workforce. Those statements were made at a meeting at the Katoomba branch of the Labor Party: I don't know who made that recording but it was lobbed into the final week of the state election campaign. There's no excuse for Daley's statement, but you would think an MP of a mainstream party would have the discipline to not make these types of statements that will cause them trouble down the track.

DL: He blew the election for Labor in that last week. In an electorate that has put Mark Latham into the Upper House, Daley loses the election on racism: it says a lot of very interesting things about the electorate. It also shows how to lose an election on one comment. It's often not the comment that the media say it is, but sometimes it is. Daley had been doing very well up until that last week.

EJ: How important is that final week of the campaign? I point that out in the context of pre-polling for the state election, which was around 25 per cent, and that's actually a very high number. As a comparison, in the by-election in late 2018 for the federal seat of Wentworth, the level of pre-polling was around 30 per cent. Whatever happened in the final week in Wentworth seemed to have less of an impact than in previous elections. Many people have pointed out Michael Daley did have a very poor final week and it's obvious that was the case. But is it similar to Mark Latham's final week in 2004 when he was the federal leader of the Labor Party with his forestry plan and the infamous handshake he made with John Howard?

DL: The final week is very important. Many people do lodge a vote before election day and the idea that you can go in before election day and cast your vote is a really good idea. There are people who for many reasons find the Saturday a struggle: old people in nursing homes, for example, shift workers; people who know that they'll be away on that weekend; people observe various beliefs and practices; and by the time of election day, one in four people had already cast their vote of the vote. Unless everybody voted one way, pre-polling isn't going to decide the election. So that last week is still important.

EJ: And the final week also influences the electoral process in so many different ways. If the leader of the party has such a poor performance in that final week, that filters through to people on the ground handing out the how-to-vote cards, it affects the psychology of everyone working on the campaign. Conversely, if you have a very good final week of the campaign—which seems to be the case for the Liberal Party, relatively speaking— that affects the workers on the ground as well: they're more enthusiastic when they hand out the how-to-vote-cards, they're more energetic. It works in so many different ways where it can also affect the media reporting of the electoral campaign but it's also a psychological process for the MPs, the leader and all the campaign workers on the ground.

DL: Many electorates seem to—and this was just going on what I could see on social media and from what people were telling me—a lot of electorates seemed to have people turning up early to vote, which generally is the sign of a landslide or a massive victory from one side or the other. In this case, it wasn't. Perhaps Saturday was just a day where everybody thought they'd get voting over and done with early and not have to think about it for the rest of the day.

EJ: And election day was a reasonably hot day, definitely in Sydney. The New South Wales state election, that's almost done and dusted. But what can be read into the 2019 federal election for either party? Scott Morrison, as mentioned, was invisible for virtually all of the New South Wales state campaign, and that's understandable on some level. But after the result was known, he was definitely there on the winner's podium on Saturday night. Bill Shorten, the Leader of the Opposition for Labor, said nothing could be read into the result from the state election. Who's right?

DL: Labor has just lost a 'drover's dog' election in New South Wales. If I was in federal Labor, I would be making sure everybody was completely disciplined, absolutely engaged on the major issues, and united on the major issues. If I was in the Liberal Party, I would be examining whether some of the things that seem to be unpopular may actually be popular, or at least not as unpopular as they seem. It would be very easy to become relaxed from a federal Liberal perspective, given that the New South Wales state government didn't really deserve to win this election.

EJ: They might not have deserved to win, but they actually did, and it all gets down to mathematics in politics. They might not have won the most votes overall, but they definitely have won the most seats.

DL: And Labor deserved to lose in the end anyway. If they couldn't beat the Liberal Party in its current state, they deserved to lose. And that's something Bill Shorten and the rest of the Labor team have to look at. A party can still lose an unloseable election, and that's a very strong message for them. And for Scott Morrison, the message is that it's possible to win an unwinnable election.

*

Scott Morrison and racism

EJ: We had the unfortunate scene in New Zealand last week, where a home-grown Australian terrorist gunned down fifty Muslim worshippers in two Christchurch mosques, all in the name of white supremacy and the so-called 'great replacement conspiracy theory'. The incident reverberated all around the world, and it has called into question the responsibility and influences of politicians who, for too long, have been too easily involved in race baiting and targeting minority groups in Australia. They've tried to create discord to boost their electoral appeal to fringe elements in the community. While they weren't the ones pulling the trigger, the two key figures that have done their best to inflame racial discontent over the years are the current Prime Minister, Scott Morrison, and Minister for Home Affairs, Peter Dutton. The events in Christchurch have focused upon the actions of Scott Morrison over the past decade. But is it fair that we place this intense scrutiny over Morrison's words and actions?

DL: He has to govern for all Australians, as does Bill Shorten if he becomes prime minister, as did Julia Gillard, Kevin Rudd, John Howard, Paul Keating, Bob Hawke, Malcolm Fraser, Gough Whitlam, right all the way back to the first prime minister, Edmund Barton. Australia has been a multicultural country since 1788—officially since 1972—and there are people from all over the world, of all different backgrounds, who live here, who vote here, who paid taxes, who obey the law here, who are good citizens. Multiculturalism has been one of the things that has made Australia great. There is an undercurrent, though, of racism here. It's a very complex topic, and racism is not necessarily just found in older generations—this is how it usually gets characterised. It's not. There are, of course, older people who think like that, there are younger people too. There are also middle-aged people who think it, who believe Australia is essentially an Anglo country and that anyone not of an Anglo background is somehow not a part of it. The big issue, of course, is soft racism, in which people say things that are racist, but they don't actually think it is racist: and many people who aren't affected by racism don't think it's racist.

EJ: The most recent drama for Scott Morrison has its roots at a 2010 Liberal–National Party shadow cabinet meeting, where all of the shadow ministers were asked to bring three ideas to improve the vote of the national Liberal–National Coalition. It just seems a little bit implausible for a shadow minister such as Scott Morrison to come into a meeting where they've been specifically asked to improve their vote, for him to claim that he wanted to improve the vote for the Coalition by trying to reduce anti-Muslim sentiment within the community. It's at odds with his actions over the past eight years since that shadow cabinet meeting, and even before—it actually goes back to a previous time when Scott Morrison was the director of the New South Wales Liberal Party, before he entered Parliament. Morrison allegedly said to a Liberal Party candidate, who was of an Afghan background: "We both hate Pauline Hanson, but the best way to destroy someone like Pauline Hanson is to express policies that make us look like her". That's a comment from 2001 around the time of the infamous Tampa election. In 2011, he complained bitterly about the Labor government paying for flights and funerals for the asylum seekers that died in the SEIV-221 disaster, where forty-eight people lost their lives just off Christmas Island. He actually announced that asylum seekers have got typhoid and communicable diseases; Australia should be fearful of them coming to the mainland. He also claimed asylum seekers were carrying guns, had wads of cash and "you would always see them with large displays of jewellery". When he then became prime minister, he talked about the "vile presence of Islam" and the so-called "shady character" at the periphery of the mosque. I could probably go on for about half an hour just getting all these quotes from Scott Morrison over the past ten years from the time he was shadow minister, then when he was Immigration Minister, when he was Treasurer and now as prime minister. Judging by his actions since that shadow cabinet meeting back in 2010, it doesn't seem to be consistent with someone who claims they were trying to reduce anti-Muslim sentiment within the community. In fact, he's actually trying his best to *increase* anti-Muslim sentiment.

DL: One of the first pieces of legislation passed by the federal Parliament in 1901 was the White Australia policy, modelled on the White American policy. What is not commonly known is that the White Australia policy was used as the model for immigration policy in Nazi Germany in the 1930s. Australia was looked upon as a way of how to manage these issues, and this is a massive shadow over any discussion of racism in Australia. Scott Morrison taps right into those people—many of whom would never say it—that think the White Australia policy was a useful policy to have. The arguments such as 'immigrants bring disease', 'immigrants bringing crime', date back to the 1850s, the 1830s and early 1800s. We could look in Australia at Chinese immigrants to the gold mines. All of this was said about them. We can look at the great Eastern European and Mediterranean migration after the second World War. It was all said about Greeks and Italians and Yugoslavs and Polish people, and it was said about the Vietnamese refugees in the 1970s and 1980s. None of it was true but it's funny how the same arguments resonate again and over again, and it's never true.

EJ: No country in the world is free from racism, it would be most unwise to think there is the perfect country and, to use Scott Morrison's words, we can't sugarcoat this and be naïve about it. Having a fear or discomfort about the 'other', that's a natural human condition. Politically, it should be more about trying to reduce the conditions for racism and extremism to exist. Australia has been one of the most successful multicultural countries in the world but historically, there has always an opportunity there for opportunistic Members of Parliament to stoke fear within the community, in the hope it will boost their profile and to be rewarded electorally. That's not only Members of Parliament, it's also the mainstream media to blame for this process. If we are going to apportion blame for heightened racism and extremism within the community, we'd have to look at Channel Seven on their breakfast program. They actually invite Pauline Hanson each week to talk about all of the issues that concern her—she has a platform every week. The mainstream media has normalised some of these extremists. There's Blair Cottrell, the racist from Melbourne and he's actually proud to be a racist. Cottrell was on Sky Television a few months ago, being interviewed by the former Chief Minister of the Northern Territory, Adam Giles. We had Milo Yiannopoulos asking a question on the ABC *Q&A* program. There was also an ABC *Four Corners* episode featuring Steve Bannon, interviewed by Sarah Ferguson a few months ago as well. These people do exist in the community, they're out there. But is it wise for the mainstream media to encourage these people? Certainly, we do need to scrutinise them: but is there a better way that we can do this?

DL: Waleed Aly is often called a 'Muslim television presenter', regardless of the topic he's talking about. If there was a debate on theology or faith, he can be presented as a Muslim, someone else as a Catholic, or a Presbyterian and that's probably okay. But if he's talking about federal government, if he's talking about the many issues they talk about on *The Project*, I wouldn't have thought his faith was relevant to the discussion. The fact it has to be pointed out, leads back to that assumption that unless otherwise stated, a television presenter is white and Anglo—and, of course, in Australia, 'Muslim' means Middle Eastern, whether you're a Maronite Christian or Parsi or any of the other religious groups that exist in the Middle East. There's racism that a lot of people wouldn't even be aware of and all the media has a big accountability in this. We have a very overtly racist media and a sanctimonious and hypocritical media too. When the Christchurch killings in New Zealand happened, who did the media blame? Twitter and Instagram and Facebook, without thinking that having Miranda Divine rile against Muslims or having Andrew Bolt tell us how terrible immigration is, might have something to do with it—Andrew Bolt was found guilty of racism in the Courts, so we can actually call him a racist.

EJ: The mainstream media has always been calling out social media, to say it's irrelevant; to say it's not part of the real process of promoting news and spreading information about political matters and related issues. They've always tried to downplay social media and its role and also the role of smaller, independent media outlets. But when the mainstream media is held directly responsible for fuelling discontent about anti-Muslim immigration and racism, they're quite happy to blame other people; they'll suggest that social media is very important, so they're trying to have their cake and eat it as well. I don't think everyone is going to accept their version of events. They're quite culpable in this process of promoting racism, as are quite a few irresponsible conservative Members of Parliament.

DL: The media point to Fraser Anning as an extremist and an outlier, but he wouldn't be there if he was the only one espousing this spectrum of views. He is more extreme than others, but it doesn't take too much media support to get to that level of extremity.

*

How recent events in Australia and New Zealand will affect the next federal election

EJ: The New South Wales election is all but over, and there are two big events coming up in federal politics: the 2019 Budget, which should be closely followed by the 2019 federal election. The Budget is due to be announced on April 2 and there will be a short period of promotion in the media about how great the Budget is and speculation about whether the purported surplus is going to be real or just a charade. Then Scott Morrison is likely to make the drive to Yarralumla to have a cup of tea with the Governor–General and call an election for May 11 or May 18. We've predicted an impending thrashing for the Coalition at the next federal election whenever it's due to be held, but does the result from the New South Wales election offer the Coalition any hope and are there other events that could have an influence in that election?

DL: The Coalition would be seeing a little bit of relief from result in New South Wales. New South Wales has shown itself to be a more conservative state than expected. In 2017, Queensland turned around the biggest majority ever for LNP Premier Campbell Newman into one almost as big, for Labor's Annastacia Palaszczuk, within one term. The Victoria

Labor Party trounced the Liberal opposition easily, in their second election as government, which traditionally sees the government lose one or two seats—they increased their majority. The New South Wales election sees the Liberal Party just scrape back in. Now how does this translate federally? If people vote for minor parties on the right, that helps the current government. If people vote for independents who lean to the right, that will also help the government. New South Wales is a big state with many federal electorates—forty-seven. Some of those New South Wales seats that even on the Friday before the state election, we might have thought were absolutely finished, have scraped through for the Coalition, meaning that we might get another minority Liberal–National government federally. It's difficult to see that happening, but anything is possible.

EJ: Many people in the media were saying, 'forget about New South Wales [in the federal election] for the Labor Party. Best look to Queensland, Victoria, or any other state'. The media tends to forget the federal government at the moment is in minority, so that would mean that they would need to win additional seats federally to hold onto government. And even if the state election results in New South Wales were replicated at the federal level, the Coalition will lose two seats, so it's not looking good for them—it might not be looking great for Labor, but it's not looking so good for the Coalition either and it might end up being a situation where there are more independent MPs to come out of New South Wales. The Coalition government, federally, they're probably hoping for a similar result to a 1993 state election in Western Australia. This is going back some time ago, the state WA Labor government lost that election, but there was only a small swing against them. The Labor Prime Minister, Paul Keating, announced the federal election on the Monday after the WA election, and the rest is history. Paul Keating won the unwinnable election against John Hewson in 1993 but the situation for Scott Morrison is different. He's not Paul Keating for a start, he's under the pump and he has a nominal minority government. In 1993, that federal election was a contest of economic and social ideas. This time around, the federal election looks like it will be a contest of competence and stability.

DL: I can't see how the Coalition can gain the seats necessary to hold onto government. I can see a potentiality where they go back to a minority government, maybe in a different configuration of seats and votes, but I still think that's a long shot, and that's maybe what they'll try for. As the New South Wales election shows, the National Party brand is, if not dead, then very sick. Key National seats went to either the Shooters Fishers and Farmers Party or to independents. One of Barnaby Joyce's state seat equivalents, the seat of Lismore, went to an independent, for example. The seat of Dubbo is still in thrall—we're talking about this on the Monday after the election—an extra 2,300 votes went to the Nationals member, but Matt Dickinson, the independent candidate, gave them a very good run and nearly took the seat from the Nationals. Dubbo is a very strong National seat but was almost lost, which shows the Liberal Party cannot rely on National Party numbers in the upcoming federal election.

EJ: There are a number of factors in other states as well. If you look at the electoral pendulum, even if the Coalition just lost one or two seats in New South Wales—or even if they picked up one or two seats —there's still a wide range of seats in other states where they need to put so many fingers in so many dikes to stop the flow. It's impossible to see the dam wall holding up for too long—all they need is a couple of seats to be lost in Western Australia, which is likely; one or two seats in South Australia; also likely. Victoria, very likely; Queensland, is a state where they already hold many seats. It's difficult to see how they can hold onto these seats, but as we keep saying; politics is a contest between two major parties in Australia so, anything can still happen. But there is one final large event coming up, and that's the 2019 Budget. Budgets don't seem to have as much impact as people think they do. The federal government, they've already telegraphed their intention to have a Budget surplus. Whether that's real or imaginary, we'll never know because they probably won't be around to see the results of their Budget. The media has had enough time to pick apart the Coalition's idea about the surplus—they probably telegraphed that too far in advance, but it should still result in a bit of a political sugar hit for a couple of days after the Budget is released on April 2. However, I can't see it having too much of an effect.

DL: The Coalition has doubled the debt since they got into office in 2013, with nothing really to show for it. There's been a lot of talk about the national broadband network, which should have been one of the world's great infrastructure projects, but has turned into a fizzer. The Adani mine in Queensland, which they claim will have no government money put into it, will be an ecological disaster and, most likely, a financial disaster. The asylum seekers being moved from Nauru to Christmas Island at large expense. It's very hard to find substantial major policy achievements from this government.

EJ: It's especially a problem for Scott Morrison, because he's only been in office since August 2018. And that's simply not enough time for a prime minister to boost their electoral standing and boost their appeal to the public. During the interview with by Waleed Aly on *The Project*, and ever since the Christchurch attacks, Scott Morrison has been floundering. His default position has always been to attack Bill Shorten, to blame Labor and the weave a message of border security and keeping Australia safe. But this time around on *The Project*, he was lost for words. His natural propensity is always to go on the attack and when he was in a situation where he couldn't blame everything on Bill Shorten, he just floundered. Compare his responses with the responses coming from New Zealand Prime Minister, Jacinda Ardern, and it's been like chalk and cheese. Scott Morrison has been severely exposed over the past week.

DL: This is where we can compare Michael Daley in New South Wales and Scott Morrison: two men out of their depth, trying to find their feet with the tide going against them. Scott Morrison, of course, was an even odder choice for prime minister than Tony Abbott. At least on paper, Tony Abbott had some qualification—whether he was a good prime minister or a bad prime minister is a debate for another day. But if you looked at just his qualifications and experience, you'd think, yes, this is someone who might be qualified for the role of prime minister. Of course, when you looked at his performance and his approach to being the prime minister, that might change your mind. But in terms of what he had achieved beforehand, there was a sense of qualification. Scott Morrison, doesn't have any of this. He had a highly unsuccessful tenure outside of politics, and he was a middling minister who had no policy achievements whatsoever and was seen as an extremist within the party. And we know seeing the fruits of this labour that he doesn't know what to do and he's not quite sure how to do it. And he's been thrown into a circumstance which is outside of all of his instincts. He claims to have done a lot of work with the Muslim community. None of these communities have stood up and said: "actually, he did help us, he was good, and we're really appreciative of it".

EJ: This week, we didn't have a Newspoll opinion poll, and it usually comes out on a fortnightly basis. They did do some work in the lead-up to the New South Wales state election—which is what they always do, of course. Perhaps Newspoll thought polling for the state and polling for federal might dilute either of those, but it would have been interesting to see what sort of effect the New South Wales election and the interview on *The Project* would have had on Scott Morrison's polls, after a week from hell for him.

DL: The next Newspoll won't be markedly different from what this one would have been in terms of polling. Morrison seems to be in terminal decline. There may be a bit of a dead-cat bounce in the next poll, but the Liberal Party has been in terminal decline since at least the 2016 election. Polling, of course, is not an election, but it's getting harder and harder to see that there's any way out of it for him. And Morrison has thrown everything they have. He can't claim to be a good economic manager—every serious economist has debunked that. He can't claim to be tough on immigration, except for being too tough on certain parts of immigration. He can't claim to be a popular leader, because he's not and he's barely known. There's a great news clip where he walks up to a man outside a football stadium, and the man asks "who are you?". Morrison answers: "I'm ScoMo", and the bemused man just walks away.

EJ: That also did happen to Malcolm Turnbull when he was prime minister, where he met an older couple on a train, and they just didn't know who he was.

DL: Scott Morrison can be held responsible for some of it: he's not responsible for all of it. As the Liberal Party has lurched further to the right, it's starting to alienate the centre. In Australia, that's always a very dangerous thing to do. The Liberal Party is losing their moderates, and it will be interesting to see what happens from now on. This might be the right thing for them to do: the current polls could be wrong and it could be that the Australian electorate is further to the right than we'd like to think.

EJ: But as we do like to say, there's only one poll that counts and that's the actual election…

*

Music in this episode
Mad World, performed by Brooklyn Duo
Bug Powder Dust, by Bomb The Bass

Budget 2019, the end of a zany Parliament and waiting for an election

9 April 2019

Eddy Jokovich + David Lewis / Podcast

In this episode, we looked at the 2019 Budget, provided a wrap-up of one of the weirdest parliamentary terms ever, and even though it hadn't been called, we decided to kick start the 2019 federal election campaign. Also in this episode, David Lewis is amateur horologist and Sherlockian scholar.

Eddy Jokovich: Everyone's been talking about 'back in black', but it could be a case of 'seeing red': the federal Budget has been predicted to be a surplus of $7 billion but very few experts feel it's still going be a surplus when the actual figures are announced in September 2020. And of course, by that time, the 2019 federal election will be well and truly over. The announcement is the first predicted Budget surplus since 2007 and it plays to the perception of the Liberal Party as 'better financial managers', even though the evidence suggests both the Liberal and Labor parties are financially competent and both apply the required fiscal discipline to manage the economy. But just like the 2016 Budget, which was also announced in the shadow of a federal election campaign, there's an element of smoke and mirrors—

which would make Archimedes proud—and there's a strong possibility this Budget will never be implemented. This Budget depends on the Liberal–National Party winning the next election and, even then, being able to have its Budget passed in full by Parliament, something it has not been able to do since the party first won office in 2013. Is this a workable Budget; is it a good Budget; is it a political Budget? And how relevant will it be to the 2019 election?

David Lewis: Many economic commentators have called it a 'smoke and mirrors' Budget. The Budget is a projected surplus, if every single thing adds up, which is highly unlikely, and much of the Budget will relate to issues which are really out of the control of the government. Budgets are always impacted by international events; impacted by national events, disasters, unexpected bankruptcies of major companies, and in the words of former US Secretary of State Donald Rumsfeld, "unknown unknowns" really come into play here. It would be like you and I claiming 'we expect a profit of $2.1 million next financial year', based on a whole range of issues we have no control over. It might happen, but in all likelihood, it won't.

EJ: Budgets are usually around 5-to-10 per cent out when the actual figures are reported, which is nine months after the end of each financial year, and there are so many issues that can happen within a 12-month period in the world of politics, within the world of finance and the economy. Many factors will need to fall into place for those Budget predictions to actually be correct, but in the government's favour, last year's Budget was actually $9 billion better off than the figures announced in the initial Budget papers. There are things that can go right; there are things that can go wrong, but it seems like this time around there's a bit of financial trickery involved. For example, there's an allocated amount of $3.8 billion from the National Disability Insurance Scheme that wasn't used up in 2018/19; there's another $1.5 billion that won't be used up in 2019/20, and that will go towards the Budget surplus figures. There's also the trickery involved of the government taking from one area of spending and putting it into another, announcing programs that will last three or four years, rather than the usual twelve months.

It's almost like subtraction and addition, and then taking away the number you first thought off.

DL: It's the spin of Morrison the marketing man, and one thing that has been shown is he's not a terribly good marketing man. Morrison keeps blaming Labor, which he could probably get away with in the Coalition's first term between 2013–16, but you can't really get away with it in the second term. The government's default position is to blame Labor for every single problem, even though they're been out of office since 2013.

EJ: One strategy the government has been trying to push—and this specifically includes the Treasurer Josh Frydenberg and Scott Morrison—is relating the overall Budget figures of government to a household budget: but managing a government and a national economy is totally different to managing a household budget. Most people understand a household budget and generally don't understand how the overall economy works. As a result, the Coalition has been pushing the message that a surplus is a virtue, and deficits are bad. And that's how the common household relates to these economic issues with the notion that a large debt is not good, and that having a surplus is fantastic. Don't get me wrong: national debt does need to be managed, and it's $550 billion at the moment. Overall, the economy does need to be managed well and, generally, governments of all persuasions need to reduce debt so it does become manageable and workable, but we're not in a debt crisis of the moment. There is that old adage that when the government is in surplus, the community is in debt. Achieving a surplus is not always good, and deficits are not always bad: it just depends on what the economic circumstances of the country are at any given time.

DL: We can see where the government's savings were made in this Budget and it shows the types of priorities they have. The government didn't gain extra tax income from big companies and they didn't cut policies that benefit already wealthy businesses and taxpayers. They took it out of the NDIS, a Labor initiative. So, the poorest and most vulnerable, through the National Disability Insurance Scheme, is where the government has got the surplus from. The number of people needing access to the NDIS hasn't gone down the last twelve months, so the government is taking money away from this scheme.

EJ: If anything, the amount of people that require access to the NDIS has gone up, and there has been an issue for people being able to access this program, and it has been extremely difficult. Governments, of course, need to be fully aware of making sure the allocation of taxpayer funds go to the people that need it the most. But with the NDIS, it seems there has been a shortfall in the administrative support services to enable people to access the scheme, and it seems that's where the government has saved a substantial amount of money. Aside from the noise about where the money savings have come from, Budgets of today don't seem to have the same impact they used to; perhaps twenty or thirty years ago, the media headlines for the Budget would continue for two or three weeks, followed by the strong discussion within the political and financial sectors and, to a lesser extent, within the community. But today, there's the big media splash when the Budget is announced on the Tuesday, there's huge headlines on the Wednesday, then the federal opposition responds to the Budget on the Thursday, and then it's almost gone. Five days after this Budget was announced, it was gone and almost forgotten.

DL: There's a few critical factors here. Treasurer Frydenberg is out of his depth, that's very clear. He's keeping his head down as he tries to explain those areas that he's not really sure how to explain. He's out of his depth, compared to Treasurers such as Paul Keating or Peter Costello, who were very much on top of all the issues they needed to be on top of. We've had a few recent Treasurers—Frydenberg, Morrison, [Joe] Hockey—who haven't been as across the economic arguments as perhaps they should have been. This government, since 2013, hasn't had a Budget passed fully by the Senate yet, and that's a really bad news story for them—their major policy announcements will probably go nowhere because they will be blocked in the Senate. Labor has been very strategic about blocking the Budget in the past to cause political difficulties for the government. They haven't blocked the appropriations of salaries and already existing contracts, so government can keep operating but after the constitutional crisis of 1975, Labor doesn't want to be tarred with the same brush as the Liberal and National parties in blocking supply. But new policy initiatives have been frozen by Labor, the Greens and the independents, for all kinds of reasons. This, of course, must be frustrating for the government, but there's not very much they can do about it, except introduce better policies.

EJ: The Leader of the Opposition always has the right of reply to a Budget announcement, and that's what Bill Shorten did on the Thursday night. But the responsibilities are different for an opposition leader; they're not in government and they're not giving out specific details about costings. The process for the Leader of the Opposition is more about poking holes in the Budget and applying a broad brush of what they intend to do if they manage to form government at the next election. Bill Shorten, has done his best to neutralise the government's Budget, matching the Coalition's plans for tax cuts but also pointing out the key policy differences in Labor's proposals: the proposed changes to negative gearing for housing and capital gains taxes, and reigning in the generous franking credits scheme. As well, he also made a key announcement about free cancer treatments, which I was surprised to find out, is not free for most people. Has Labor done enough to offer the electorate key policy differences when compared to the government, or do they need to do some more work in this area?

DL: If the polls are right, it's almost at the stage where Bill Shorten could say his policy is to burn down orphanages, close down the RSPCA and bulldoze children's hospitals, and it still wouldn't matter—if the polls are right—and there have been many polls over the past three years suggesting the federal government is very much on the nose. Free cancer treatments was a very clever announcement because it wasn't something that was on the radar. Cancer is one of those things that everybody is affected by, either directly or indirectly: one in three people will have some form of cancer over their lifetime, whether it's a relatively curable and treatable form of the disease, for whether it's more serious. Everybody knows someone who has needed treatment, so it's one of those areas that will resonate with a large number of people in the community who have either had treatment, will need treatment or will know somebody who has—pretty much 100 per cent of people. This was probably a very smart move, and it's taken the attention away from the other debates, which the government has many talking points on.

EJ: This Budget announcement really is the last roll of the dice for this government. Throughout the next election campaign, whenever that's called, they'll be able to use all of the key points from the Budget. But the biggest factor is whether the Budget is going to be enough to pull them over the line, or get them closer to the line during the election campaign. The Budget is being used as a stepladder to get back into the political game and then see how it all goes. And in an election campaign, anything can happen.

DL: Anything can happen in an election campaign, and usually does: just ask Michael Daley in New South Wales. The other point about equating federal budgets to household budgets dates back to at least the early 1930s. Joseph Lyons, who had been a Labor Treasurer, defected to the other side of politics and then became prime minister, said that his Budget was much like the mothers of Australia, who had to make one shilling do the work of two. The statement didn't work for Joe Lyons then—Labor was forced out of office at the next election. Of course, this was in the midst of the Great Depression, which was caused by international factors well beyond the control of the Australian government.

EJ: It's just a question of whether these types of tactics will resonate in 2019. Politicians of all persuasions will try different strategies to make their policies and economic practices more relatable to people in the electorate—which includes simplifying complex economics to the level of the household budget. We'll see if that's enough in a few weeks' time when the election campaign commences.

Continuing corruption in politics, the politician who shall not be named, and a fine way to end the 45th Parliament

EJ: There were only a few sitting days of Parliament last week—the last sitting days before the election—but it seemed that aside from the time taken up with the Budget, there was enough time to witness some more corrupt practices in politics. We found out more about One Nation and its relationship with guns, and we had a censure for the politician the media doesn't care to name anymore: Fraser Anning. Also, a Liberal minister was caught allocating grants to the community, even though the application date for this grants program hasn't even opened yet. The Qatar-based Al Jazeera network called out One Nation's James Ashby and Steve Dixon in an undercover sting developed over a three-year period, and Fraser Anning was censured by the Senate for being racist and subhuman. The 45th Parliament doesn't officially end until the day the election is called, but this final week was a reminder of just how dysfunctional this term has been: we've seen the removal of a prime minister, a descent into minority government, and a motley collection of very strange people sitting in the Senate. That's all quite amusing to watch, but there is a feeling of being short-changed by this Parliament, and the public does expect better.

DL: It's a Parliament that has been very much run on the agenda of the Institute of Public Affairs. We've witnessed fewer sitting days, cuts to social services and shovelling money to the rich and famous. On the weekend, we saw how Barnaby Joyce allowed a phone tower to be put onto one of Gina Reinhart's properties, where she'll receive a fee for hosting the tower. This is very symptomatic of how this government has been behaving. The Senate is a mess, and that is the fault of the major parties for not really being inspiring enough, and people deciding to turn to vote for other smaller parties.

EJ: It's also a result of the changes to the Senate voting rules and the double dissolution election in 2016, which made it easier for fringe parties and fringe Senators to be elected. And the quality of ministers hasn't really helped this Parliament reach any great heights.

DL: Usually, the position of worst minister in any government is easy to determine, and they usually don't last long. But I couldn't tell you who the worst minister in Parliament is at the moment, because each time you think 'oh yes, it's definitely this one', someone else pops their head up. Greg Hunt, Peter Dutton, Melissa Price, Michaelia Cash, Josh Frydenberg...

EJ: Generally, the public just wants to see good government in action, irrespective of what their political persuasions are. Whether they are generally Liberal voters, or Labor voters, or a swinging voter, or a Greens voter, whatever the case might be, they want good governance, and we just haven't had very much of good government during this past term. Two Liberal Party prime ministers have been thrown out since the Liberal government was first elected in 2013 and now we're onto the third prime minister with Scott Morrison. The machinery of government still continues, irrespective of how poor the Parliament might actually be, how poor the prime minister is, or how poor those ministers are. The operation of government is pushed forward by the public service, and that all goes on behind the scenes. But electorally and publicly, we're not seeing very much of a good performance by this government.

DL: I think the baseline question for any political leader should be: "are they going to embarrass us when they go overseas?". We knew when Malcolm Turnbull went overseas, he was sophisticated enough to not embarrass the country, even if we didn't agree with what he was doing. We can't really say that about Scott Morrison, and we couldn't say that at all with Tony Abbott—that's not to say Malcolm Turnbull was a great prime minister, but he did at least achieve that baseline.

EJ: When Members of Parliament or any political representatives go overseas, we definitely don't want them to embarrass the country. But we had a lot of embarrassment through the One Nation party. Steve Dixon is the One Nation representative in the Queensland Parliament, and James Ashby is the Chief of Staff for Senator Pauline Hanson. A three-year sting instigated by Al Jazeera resulted in the 90-minute documentary 'How To Sell A

Massacre'. It was broadcast on the ABC's *Four Corners* program, and we found out all of these things that were going on behind the scenes: those One Nation members [Dixon and Ashby] were trying to access money from the National Rifle Association in the United States for their political campaign work; weakening Australian gun laws—not immediately, but eventually through obtaining funding and strategic advice from the NRA. MPs and political apparatchiks should not be embarrassing Australia overseas but, in this case, One Nation did embarrass Australia quite severely.

DL: It is this far right-wing American funding that comes from people like the Koch brothers, and Rupert Murdoch through the Institute of Public Affairs—there's a pattern of this funding. The Australian Association for Cultural Freedom, which does things like fund *Quadrant* magazine—in the 1960s, it was actually funded by the CIA. This is on the historical record and has been admitted by key people within the organisation. Richard Krygier was one of the founders and it was designed to undermine the threat of communism by having intelligent debate leaning to the right, with projects such as *Quadrant*. They also organised modern art exhibitions because some communists, particularly Stalinists and Maoists, didn't like modern art. The strategy was to divide the left in such a way that the more progressive leftists would find it difficult to align themselves with the hard left. These days, funding doesn't come from the CIA: it's coming through private institutes, like the Koch brothers' foundations that help fund the NRA and neoliberal organisations, with the idea of stripping back the power of government, mostly to reduce taxes and reduce wages, and to come back shovelling money upwards using the long discredited, trickle-down supply side economics model.

EJ: The Al Jazeera documentary on One Nation has been regarded as the 'sting of the year'—the year is only three months old, so far, but it would be hard to find anything that will outdo this. It was absolutely riveting and fantastic journalism, but there was a question about whether it was ethical using an actor to entrap the two people from One Nation. There is a public interest story here—the National Rifle Association is a very secretive organisation and it's very difficult to get inside information. But an international organisation that tries to intervene in domestic affairs, such as weakening Australian gun laws, is an activity we need to be aware of. The way Al Jazeera obtained the story, on the surface, might have been unethical but the public interest has been served quite well.

DL: The people claiming the documentary was unethical were mainly those in commercial media, those that are involved with news and media outlets that entrap dodgy tradespeople and dodgy financial people in much the same way. It was almost a case of 'if we do it, it's okay, but when others do it, it's really terrible'. If you're a politician and doing the right thing, there's nothing to be worried about. If the NRA had got in contact with the two One Nation people and they said: 'no, we're not interested, thanks very much but go away', there wouldn't be a story about One Nation soliciting foreign money—which should be made absolutely illegal anyway. We probably just should have fully publicly-funded elections, and we are close to that. At the moment, if a candidate achieves at least 4 per cent of the primary vote, they receive $2.77 per vote from the Australian Electoral Commission, which is a good thing. It's a system that helps smaller parties keep a profile, and we need smaller parties as much as we need the larger parties, even when we don't agree with those smaller parties. It's a system that's fair and we also know exactly where the money's coming from. We should probably ban private donations to elections and political parties completely.

EJ: One recent development in politics is the hand-over of celebrity cheques and ministers announcing grants that haven't actually been authorised yet. We did have the spectacle of Minister for the Environment, Melissa Price, and the Liberal MP from Victoria, Chris Crewther, announcing grants of up to $20,000 in key marginal seats, including recording videos of themselves with the recipients of these grants receiving the large celebrity cheques, and posting those videos on social media. This is all well and good—MPs are allowed to actually announce grants and grandstand about it, but the only problem in this case was the applications for these schemes hadn't actually been opened—so grants were provided to recipients, even though they hadn't applied, and the scheme hadn't been formally announced: that's a new level of pork barrelling. There's also one other tactic that's quite new, and the prime example was Georgina Downer, the Liberal Party candidate in the South Australian seat of Mayo. She was on cue with the photo-opportunity, turning up with celebrity cheques, and making it seem like she was the actual MP responsible for delivering these programs, even though she's not even an MP—the actual MP is her opponent, Rebekha Sharkie from the Centre Alliance. And we've seen this happen in quite a few seats, where the celebrity cheque comes out, the local candidate for the Liberal Party is there to announce the hand-over of the money—even though they're not an MP, and they're not even responsible for obtaining the funding. I've checked to see whether this is legal or not according to the Australian Electoral Commission—it is legal, but it's certainly not ethical political behaviour.

DL: It shows the level of desperation of the Liberal Party. Georgina Downer should have a fairly high profile in the seat of Mayo, which is where she grew up and her father, Alexander Downer, was the local member for many years, was a very senior member of the Liberal Party and had achievement—he was Foreign Minister, the UK High Commissioner, and a former federal leader of the Liberal Party. She moved out of South Australia many years ago, and then tried to parachute into the seat of Mayo. Rebekha Sharkie easily won that seat in last year's by-election and probably will win it again at the upcoming election. And it seems these stunts of having Georgina Downer presenting the grants hasn't gone down well with the local constituents.

EJ: The Liberal Party's process of trying to maximise every single, undeserved opportunity has been the feature of this Parliament, and with this type of approach there are other consequences that arise. Instead of focusing on development of good policy which will benefit the electorate—which ultimately would give them a good outcome at the ballot box—this government has focused on political games, and this has caused the high level of dysfunction. But what epitomises that high level of dysfunction in this Parliament is the story of Fraser Anning: he's an accident of history and he shouldn't be in the Senate. He became a Senator after One Nation's Malcolm Roberts was found to be ineligible after the 2016 election. Roberts only received seventy-seven primary votes at the 2016 election, and Anning actually received even less—nineteen primary votes. Anning's vote probably will probably increase in the 2019 election, because he has become more prominent, but he's very unlikely to win his Senate seat again, and it will be good riddance to bad rubbish.

DL: Anning is a total and utter disgrace. The Senate was right to censure him and Senator Mathias Cormann should be congratulated for moving the motion in the Senate and allowing Penny Wong to second it, allowing for a totally bipartisan motion. The feeling in the Senate was very high. Anning has shown himself to be a bully and a coward, when he famously slapped 'Egg Boy' [17-year-old Will Connolly, who cracked on egg on Anning's head] at that media conference. There's that moment where he sizes Egg Boy up and thinks: is he going to be able to slap this kid? It wasn't a natural reaction to an attack on the body, there was a calculation that once he realised he was bigger and stronger than the kid, he just slapped him. That's just cowardice, that's just bullying, and then his henchman jumped on top of Egg Boy. That was a disgraceful display of the misuse of force. Had they taken Egg Boy away: yes, fair enough, and had there been an instinctive swing from Anning, because he'd been hit with an egg on the back of the head, maybe. But it's still not right. Fraser Anning is a disgraceful figure, whose opinions are appalling and even members of One Nation find his opinions appalling. Anyone who has ever been to an ANZAC Day commemoration should understand why Fraser Anning's views are so abhorrent.

*

The ongoing wait for the election date

EJ: How long do we have to wait until the next election? The date of the election should have been set by now, but we're still waiting and waiting and waiting, and it's almost like *Waiting for Godot*. Scott Morrison is trying to catch Labor with its pants down but there's not too many surprises available to the Prime Minister. Realistically, there are only two dates available: May 11 or May 18 and we're beginning to wonder what the delay is all about. Of course, holding off for as long as possible means there's more access to government-funded advertising, more time to enjoy the trappings of office and more time to use the shredders to destroy sensitive departmental material that could come back to bite the Liberal Party in the future. But for a government that is running out of options, delaying the election date does mean there's always a possibility that something unusual might appear on the horizon that totally changes the dynamics of politics and deliver an unlikely victory. But based on what we've seen over the past three years, a victory for the Liberal Party is still unlikely. Why is Scott Morrison holding off calling the election?

DL: With most political leaders in most situations, you can eliminate the really stupid ideas but with the current government, you can't, and I'm wondering if Morrison is trying to work out if he could hold a half-Senate election in May and then try and hold out for a House of Representatives-only election in October or November. There's not very much chance of this happening—I think calmer heads will prevail—but I'm wondering if Morrison is looking at that option to try and get that knockout blow that he's been waiting for. Some commentators have suggested he's delaying the campaign through government announcements that are paid for by the public and doing that as much as possible. The federal Liberal Party is $3 million in debt—essentially bankrupt—and what better way to offset that problem by getting the public to pay for your advertising in a *de facto* manner.

EJ: Of course, governments will look at every possibility, such a calling an election on May 11 or May 18, or even extending it to May 25, which is constitutionally available. And even looking at a half-Senate election before May 18 and then holding off the House of Representatives election for as long as possible—the absolute latest for this would be November 2, 2019. But it just gets down to what will be the net result of making such a decision. Scott Morrison has only been prime minister since August 2018 and a prime minister wants the electorate to feel like they're part of the furniture; that they're familiar. That would be the only advantage of delaying the election day—he would feel more like a prime minister, and develop a sense of incumbency. But the trade-off is, according to the polls, that people have just been waiting to throw this government out of office for a very long time. That's what the opinion polls have been suggesting since August 2016, where 165 consecutive polls have placed the Liberal–National Party behind the Labor Party and in a very poor position, and it's hard to see how that would change over the next two or three months. Political circumstances do change and when they do, they sometimes appear out from nowhere. It's possible to look out over the political horizon and wonder where an event will arrive that will change the dynamics of an election—and then, all of a sudden, an issue arises which, in hindsight, everyone points to as the event that changed the election. With reduced time available, and reduced options, perhaps that's what Scott Morrison is waiting for.

DL: The results in the recent New South Wales election will hearten the Liberal Party. *The Australian* is suggesting this, despite the fact that the aggregated polling puts the government behind at 47-to-53 per cent in two-party preferred voting. *The Australian* has also suggested the government is within striking distance of an election win. This is possible, when taking into account the entirely negative media campaign against Bill Shorten ever since he became Leader of the Opposition, and the push to make Shorten seem like an unelectable leader. And then there was the Royal Commission into Trade Unions to try and discredit Shorten and Julia Gillard—nothing came up. The worst to arise from that Royal Commission was that Gillard should have kept 25-year-old records for another job that she was no longer in, which hardly seemed to be a damning judgment. Shorten is relatively clean—of course, there are dirt units on both sides of politics digging up material from the past, and it may be a case where these units find something, if not about Shorten, then on one of the other Labor frontbenchers.

EJ: One advantage of being Leader of the Opposition for such a long time is that your opponents have found all the dirt that can be found and they've thrown it all. The kitchen sink has been thrown at Bill Shorten over the past five-and-a-half-years. That has been enough time for him to divert all the negative material that has being pushed by his opponents in the media and there's probably nothing new that could be found to further damage him. Shorten, however, is still an unpopular leader as far the opinions polls are concerned, but in the same way that the electorate put aside their questions about Tony Abbott when they voted in the Coalition in 2013, it seems like the electorate is on the verge of repeating that step and voting in an unpopular leader as prime minister.

DL: Shorten was involved in the removal of two prime ministers, Kevin Rudd and Julia Gillard, but that's how the Labor Party works and, of course, the Liberal Party has its own very similar processes for removing prime ministers. We have to remember Mathias Cormann, who it was said was the only person ever [in the Liberal Party leadership spill in August 2018] who has supported three potential prime ministers in the one day—Malcolm Turnbull, Peter Dutton, and Scott Morrison. If Shorten does get torn down, I suspect it will be within Labor, and that will be to do with his popularity levels.

EJ: Despite what politicians say, they love opinion polls and there has been a slight poll movement in the Newspoll for the government, but they're still lagging at 48-to-52 per cent, and the latest Ipsos–Nielsen poll, which came out on the same day, actually showed a weakening of their position, down to 47–53 per cent. So, the government has received some good news and some bad news on the same day. And these fresh rounds of opinions polls will feed into the ongoing speculation about when the election will be called. And this speculation has also brought up the issue of four-year terms for federal governments—it currently feels like a game of cat-and-mouse and a pantomime act, and this process of waiting for prime ministers to call an election date seems quite archaic. Every state and territory in Australia, except for Tasmania, has fixed-term elections, so why can't we do that for the federal elections?

DL: The prime minister's pleasure of advising the Governor–General can and has backfired in the past. It's a process that creates confusion, it creates all kinds of problems, so perhaps we should just move to three- or four-year fixed terms: three years is probably not quite long enough, five years is too long, perhaps four years is the optimum, which is the amount of time most parliaments around the world are given. We'd also need to rethink how the Senate is elected as well, but to have a Fraser Anning in the Senate, or a David Leyonhjelm in the Senate, radical leftists, who don't really represent the view of mainstream Australia and exist on the extreme fringes, is not a good look.

EJ: Some of those views should be represented in Parliament, but there needs to be a mechanism where we don't end up with 'accidental' Senators. Four-year fixed terms for the House of Representatives would practically mean eight-year Senate terms under the current rules, and there would need to be a constitutional fix to get around that. And I'm sure it could be done.

DL: Yes, eight years is a long time for a Senator term, but then again, the Senate is a brake on the excesses of the House. It will be sorted out at some point.

*

Music in this episode
Under The Sea, Digby Jones

Maths and media: where the election will be won and lost

12 April 2019

Eddy Jokovich

It's always unwise to make predictions about who is likely to win any election, but if Scott Morrison does end up on the victory podium on the evening of 18 May, it will be one of the most unlikely victories seen in Australian politics.

Not quite as unlikely as the Labor victory in the 2015 Queensland election, where a rump of a party managed to win an election against the Newman government after just one term, but probably on par with Paul Keating's 'true believers' victory in 1993, where Labor managed to turn around very difficult polls and trump John Hewson and the Liberal–National Party to win by eleven seats.

But the 1993 election was a contest of ideas, with Hewson's *Fightback!* package providing many targets for Keating to attack. In 2019, it's a contest of stability against instability, and competence against incompetence—the LNP has removed two leaders since 2013, whereas Labor has kept its leadership team intact during this time.

Not much has been said about this in the media, but the Morrison government has been in minority since the Wentworth by-election in November last year. Perhaps it's because this occurred relatively late in the term and the expectation an election was due to be called soon, but it's interesting to compare the rabid media during the final months of the Gillard–Rudd government—the previous time we had a minority government—with the tepid media response when the LNP found itself in exactly the same position.

The LNP's two terms of government since 2013 have been littered with political incompetence, navel gazing, corruption and policy quagmire. It denied the need for a Royal Commission into banking and has made its time in government a continuation of the Howard era of Liberal Party, rather than create a form of leadership that is relevant in today's world.

For all of the faults of the Labor period between 2010–13, at least they can argue they had the global financial crisis to contend with and their differences were based around their dislike of Kevin Rudd as a personality, rather than policy matters.

The divisions with the LNP have been far worse—a divide between personalities, but coupled with a severe schism in the party about climate change and renewable energy. It's almost as though they've been at war with everything, including themselves. And electric cars and veganism.

As John Howard loved to say when he was prime minister, elections and politics are all about arithmetic, and the measures required for the LNP to win the 2019 election will be difficult to achieve.

The first path to victory

First of all, the Liberal–National Party is currently in minority, holding only seventy-four seats of 150 seats, notionally, only seventy-three of 151 seats. This means to govern in its own right, the LNP will need to make a net gain of three seats. Just based on numbers alone, it's hard to see this happening.

There are a few seats that can be easily identified as potential wins—Wentworth, Indi and Lindsay. Wentworth and Indi were LNP-held seats until Cathy McGowan took Indi in the 2013 election, and Kerryn Phelps took Wentworth in the November 2018 by-election. McGowan is retiring from politics, and there are suggestions that away from the national spotlight a by-election commands, Wentworth will return to the Liberal Party.

The Liberal Party confidence in Lindsay is based on their performance in the recent NSW election, where they managed to hold on to the seat of Penrith, but internal party polling suggests the seat will be held by Labor's candidate, Diane Beamer.

There are three ultra marginal seats held by Labor, all held by first-time MPs. The Queensland seat of Herbert is held by Cathy O'Toole, and this is the most marginal seat in the country, separated by only thirty-seven votes.

Anne Aly took the WA seat of Cowan by just over 1,000 votes in the 2016 election, and is up against a political novice, Isaac Stewart, who currently works as a community development officer.

Ged Kearney holds the seat of Cooper, but the contest in this case is between Labor and Greens, and is out of reach for the LNP.

The seat of Dunkley, although notionally a Labor seat, is actually held by the Liberal's Chris Crewther, but he will need a swing of 1.3 per cent towards him to hold the seat.

The renamed seat of Macnamara (previously known as Melbourne Ports) is held by Labor, but Michael Danby is retiring, and this seat is in contention—but for the Greens, not for the Liberal Party.

These are the only seats that present themselves as low-hanging fruit for the LNP, and they would need to win three of six winnable seats to win the election. And, if they did, they'd only be back to the precarious one-seat majority they found themselves with after the 2016 election.

The second pathway to victory

But this is only part of the first equation, and assumes the Coalition holds all of its other seats. How likely is this? There are four ultra marginal seats held by the Coalition: Corangamite, Capricornia, Forde and Gilmore.

The Victorian seat of Corangamite is held by Sarah Henderson. She won the seat in 2013 and again in 2016 by a margin of 3.13 per cent, but a redistribution has the seat notionally on 50.0 per cent. Given the large anti-Liberal swing in the Victoria election in November 2018, and the home-town factor for Bill Shorten, this is one seat that is likely to fall.

The two Queensland seats of Capricornia and Forde are held by Michelle Landry and Bert van Manen respectively—of the two, Forde is the more likely to fall. Incumbency will play a large part here, and with lesser-known candidates in these seats, Labor will be hoping for overall swings against the government in Queensland for one or both of these seats to fall.

Gilmore in the Shoalhaven area of New South Wales is another seat that is delicately balanced, and is held by the Liberal Party by just over 1,100 votes. The sitting member, Ann Sudmalis, failed in her preselection bid against Grant Schultz who, in turn, was turfed out when Scott Morrison decided to parachute former Labor leader, Warren Mundine, into the seat.

It's not quite clear what this episode was meant to achieve. After her disendorsement, Sudmalis has failed to provide any support to the Liberal Party in the lead-up to the election—why would she—a disgruntled Schultz is running as an independent candidate, and Mundine has no connection to the area, and was only preselected in February.

Of these four ultra marginal seats, three are very likely to fall. Even if only one of these seats was to fall and the LNP managed to gain the three seats mentioned above, it would still be in a minority position, and depend on support from independent MPs to form government.

Other seats in a losing position

The mathematics in the position of having to gain three seats, while holding four ultra marginal seats is already difficult.

On top of this is a swathe of LNP-held seats all over the country that are delicately poised. In Queensland, the seats of Petrie, Flynn and Dickson are held by less than 2 per cent, and in Western Australia, the Liberal Party is not polling well in the seats of Hasluck, Swan or Pearce.

In the inner west Sydney seat of Reid, the Liberal Party only preselected Fiona Martin as their candidate last week, after the departure of popular MP, Craig Laundy. The seat is held by 4.7 per cent, but Laundy's departure and the invisible nature of Martin's campaign means this seat could also fall.

The media is here to help

Clearly, the mathematics are against the chances of the Liberal–National Party securing a third term of office. The reason why governments usually face difficulties securing third and subsequent terms is that the electorate has a track record of a two-term government they can use to assess what they are likely to do in the future. And the signs for the LNP are not good.

The main issue for the LNP is one of political competence and management, and for a party to have three prime ministers within five years is a clear sign there are troubles within its ranks, just as there were for the Labor Party during 2010–2013.

The LNP in 2019 finds itself in exactly the same position as the Labor Party when the 2013 campaign commenced, but with one notable difference: the media.

The media constantly tells the electorate Bill Shorten is unpopular but, according to opinion polls, it seems the electorate will put that to one side and vote in a Labor government.

Already, the mainstream media has swung into action behind Scott Morrison, and started to hammer Bill Shorten and the Labor Party. 'Why are you so unpopular', they ask Shorten, seemingly unaware according to many polls, Morrison is equally unpopular. Shorten does have an average disapproval rating of 51 per cent, but Morrison is not that far behind on 45 per cent.

Why is Morrison never asked by the media about why he is so unpopular?

Why are Morrison or Treasurer Josh Frydenberg never called out for the misrepresentation that Labor will increase taxes by $387 billion? Or that Labor's negative gearing changes will make 'property prices go down and rents go up'? Or Labor's proposal changes to franking credits rules is a tax that will hurt pensioners, even though 80 per cent of those people affected have share assets of well over $1 million?

And now we have, not even two days since the election campaign was announced, *Sydney Morning Herald* journalist Peter Hartcher claiming the election is already a 'depressing contest' between an 'angry dad figure in a baseball cap and a sad sack who looks like he learned public speaking at a funeral parlour'.

It's hard to know what amuses the media when it comes to election time. All elections are fascinating, although for different reasons, and for political journalists to downplay an election is sad indictment of where the mainstream media sits today.

Elections are important, the 2019 federal election is perhaps more important than most. It pits one unstable and ideologically-divided side that is so set in the past and thoroughly undeserving of re-election, against another side that has provided stability in opposition and released a steady flow of policy ideas that offer a fairer and more equitable future.

If elections don't matter to these over-paid journalists who manage to somehow survive in a dying industry, it's best they retire to other pastures and give up on the trade, because they're not doing anyone any favours.

Labor is strongly favoured to win the election on 18 May but in a two-party race held over thirty-five days of campaigning, many issues still need to fall into place for either side, albeit, many more factors need to fall into place for the Coalition, than for the Labor side.

*

Captain GetUp: The lost avenger?

13 April 2019

David Lewis

Some election campaigns are fairly straightforward. The prime minister sets a date, and both parties sell their policies. There's a lot of talk about economic management, fairness, justice, some international relations and, maybe some specific issue concerning the electorate. The major candidates tend to be pretty honest and the public makes a choice one way or the other, usually returning the government of the day. Every now and then, though, a campaign has something happen that overturns *everything*. In recent memory, the Tampa crisis in August 2001 was one of these election-changing events.

The current electoral cycle will be remembered for its bizarre events. In the week of writing, we've had the federal government approve a mine no-one really wants; a weird debate on electric cars; a senior Liberal Senator imply all people of Asian descent are related; and the launch of Captain GetUp, a character developed by Advance Australia, the conservative rival to GetUp!

Of all the tin-eared, out-of-touch maneuverings of the current government, it's hard to think of a more inept attempt at using comedy to sell a message. Captain GetUp is a costumed superhero who is travelling round Australia. Why? Well, to look at him, you'd think he was a part of GetUp!, the progressive movement. After all, he is named after them—he is muscular and has a chiselled jaw. He is reminiscent of most superheroes. So, he would, for most people, at least provide a positive reaction.

So, why is he actually an anti-GetUp! message? He claims that he's there to stop political correctness, and Labor/Greens, independent candidates and union collusion. Okay... He further claims to be the son of Labor leader, Bill Shorten. I am not making any of this up. And that he has spent fourteen years locked in the office of GetUp!, learning their ways, so he can tell people all about what they're doing. He has certainly provoked laughter, but we all know the difference between being laughed at, and being laughed with.

There is a misunderstanding of comic superheroes here. As parody, it fails, because we are getting mixed signals. He is strong, positive and has a pleasing physical appearance. He has Labor, Greens and independents on his cape—which at least in a large minority of people (and if the polls are any indication, a majority) give a slightly-to-significantly positive image.

On the second day of his reveal, he introduced 'Freddie Foreign Money'. Most superheroes have an arch-nemesis. Some have a sidekick. Freddie Foreign Money looks like and is named like an arch-nemesis. He's not. In a month in which troubling allegations of foreign money interfering on the right wing of politics have aired, this is beyond ridiculous.

To say this is a risky strategy—attacking Labor, the Greens and independent candidates for obtaining foreign money—is like skating on paper thin ice on a hot day. No doubt there is something there, at least in some cases, but after the revelations of the last few days about Peter Dutton's relationships with members of the Chinese Communist Party, I'd think the strategy is, at the very least, courageous—in the *Yes, Minister* sense.

So why else does he fail? Apart from the mixed messages, he is ridiculous. He fails as satire. What is he satirising? GetUp!? Bill Shorten? The Greens?

Why is it funny that Bill Shorten is Captain GetUp's father? Generally, families are off limits. Did Captain GetUp gain his superpowers from Bill? If so isn't this a good thing? Or are superpowers bestowed only to certain Liberal Party members?

Superheroes have a clear origin story. Superman came from the destroyed planet of Krypton. Batman's parents were murdered, giving him a pathological need for revenge. Peter Parker was bitten by a radioactive spider. Captain America was given a super serum. Stories about the origins of a superhero don't need to exist in the real world. But they should make sense. Captain GetUp seems to be an office administrator, but with that physical build? What is his motivation for telling the 'truth'?

Precisely what has Captain GetUp gained from his origins? He knows how a progressive political party works. But doesn't seem to understand that the various groups he claims are in cahoots with each other are actually separate and often at odds. Yes, political alliances can be formed but Labor is the parliamentary wing of the union movement. That's not a secret and it means that unions get to have a say in Parliament. Whether this is a good thing or not depends on your politics but it's not a secret conspiracy. Most independent candidates seem to be disaffected or ex-Liberal Party members and they are mostly centre- or right-leaning.

At a time where superheroes are prominent—look at the roaring success of the Marvel Cinematic Universe, for example—Captain GetUp fails. And at a time where we need more satire in public and political life, Captain GetUp fails again.

Many of the more prominent independents running in the 2019 election lean to the right of politics. How they are suddenly Labor Socialists or Greens activists hasn't been explained. Of course, half a second of thought on Captain GetUp leaves more questions than answers.

It is possible Captain GetUp might gain some traction in the electorate. He may be able to cut through his mixed messages and convince skeptical voters that GetUp! is a Labor, Greens and independent front. The national director of Advance Australia, Gerard Benedet, has claimed Captain GetUp has been a massive success.

I'm a bit pessimistic on Labor's chances in the upcoming 2019 federal election and I think it's possible we'll get another three years of the incumbent Liberal–National Party. As someone who loves politics and popular culture, I'm in the mindset of 'whatever' the final outcome ends up being; however, I suspect Captain GetUp won't be back in a hurry.

*

Divided Opinions: Eddy Jokovich + David Lewis

On water matters set to sink Morrison

22 April 2019

Eddy Jokovich

It's the end of the first week of the federal election campaign and, already, we have the mainstream media telling everyone within earshot that this is a 'boring' campaign, and the electorate is 'disillusioned' and 'jaded' with the two main political parties.

But what are they expecting? What amuses these seasoned journalists that have probably been around for far too long? Would they like to see candidates playing saxophones, just like Bill Clinton during the 1992 US presidential campaign? Live twerking, just like Clive Palmer demonstrated in 2013? Even when a grand scandal is brewing just under their noses, they refuse to take the bait, so we're left wondering what does it take for journalists to hold a conservative government to account?

This 'the-election-is-boring' mantra is a tactic to have voters switched off from the main issues and remain disillusioned with politics, in the hope that a conservative government remains in office. It's a tactic used by Fox News in the US, but it's a standard now used by the Australian conservative media.

Aside from the boredom factor, we've also been told the Prime Minister, Scott Morrison, is an excellent campaigner—after just one week—is more 'wily' than his predecessor, Malcolm Turnbull; and

Labor leader, Bill Shorten, now has 'every reason to be nervous' about his election prospects, according to political journalist Michelle Grattan.

Others in the media are suggesting Labor's attempts to win government have much greater obstacles in 2019, when compared to 2016. Some are reporting the pathway for the Liberal–National Party to return to government is becoming clearer, without outlining how the LNP is going to overturn almost three years of negative polling, change the perception they're a divided political entity, or overcome the lack of real policy solutions for the future, especially on climate change.

We've also been told by *The Guardian Australia* that Morrison is 'master of the middle', and is "closing in on Bill Shorten and unsettling the Labor leader". As with most of these statements, no evidence is provided to support the claims, just aimless ramblings and endless unsubstantiated opinion, just like all of those inane and inaccurate opinions proffered during the 2016 election campaign.

And most in the mainstream media have commenced their interviews with Shorten by asking him about his low popularity, a question never asked of Morrison, even through his levels of unpopularity aren't far behind. In the latest Newpoll survey, Shorten's disapproval rating is 51 per cent, while Morrison's is slightly lower at 45 per cent.

Shorten is unpopular, because the media wants him to be, and it's a narrative they've been constantly feeding ever since he became Leader of the Opposition in 2013. Labor is 'stumbling', because there any many in the media who actually want Labor to stumble. In the 2016 election, the media constantly told us the amount of seats to be won by the Turnbull-led Liberal–National Party would have an '8' or '9' in front it, even though polls were consistently suggesting a much closer race, some polls even having Labor ahead with a slight lead.

In the last week of the 2016 campaign, Laura Tingle from the *Australian Financial Review* wrote that "the sense that Labor is a serious challenger has faded"; *The Australian*'s Dennis Shanahan suggested "Malcolm Turnbull is coming home with the wind in his sails, Bill Shorten is running out of puff"; and the *Daily Telegraph*, claimed Malcolm Turnbull was on the "brink of victory".

The LNP did win the 2016 federal election, but it won just seventy-six seats, a bare one-seat majority, not the expected landslide the media wanted.

Many in the mainstream media refused to read the writing on the wall then, and we're seeing a repeat of this in 2019, even though we're only at the end of the first week of the campaign.

Let's compare the respective low points of the week for the LNP and for Labor.

Disability is an advantage

The Minister for Home Affairs, Peter Dutton, started the week with a terrible slur on his opponent in the seat of Dickson, Ali France, claiming she was using her disability as an excuse for not living within the boundaries of the seat. The day after, instead of apologising for this slur, he doubled down, claiming he was just "representing the views of his electorate", before apologising for his comments, three days after he first made them.

As it turned out, this was spectacular own-goal for the Dutton campaign: France was able to outline her story of how she lost her leg—protecting her young child while a car reversed into her in a shopping centre car park—as well as outlining the difficult factors involved in finding suitable accommodation for people with disabilities. France lives at a location which is a seven-minute drive outside the seat of Dickson, compared with Dutton's primary place of residence on the Gold Coast, almost 100 kilometres away. What is Dutton's excuse for not living within the boundaries of his own seat?

Dutton holds the seat of Dickson by a margin of 1.60 per cent, and needs everything to go right over the next four weeks to hold. But in his attempts to score cheap political points, he has only offered a greater platform to his opponent, and is likely to lose the seat.

Love and the iPad in Manila

We also had revelations about the Liberal–National Party member for Dawson, George Christensen, that he'd spent at least seventy days in each of the past three years visiting his fiancé in the Philippines. Christensen spent 294 days between 2014–2018 travelling to Manila, the equivalent of nine weeks of paid holidays each and every year.

We haven't heard from Christensen about this matter, but fellow LNP MP, David Littleproud, tried to downplay the episode by claiming "everyone is entitled to love", and Christensen could easily carry out his parliamentary duties from the comfort of his iPad.

We can try to overlook all the security issues that would arise from an MP carrying out their electoral work from an iPad in one corner of a Manila district through an unsecured internet service provider, but to suggest parliamentary work can be performed primarily with a mobile phone and iPad in a foreign country is ludicrous.

Littleproud's claim is also in contrast to reports of Christensen missing one-third of the important hearings of the Inquiry into the Development of Northern Australia, because he was in Manila, where he neither called in remotely during these times, or engaged with the inquiry.

Dawson is one of the poorest electorates in Australia, starved of economic and employment opportunities. For Christensen to miss one-third of a forum that is critical to the future prospects of the region, as well as engaging in a love-fest overseas junket for three years is certainly not going to impress the voters of Dawson.

On water matters

But the biggest news of the first week of the election campaign has been the revelations of the 2017 water buy-back from Eastern Australia Agriculture, for the sum of $79 million. There are many questions that need to be answered in this deal.

For a start, EAA sought a water buy-back twice during Labor's time in government between 2007–2013, but was refused on both occasions; one of the establishing directors of EAA was Liberal MP Angus Taylor, who is now Minister for Energy and member for Hume; EAA is a company registered in the Cayman Islands, shrouded in a cloak of great secrecy; EAA made a profit of $52 million from this one transaction; and Barnaby Joyce was the Minister for Water at the time.

This is not a new story, but has been bubbling just under the surface for some time on Twitter through a story thread provided by @MsVeruca (since removed by Twitter, under malicious legal threats from Taylor's lawyers, Mark O'Brien Legal). Despite the allegations of mismanagement and corruption, the mainstream media refused to become involved until Channel 10's *The Project* presented a video story on 18 April.

Others in the mainstream media then started to ask questions of the Prime Minister on Easter Saturday about whether there was any impropriety in the EAA water buy-back. While the questioning of the Prime Minster was strong, the follow up was poor.

Morrison's initial response was to say the buy-back was initiated by the Queensland Labor government, and that the federal government has been very transparent. But a document released in 2017 proves the Queensland Government had nothing to do with the transaction, and documents released by the federal minister had 70 per cent of its content redacted. So much for transparency.

Perhaps journalists at Morrison's media conference were flummoxed by his statement the Queensland Government was somehow involved with a federal government transaction, but no one had the wherewithal to ask for proof from the Prime Minister, or which Queensland minister they could contact to verify his statement.

Or perhaps they were more worried their invitation to watch the second episode of *Game Of Thrones* in a cosy home theatre with the Prime Minister would be revoked if they asked questions deemed to be too difficult.

A horror week for the LNP but, somehow, Labor still loses

Despite all of this, the mainstream media decided the Liberal–National Party had won the first week of the campaign and, according to Channel Nine's political correspondent, Chris Uhlmann, "Labor was seen to have a fairly bad first week".

And how did journalists arrive at this conclusion of Labor having a 'bad first week'?

Because Labor leader, Bill Shorten, was tripped up in a 'gotcha' moment when asked about his superannuation policy. The question, asked by Sky News reporter, James O'Doherty, had the hostility of an attack Rottweiler on steroids, and Shorten responded by saying Labor had no plans for new taxes on superannuation, even though he previously announced there would be superannuation reform if Labor was elected to government.

Did Shorten mishear, or did he not understand his own policy? It seemed more like a stitch-up by a Liberal Party operative than a serious political query. Labor released their superannuation plan to curb tax concessions on superannuation contributions from high income earners towards the end of 2016—three years ago. Why would O'Doherty ask the question on a long-existing policy if he wasn't planning to trip Shorten up?

The media had a field day when Bill Shorten was tripped up on a question about superannuation. But was it a set-up?

Needless to say, the mainstream media ran with this story for the rest of the week, promoting endless stories about Shorten not understanding his own policy work, that somehow this was the turning point of the election and would give ample opportunity for the LNP to surge ahead in the polls.

Intelligence is usually in short supply among the media throng during election time, and it seems it won't be any different this time around. Journalists are 'bored', they report about how 'jaded' the electorate is, they question why Bill Shorten is 'so unpopular', and report with alacrity when Shorten misunderstands a question designed to fail him.

Some in the media are even suggesting that more pressure is being placed on Labor because they now have a suite of policies that can be scrutinised, while the LNP has none. For years, journalists have bemoaned the lack of policy from all sides of politics but when one side of politics releases a swathe of substantial material, it's reported as a political disadvantage?

And, supposedly, as a result of this pressure and scrutiny on Labor policies, the electorate will return to the LNP, even though they have an absence of policies.

It's this kind of logic that often makes me wonder how on earth journalists get their jobs in the first instance. They complain about elections being dull and boring because they're cocooned from the results of whichever government is formed. But for working people, elections are important events and consequences from government decisions can be life changing. Elections do matter. It's just a pity the media sees it all as an entertainment sideshow.

And the real winner was…

Whoever the winner was during week one of this campaign, it's not really of great consequence. The mainstream media collectively agreed Malcolm Turnbull was the winner of week one of the 2016 election campaign, even though he ran one of the poorest campaigns since Billy McMahon in 1972, and ended up with a slim one-seat majority. Sure, he still won the election, but the tight result was against all media expectations, and caused Turnbull so many problems throughout the term, until he was finally ousted by his own party in August 2018.

Week one is when both campaign machines get their wheels in motion, clear their throats and start road testing their election scripts. Many people in the electorate aren't even aware an election is being held on May 18: they're still consumed with the long weekend, and worried about what to do with their kids during the school holidays. And the other big factor is, they may have already made up their minds about who'll they'll be voting for and the campaign will be immaterial to their selection on election day.

But whatever the case, week one was not even a nil-all draw: the main game hasn't started yet. Let's see what happens after ANZAC Day to get a better perspective of how the campaign is being played out.

*

Sweet election victories from the 1990s

25 April 2019

Eddy Jokovich / Podcast

T he date of 2019 federal election has been announced and all sides of politics are veering through the first stages of the campaign, driving their buses and flying their planes with the media pack joining them, testing out their election scripts and trying to navigate a path towards an election victory on May 18.

According to all the polls and betting agencies, Labor is set to win this election and Bill Shorten will become prime minister, but it's never as clear cut as the evidence suggests: we only have to look at the election of Donald Trump in the 2016 US presidential campaign and Brexit in the UK to see how results can be quite different to expectations. No-one really believed those results until they were clearly confirmed.

Elections, of course, are never the same and always play out to different campaign songsheets: each election is made up of different politicians, different candidates and different circumstances, but scanning through the archives has shown there are elections from the past that can provide us with some insights for 2019. And there are two particular elections to inspect: one in Britain, and one in Australia.

*

It's 1992 in the United Kingdom, almost eighteen months after Prime Minister Margaret Thatcher was removed as the leader of the Conservative Party, their new leader, John Major, hadn't quite captured the imagination of the electorate: the popular consensus was that he was a stop-gap leader who was likely to lead the Conservatives to an election defeat, after which they'd elect a new leader and lick their wounds sitting on the opposition benches.

Neil Kinnock was the leader of the British Labour Party—now into his ninth year as party leader—and with his nemesis Margaret Thatcher out of the way, Kinnock was expected to comfortably lead Labour back into office after thirteen years of Conservative rule. Here is his confident address to the Labour faithful, a few weeks before the election:

Neil Kinnock: We're alright! This is the Labour Party, this is the party that is going to win the election and win for our country! British people want a country with a sense of community, they want a Britain that is whole, and fair, and free; a sense of duty towards all of the people. That... is... a Labour government!

Kinnock and the Labour Party had good reason to be optimistic: the Conservatives were seeking a fourth consecutive election victory—always difficult in Western democracies—there was a deep economic recession in Britain, and there had been a sharp rise in unemployment over the past year.

Labour had been ahead in opinion polls for most of the previous three years, and even the conservative newspaper, the *Financial Times*, was backing a Labour election victory, and there was a strong mood for change in the electorate—or, so the electorate was told. But, as it turned out, there wasn't enough of a mood for change. This is what happened on the election night in 1992:

BBC announcer: Here are the scenes at the Conservative Party headquarters, as John Major, the Prime Minister, arrives back, as Mrs Thatcher arrived back in 1987, with another victory to give them... a fourth term in office.

John Major: We've won tonight, a magnificent victory, a victory many people thought was beyond our grasp, but one which the Conservative Party always believed was there for the taking. And as a result of that victory, we have five years to put into place those items of policy we outlined in our Manifesto, those dreams of our future...

John Major and the Conservatives were returned to office with a small majority, and Labour didn't reach the victory most people expected. There had also been a vicious campaign against Labour by the Murdoch-backed media, which also wouldn't have helped their cause, but it seemed whatever people were telling opinion pollsters for three years in the lead-up to the election, it wasn't the same as what they were prepared to mark up on their ballot papers. Neil Kinnock was unelectable.

The 1992 British election result was very unusual and caught most people by surprise, but an even bigger upset was coming up just around the corner...

*

In 1993, Australia was still recovering from the effects of a deep recession; unemployment had reached a post-war high of 11 per cent and the Australian dollar was only worth 66 US cents on the international money markets. The Labor brand was on the nose in most parts of the country, and the party had just lost state elections in Victoria and Western Australia.

Labor had been in office federally since 1983, had made fundamental changes to the economy and the workplace through the Accord processes, and was seeking a fifth consecutive term in office. It had barely scraped through to victory during the 1990 election on the back of environmental preference deals with minor parties and, after the election, Bob Hawke's leadership of the Labor Party became more and more tenuous.

While it had been a successful government for some time, reform fatigue had set in and the observation from Treasurer Paul Keating that "this is the recession that Australia had to have" became a millstone around his neck, and the Coalition was very keen to weigh him down with it.

After the 1990 election, there was a newcomer on the scene—John Hewson became the Leader of the Opposition, and released his *Fightback!* manifesto in 1991—a radical free-market proposal with the goods and service tax as its centrepiece. Soon after Hewson released his *Fightback!* package, Paul Keating challenged Bob Hawke for the Labor leadership:

Bob Hawke: The question of who will be leading this party and who'll be prime minister of Australia will be decided by my party in a ballot at 6.30 this afternoon.

Channel 9 newsreader: Bob Hawke to resign, opening the way for a leadership ballot.

News reporter: Paul Keating confirms he will challenge, and followers say he has the numbers.

As it turned out, Keating did have the numbers and became the new prime minister in December 1991. For most of this parliamentary term, John Hewson was the preferred prime minister in all opinion polls, and had the Coalition leading the Labor Party in forty-nine of the preceding fifty-four Newspoll surveys. Just one month before the 1993 election, the Coalition was leading by 53 to 47 per cent in the two-party preferred vote.

Keating had a high disapproval rating for most of the time since he became prime minister, and questions about the election were mainly about how many seats Labor would lose, and even whether Labor could survive as a political party. And then, ten days before the election, Mike Willesee interviewed John Hewson on *A Current Affair*, during prime time television:

Mike Willesee: If I buy a birthday cake from a cake shop and GST is in place, do I pay more or less for that birthday cake?

John Hewson: Well, it will depend whether cakes today in that shop are subject to sales tax, or they're not—firstly. And they may have a sales tax on them. Let's assume that they don't have a sales tax on them... then that birthday cake is going to be sales tax free. Then of course you wouldn't pay—it would be exempt, would, sorry—there would be no GST on it under our system. If it was one with a sales tax today it would attract the GST, and then the difference would be the difference between the two taxes whatever the sales tax rate is on birthday cakes, how it's decorated, because there will be sales tax perhaps on some of the decorations as well, and then of course the price—the price will reflect that accordingly. But the key point is that there, the average Australian will have more money in their pocket.

MW: No, but just on the, just on the birthday cake, because I'm trying to pick up a simple example. You tell us in what you've published that the cost of cake goes down, the cost of confectionery goes up, there's icing and maybe ice cream, and then there's candles on top of it.

JH: That's right, now that's the difficulty—that's what I'm addressing in the question. To give you an accurate answer, I need to know exactly what type of cake to give a detailed answer. I mean if it's just a cake from a cake shop that is not presently subject to sales tax, it will not attract the GST.

MW: But isn't that...

JH: If it is a cake shop, a cake from a cake shop that has sales tax, and it's decorated and candles as you say, that attracts sales tax, then of course we scrap the sales tax, before the GST is...

MW: Okay—it's just an example. If the answer to a birthday cake is so complex, you do have an overall problem with the GST, don't you?

This interview was a disaster for the Coalition and although the polls tightened dramatically in the final week of the campaign, the Coalition was still expected to win. Even on the day of the election, John Hewson was highly confident of getting the Coalition back into government, even detailing the conversations he'd be having with Treasury, after he won the election:

Newsreader: Though he won't predict the margin, Doctor Hewson seems to have no doubt about the result tomorrow.

John Hewson: We believe so [that we will win].

N: He says he will carry out all the commitments he's made and won't cry foul once he's in office.

JH: We aren't going to go into government and change our mind; we aren't going to go in and say 'look, things are worst than we feared'. We feared the worst, we know we're going to find it.

N: He says he'll start work on Sunday, getting Treasury briefings on the state of the economy.

But on election night, the result was quite different. Here's John Hewson again, speaking at the Liberal Party election night gathering, at Sydney's Hotel Intercontinental:

Clearly it was a tough campaign, clearly it's close, something like fifteen or sixteen seats still in the balance but you'd have to say the probabilities are that the government will win.

From the halls of the Bankstown Sports Club, the Prime Minister, Paul Keating was more definitive about the result:
Thank you ladies and gentlemen. Well, this is the sweetest victory of all. This is a victory for the true believers.

There were an incredible eighteen seats that changed hands from one side to the other—eleven seats were picked up by Labour, seven by the Coalition; Labor picked up a swing towards it of 1.5 per cent and made a net gain of two seats, winning the election with a majority of fifteen seats. Somehow, Labor had managed to win the unwinnable election.

*

In hindsight, the 1993 election was a Pyhrric victory for Labor: it lost government in a crushing defeat at the next election in 1996, and the Coalition under John Howard introduced most of the contents of Hewson's *Fightback!* package between 1996 and 2007. But still, the 1993 election result is the most unlikely of victories in Australian political history.

Looking at these historical elections, Bill Shorten will be hoping to avoid what happened to Neil Kinnock in the 1992 British election, and ironically, Scott Morrison will be looking to emulate Paul Keating from the 1993 Australian election. But Morrison is not like Keating and, unlike Labour in 1993, the Coalition in 2019 is a divided party and they're trying paper over a long list of corruption allegations.

But in a two-horse election race anything can happen, and the usual clichés we'll be hearing over the next few weeks are: don't believe the polls; it's not over until it's over; and, the best one: the only poll that matters is the one on election day.

*

Music in this episode
Sweetness and Light, Itch-E & Scratch-E
The Holy Grail, Hunters and Collectors
I Am Resurrection, Stone Roses

A most exciting 2019 election campaign continues

3 May 2019

Eddy Jokovich + David Lewis / Podcast

In this episode, we looked at the progress of the 2019 election campaign; the sinking feeling of the politics of water; and we assessed the role of the mainstream media and how they are affecting the election campaign. Also in this episode, David Lewis appears as President of the Cayman Islands Chamber of Commerce.

Eddy Jokovich: We're into the third week of the 2019 election campaign, and real votes have been already lodged in pre-polling booths all around the country. It's been an up-and-down campaign—so far, we've had the revelations of the water buy-back scandal involving Angus Taylor and Eastern Australia Agriculture; a range of policy announcements from one side of politics but from the other side, we've had beer swilling, sheep-shearing, lawn bowls, and football. But the real question is, have people started listening in to the campaign, or will they wait until the final week to start focusing their attention on the election? And will they start taking notice of the various scandals building up in the Liberal Party?

David Lewis: The Liberal Party is too obviously in the pockets of vested interests that aren't necessarily in the best interests of Australia.

The last time this level of scandal happened was in about 1940, with what was then the United Australia Party—no relation to Clive Palmer's current day version—it collapsed in 1943, and was nearly wiped out of office in 1944. The UAP then restructured itself as the Liberal Party and then went on to have great electoral success in 1949. Whether the current day issues for the Liberal Party are affecting this campaign in this sort of way is difficult to say. I do think most people have already made up their mind about this election. There's one opinion poll indicating 73 per cent of the electorate has already made up their mind about who they will vote for, which suggests much of this election campaign is becoming redundant. That still leaves 27 per cent of the electorate that are still unsure, so it's too early to say.

EJ: It has been a very unusual campaign timewise, because there was the Easter holiday break; then there was the ANZAC Day holiday and it has also been wedged in between the school holidays, so it's almost like the first two weeks of the campaign were like a staggered warm-up lap: both sides have been clearing their throats, testing out different messages and different ideas, and because of the breaks due to the range of holiday periods, it's almost like the first two weeks didn't really matter, the electorate was focusing on other matters in their lives.

DL: Every week of the campaign is important, but some insiders have been worried about Labor's campaign strategy. Labor tends to do better electorally with charismatic and popular figures: Bob Hawke, Paul Keating, Kevin Rudd and Julia Gillard, but Bill Shorten is not one of those people. In comparison, the government's campaign so far has been poor. Probably the most entertaining and most disturbing interview of the last ten years was Barnaby Joyce on Radio National, interviewed by Patricia Karvelas: half-panicked, half-paranoid, bluff and bluster, jumping around trying to defend the indefensible water buy-backs. It was a very strange interview which we'll discuss later.

EJ: The overall process for the Liberal–National Party in this campaign would have to be a 'save-the-furniture' strategy. That would be corralling their base supporters so they don't start thinking about sending off their preferences to One Nation or the United Australia Party, with the chance of that vote going over to the Labor side.

Just recently, over the past week, there has been a tightening of the opinion polls which, of course, can be read in so many different ways. Consistently, it's been 52–48 per cent in the two-party preferred vote in the favour of the Labor Party for a long time. But two polls over the past week: Newspoll, which showed a tightening of 51-to-49 per cent, and there was also an Essential poll, which showed similar figures as well. We've been consistently saying the Liberal–National Party will be wiped out in this election campaign but with the narrowing of the polls, do you still think that might be the case?

DL: We might be looking at another term of Liberal–National, to be quite honest, and it's going to happen through preferences. Labor may win the primary vote, but in those marginal seats where people will vote for independents, One Nation, or United Australia Party, preference flows will go to the LNP, and we might also be in for another term of minority government, or close to it.

EJ: In yesterday's leader's debate broadcast on Channel 7, Scott Morrison did say federal election campaigns and elections are usually quite close and numerically speaking, he's quite correct. An election result of 53-to-47 per cent in the two-party preferred vote might sound numerically close, but it's actually a landslide victory in Australian politics: 52-to-48 per cent can also be a landslide as well. But the last election in 2016 was close to 50:50. In the 1998 federal election, the Liberal–National Coalition achieved a two-party preferred vote of 49.02 per cent and managed to win the election by thirteen seats. In the Australian political system, elections are not necessarily all about the two-party preferred vote: it's all about how many seats you win. But would it would be possible for the LNP to win the election, overall, with a two-party preferred vote of 49 per cent?

DL: There are many marginal seats in Sydney's west; in Melbourne's west; the outer suburbs of Brisbane; in some rural seats, there are strong independent candidates. I don't think there will be too much 'strategic' voting. There probably will be exceptions—in the Wentworth by-election in 2018, for example, there was some discussion throughout the community about how to manage the vote to ensure the independent Kerryn Phelps could win the seat, after Malcolm Turnbull resigned. But that was a one-off, and that particular by-election has a great deal of attention thrust upon it. That won't happen in many seats during a general election. Many people, of course, don't fully understand how the preference system works. It's actually a very fair system, but you have to know how it works to make sure it works properly. Some people will 'donkey' vote, just place 1-2-3-4-5 down the ballot paper; they might recognise the name of a candidate, or specifically vote for a recognised party. Most people don't think much beyond their first preference vote.

EJ: In this election, there is a new United Australia Party—not the party from the 1930s, but the party created by mining magnate, Clive Palmer, and there has been a preference deal between the Liberals and the United Australia Party. But Palmer's name is mud in Queensland—people might have short memories about this, but not so short. He does currently owe the Australian Taxation Office around $67 million, through one of his nickel mines—Queensland Nickel—and also owes workers of that nickel mining company around $7 million in unpaid entitlements. This preference deal could backfire and, turn out to be quite a mistake, based on these unpaid entitlements.

DL: On YouTube and other social media channels, every second or third advertisement is one for the UAP, usually showing the unknown James McDonald. It used to be Clive all-the-way, but someone has obviously thought Clive Palmer might not be the best face to front the campaign, and the UAP has enlisted all kinds of people as candidates. There is a Chinese woman talking about how the UAP will stop racism, which I thought was a very interesting strategy and I hope it's a genuine one. There's a wide range of other candidates jumping in as well. The point is, Clive Palmer has thrown a lot of money into this campaign: whether Australians will be swayed, it's hard to tell at this stage. Palmer is announcing policies: high-speed rail lines which everybody seems to want but nobody seems to want to commit to. Announcements like this may swing votes in some parts of the country but, then again, the public might say: 'yes, it's Clive Palmer, we can't trust you'. He was also bragging on the *Sunrise* program on Channel 7 that he was worth "four thousand million dollars" and it's hard to see how comments like this will be beneficial to his campaign.

EJ: At the least, you would expect someone that is worth "four thousand million dollars" should be able to find $7 million to pay out the worker entitlements owed by Queensland Nickel. Clive Palmer has been a one-man show during this campaign, but Scott Morrison has also been a one-man show, almost like the Marlboro Man. The only trick Morrison hasn't attempted so far is ride horseback without a shirt, in the style of the Russian President, Vladimir Putin. Aside from this, he's been sheep-shearing, he's been doing a lot of different campaign stunts like that, but always by himself, as if he hasn't got much of a political team behind him. Whereas Bill Shorten comes with the team: he's on the campaign trail with Tanya Plibersek; he's out there with Chris Bowen; he's out there with Penny Wong; he's out there with a whole range of different Labor MPs beside him. Of course, that could be a strategy to shield some of the perceived levels of Shorten's unpopularity, but it does seem to be the key difference between campaigns: the individual on the Liberals' side and the team approach on the Labor side.

DL: Penny Wong has been a high-profile candidate for Labor, and a bit of a political headkicker. Tanya Plibersek. Chris Bowen. Tony Burke. These are high calibre people and, for Shorten, it shows a confidence in his potential ministerial team. For the Liberals, where is Josh Frydenberg; where's Mathias Cormann? Senator Mitch Fifield was on the ABC's *Q&A* last night and, based on this performance, he won't be back on television for a repeat appearance.

*

The politics of water buy-backs

EJ: In 2017, Barnaby Jones was the Minister for Water and authorised a $79 million purchase of water rights from two properties in Queensland, and the details of this deal have only come to light recently. The properties are owned by Eastern Australia Agriculture and the Minister for Energy, Angus Taylor, was an establishing director of this company. Taylor did resign from the company when he entered Parliament in 2013 but there are still many questions that need to be answered. The company is registered in the Cayman Islands, so we don't have any details at all about ownership structures, and there's no way we can find out. There were no tenders for this purchase of water rights, so we don't know the background to the deal; the company made a $52 million profit on the transaction, and the deal is for access to flood water, which means the Commonwealth has access to water that, on average, only arrives once every decade. On face value, it doesn't seem like it was a very good deal for the taxpayer.

DL: It's not a good look at all. If there's anything dodgy going on in politics, Barnaby Joyce doesn't seem to be too far away from the action. This water was initially valued, at most, $24 million. How it then gets sold for $79 million has not been explained at all. We can't say, as this stage, if Taylor personally benefited, and it's likely that he didn't. But it's still not a good look if a company that he set up and was a director of, and one that is based offshore in the Cayman Islands, profits from these types of transactions.

EJ: The critical factor is that because the company is registered in the Cayman Islands, we just don't know anything at all about the company. There's nothing illegal about setting up this type of company, but the combination of massive profits and company secrecy makes it seem like it's a very dodgy deal.

DL: It's not the type of deal most governments would do. Generally, government tenders have a very clear and open paper trail: this one has no paper trail and more questions need to be asked. Barnaby Joyce has been an irrelevancy since he lost the leadership of the National Party, his political career is dead and if there was any doubt about his leadership career being over, this water buy-back deal confirms it.

EJ: He did actually receive the Water portfolio when Malcolm Turnbull became prime minister in 2015...

DL: ...he actually demanded the Water portfolio, as part of his purview as Deputy Prime Minister, under the Coalition agreement...

EJ: The Coalition agreement is between the leader of the National Party and the leader of the Liberal Party, when the two parties are in government, but it's a secret agreement and that just adds to the level of secrecy of the water buy-back scheme. The public has no idea about the deal between the Prime Minister and the leader of the National Party, we don't know what's in there. But Joyce did actually demand the water portfolio, and with all the revelations about the water buy-back scheme coming out, we're finding out the reasons why he wanted it so much.

DL: Barnaby Joyce is probably one of the most corrupt federal Members of Parliament we've ever had: I should qualify that by saying there could be some very straightforward and honest explanation as to how the buy-back scheme has been going in this particular way. The public hasn't heard the reasons yet, but the more he tries to defend himself, the deeper he digs his own hole.

EJ: Joyce's defence of the water buy-back deal and whatever happened during the time when he was the Minister for Water is quite bizarre. There was *that* interview between Patricia Karvelas from the ABC and Barnaby Joyce—here is just a small sample:

> PK: In terms of the beneficiaries on the Cayman Islands, you said you didn't know. But you know now...
> BJ: [interrupting] ...no, no, hang on...
> PK: [continuing] ...who they are, who are...
> BJ: [interrupting] ...it's the same beneficiaries as the Queensland Labor government should have known about!...
> PK: Okay, do you know where they are now?...
> BJ: [interrupting] ...maybe state governments just aren't up to the job...
> PK: Okay, I'll ask again. Do you know who they are now?
> BJ: [shouting] Maybe the Queenland Labor government, who recommended this to us—the Queensland Labor government—Labor-Labor-Labor-Labor-Labor government—who recommended this to us...
> PK: Do you know who the beneficiaries are now?
> BJ: [interrupting and shouting] ...are you saying they're incompetent and don't know what they're doing...
> PK: Are the associates...
> BJ: [interrupting and shouting] ...are you saying they're incompetent and don't know what they're doing...
> PK: ...I'm asking you a question.

EJ: And on it went, for thirty minutes, and it's being described as one of the most bizarre interviews ever between a radio journalist and a politician. I'd go one step further: it's just the most bizarre interview between anyone I've ever heard on radio. There was no defence of the decisions Joyce made when he was Minister for Water, he was just talking over the top of Patricia Karvelas; there wasn't any sense behind what he was saying. It seems like Joyce and his brand of retail politics is going to end up in the bargain basement bin: it seems like it's not going anywhere for now. Many journalists in the media seem quite amused by someone like Barnaby Joyce—he comes across as the political joker within the system: part Joh Bjelke–Petersen, part comedian, and part something else. But Joyce is not a clown, he knows exactly what he's doing. Whenever a National Integrity Commission is created, hopefully sooner rather than later, he's likely to be one of the first people appearing in there.

DL: Joyce is basically a small-town mayor with a federal reach and access to a federal budget. All politicians do favours for each other and use those lines of influence to push policy. It's a question of whether a politician is doing that for the greater good or whether they're doing it for personal gain. In this case, it seems he's clearly done the favours for personal gain and he's clearly in the pocket of big mining and big farming. The current leader of the National Party, Michael McCormack had a media interview that has been completely overshadowed by the Barnaby Joyce radio interview—fortunately for him—where he couldn't actually point out a recent policy of the National Party that favoured farmers over mining interests. With Joyce, it looks like he's on track to win the seat of New England again: I don't know what they put in the water in New England, although the independent, Adam Blakester, is being mentored by Tony Windsor, so that could have an effect on the vote. At this election, we might see Joyce be returned with a much reduced margin, or pushed out of office, unlikely as that might be. The ABC interview with Barnaby Joyce was quite odd, and many people thought he was drunk: if I was a betting man, I'd probably put money on it, just because the odds would be in your favour. But Joyce was clearly a man who was panicked and came across as a man who at least thought he might have something to hide. The notion that a minister would let negotiations of that size go on at arm's length is astonishing.

EJ: Compare Barnaby Joyce with someone of the calibre of Ian Sinclair, who was the leader of the National Party, and actually held the seat of New England for thirty-three years. Sinclair had a fine sense of public service and being a politician in the public interest and the public good, but you look at someone like Joyce and then Michael McCormack, the current leader of the National Party, and it seems like the Nationals have fallen so far since those times of Ian Sinclair.

DL: 'Blackjack' McEwan, Tim Fischer. The National Party survived for so long because it had substantial people running the party who were basically honest, who basically had the good of Australia at heart. You didn't have to agree with these leaders, but at heart, they wanted to advance Australia in the way they thought best. I can't see this ethic from either McCormack or Joyce.

EJ: Water will be one of the big issues in the regions of Queensland and New South Wales in this election, and there are independent candidates in the regional seats of Farrer, Mallee and Cowper with a strong chance to win those seats, and a distant possibility in New England as well. These seats could be the real surprise of the election—there's great focus on marginal seats, there's great focus on what the Prime Minister is doing, and what Bill Shorten is doing. But, quite often, the election surprises happen when no one is looking. The seats of Cowper and Mallee are held by the Nationals, and Farrer is held by the Liberal Party—that's Sussan Ley's seat. They're up against a few strong independents, and these could be the big surprises on election night.

DL: The Shooters, Fishers and Farmers Party looms large as well. They turned the New South Wales state seat of Orange from a 30 per cent margin for the National Party, into their own seat. Anything can happen, and the National Party is on the nose. In some electorates in New South Wales, rural people are seeing large-scale fish deaths, and they're seeing a worsening drought, made worse by poor water management. The town of Walgett has no water, they have to truck water into the town; and in twenty-first century Australia, this is appalling. That town has had flowing water since its inception, right up until the recent fish kills in the area—there was also another fish kill that wasn't widely broadcast. And the people who are upset about it just aren't inner-city greenies: it's the farmer and rural people that are frustrated and upset, and know something is desperately wrong in these regions. These are the people concerned about the environment that have bucked that traditional perception of what an environmentalist looks like.

EJ: The water buy-back scheme, and in particular that $79 million transaction with Eastern Australia Agriculture, has been referred to the Auditor–General, in the hope the issue blows over during the election campaign, but there will be more focus on it after the election. The former Australian Federal Police Commissioner, Mick Keelty, has suggested there are so many gaps in the government's water buy-back scheme, and there are so many undeclared conflicts of interest, that it's wide open to corruption. But the water buy-back scheme also fits into other areas of perceived corruption from the LNP: there's the Helloworld incident with ministerial travel, there's Parakeelia and electoral money, there's Paladin and immigration detention. There's other allegation of corruption relating to Barnaby Joyce, with plans for the inland rail in New South Wales, there's the gas fields in Narrabri—both near properties owned by Joyce—there's the Great Barrier Reef Foundation receiving funding of $444 million without a tender. There are many allegations of corruption, and the water buy-back scandal may be the final straw for many people, certainly in Queensland and New South Wales.

DL: There is an understanding that, sometimes, ministers are put into portfolios they're not suited to, but they're supported by an excellent public service. It was the case for many years, and could still be the case today; staff from the Department of Agriculture used to vote solidly Labor, because they'd rather work with a minister who grew up in, say, Woolloomooloo, who knew nothing about agriculture but could be taught, rather than a National Party hack who was actually a failed farmer, who thought they knew everything about farming. This would create headaches for the Department of Agriculture. It's not so much that ministers are out of their depth—we don't like it when it happens, but we do understand that's how the Westminster system operates. The problem is when the corruption comes in, and that's what the public doesn't like. I suspect there may be some kind of electoral reckoning from all of this, but what form that takes on; whether it's a major drop in votes, or a loss of seats, it's hard to say. And if a National Integrity Commission is introduced, there's going to be a lot of sleepless nights for certain members on both sides of politics.

*

The media coverage of the election campaign

EJ: Winning election campaigns is based on how well political parties engage with the media and there's a number of different techniques used to attract voters. There's social media such as Facebook, Twitter, Instagram, and overseas platforms such as WeChat and Weibo are being used to engage Mandarin-speaking communities in different electorates. Despite the growth of alternative media, most political information is still disseminated through journalists from the mainstream media, and that's television, radio and print. And it's these journalists that are usually embedded within the respective campaign teams, hoping to gain enough information from the politicians to produce the content they need to achieve their deadlines. But most of the media reporting so far has been looking at slip-ups from politicians on the campaign trail, journalists trying to be the star reporter that captures the classic 'gotcha' moment, and they're more interested in providing a dream run for the Prime Minister through uncritical media questioning and the broadcasting of positive images on television. I've actually lost track of how many pubs and drinking environments Scott Morrison has visited during the campaign, and I'm actually beginning to wonder if he might have a problem with alcohol. So far, the Prime Minister has evaded much scrutiny, he's evaded much of the truth and continuously deflected away from the performance of the Liberal–National government over the past three years, and instead, much scrutiny by the media has been placed on the Leader of the Opposition, Bill Shorten. An aspiring prime minister does need to have the blowtorch applied to them if they want to become the prime minister, but have we seen too much scrutiny placed onto Bill Shorten and not enough on Scott Morrison?

DL: Scott Morrison is a very strange candidate for prime minister and he has a lot of question marks hovering over his own performance. Nobody has publicly explained why Malcolm Turnbull was rolled by the Liberal Party—we know it's because he lost internal party support and annoyed a sufficient amount of Liberal Party donors that didn't support the party anymore, even though, of course, Turnbull was one of the biggest donors—but Scott Morrison has never adequately explained why Turnbull was removed, and the media has given up too easily on this question. Morrison's own winning of his seat of Cook back in 2007 is shrouded in mystery—he had lost quite badly in the initial preselection and his Liberal Party opponent, Michael Towke, was basically run through the Murdoch media with its worst tendencies for character assassination. Scott Morrison never looks comfortable; he never looks like he's in control of the situation. There was that video making its way through social media, of Morrison skolling beer with a group of Young Liberals and they start chanting: "he's no Bob Hawke", referring to Hawke's drinking antics before he became prime minister. Tony Abbott, of course, received derision for skolling a beer. Many people felt that it wasn't very prime ministerial. Scott Morrison takes a mouthful and he looks like someone who doesn't like the taste of beer. Australians aren't interested in the big drinker anymore; they just want their prime minister to be competent and in control of the situation.

EJ: That's one reason why I do find the campaign imagery of Scott Morrison quite bemusing: he's walking into a pub; he's drinking beer with a mate; he's drinking beer in a crowed hall with other people drinking beer, many of whom seem drunk as well. He's shearing a sheep; he's lawn bowling; he's hitting a cricket ball; he's kicking a football. I've noticed many journalists out there reporting from field are saying the election campaign is quite boring, and I'm wondering why that is, because there's so many things they could be looking for. Instead of following Scott Morrison and recording him shearing a sheep or drinking yet another beer, they should be asking him decent questions about what his actually policies are. The electorate doesn't really care if a prime minister can shear a sheep or not, whether they can drink beer or whether they can hit a cricket ball or kick a football. What they are really interested in is the policies they're putting out in the public domain, whether they can introduce and implement those policies and how competent they will be if they manage to form government.

DL: Paul Keating, who was less electorally successful as a prime minister, but still managed to become prime minister and win one election, was not a sports fan and not a big drinker. These are not tastes aligned with what is perceived to be mainstream Australia. John Howard loved sport, and had a genuine love particularly of cricket, but used that as a side issue rather than the major focus of his electoral appeal. I'm not sure how many people in the electorate will think: "this person is just like me, so I'm going to vote for them", without some kind of policy appeal they can also vote for.

EJ: The two major parties have their respective campaign buses travelling around Australia, with journalists piling onto the bus and taken out to a secret location they don't know about until they actually arrive. It's similar to the embedded journalists during the Iraq War in 1991, where if a journalist's life depends on the protection of the military, that journalist is not likely to ask the serious questions that might be critical of that campaign. The same situation arises with journalists travelling on the campaign buses with the Prime Minister or the Leader of the Opposition. If a journalist asks too many tough or critical questions which results in negative press, they're likely to be booted off the bus and left in the middle of nowhere. If too many difficult questions about policy matters arise, that journalist is probably not going to be invited to the Prime Minister's special screening of *Game of Thrones*—an event which actually did happen—and their access will be denied. And this cosy relationship with the media has led to Scott Morrison not being asked the serious questions, or Morrison being able to just deflect most issues by claiming they're in the 'Canberra bubble', simply ignore them, claim that he's already answered the question—when he hasn't—or just assert that it's not of interest to the electorate. The media keeps telling the public that Morrison is a more 'wily' campaigner than Malcolm Turnbull, but this is a code word for being loose with the truth and avoiding the key questions.

DL: Scott Morrison doesn't come across as a great intellectual. The media does claim that he's wily—maybe in the Wile E. Coyote sense of the word—in that every time he tries to set up a bomb for the opposition, he walks into it himself, and ends up falling down the cliff again. And he has escaped a great deal of media scrutiny, whereas most of the pressure has been placed on his opponent. The media makes too much of the little things: Bill Shorten didn't have quite complex figures of superannuation at his fingertips when asked by a journalist, and this was reported as a terrible blunder by the media. Whereas Morrison doesn't say very much at all, and this is reported as great campaigning—and perhaps it is. But something has changed within the campaign: four weeks ago, even the Liberal Party seemed to think they were gone for all money. Now there's a feeling within the party that they're going to win. As I mentioned previously, there is a fairly good chance the Liberals are going to win the election. I'm not quite sure exactly what has changed, except Bill Shorten couldn't quickly answer a fairly complex question, and the media made a big deal about that. Also, the habit for Shorten is, whenever he is asked a complex policy question, he'll often hand on the question to the shadow minister responsible for that area. And there's nothing wrong with that: why bumble through the answer yourself when can you give it to the person who has been on top of the issue and probably wrote the Labor report on that policy area?

EJ: Whether that process of not being able to directly answer a question is good or not, the media will always pick up on a politician's response: it's considered an issue of competence. If a politician who's aspiring to be the prime minister, if they can't answer a question off-the-cuff or answer a difficult question they didn't see coming, that's seen as incompetence, and generally, it has always been that way. And that's why the media is always looking out for the 'gotcha' moment with Bill Shorten, but not so much with Scott Morrison. The potential prime minister does need to be carefully scrutinised by the media but there has been so much scrutiny placed on Shorten and not enough on Morrison. I've lost count of how many journalists start off their propositions or their questions—whether it's directly to Bill Shorten or whether it's an introduction to a political panel on television or radio, or a direct question to voters in vox pops: "why is Bill Shorten so unpopular?". Quite often, this question is asked by journalists without realising Scott Morrison is also unpopular—in opinion polls, he actually has a negative net approval rating, which means his disapproval rating is higher than his approval rating. There's no dispute that Shorten does have a high disapproval rating in many opinion polls: his disapproval rating is 51 per cent but Morrison has a disapproval rating of 45 per cent, not too far behind. For sure, Shorten's disapproval is higher, but we never hear the question asked by journalists: "why is Scott Morrison so unpopular?".

*

EJ: The media was also making a big point about the amount of debates that should be held during the election campaign—in American politics there are debates left, right and centre in the primaries and during election years. There is a Commission on Presidential Debates in the US that moderates debates and there's a minimum amount of debates that take place in US presidential campaigns. In Australia, there's no such official body, but there is an expectation there will be three debates during the election campaign, although there's no specific rule about how many there should be, or where they should be held. There's already been one debate so far in this campaign, and that was jointly hosted by Channel Seven and *The West Australian* newspaper in Perth. Bill Shorten won that debate quite easily—it was 25-to-12 in Shorten's favour and eleven people undecided in an audience of forty-eight. Many in the media were quick to downplay this victory though, claiming those forty-eight people were hand-picked to sway the result and it was just a small sample of people. Yes, the group was hand-picked, but they were hand-picked by a professional research company that specifically looked for people that were not affiliated to any political party and were deemed to be completely neutral.

DL: I dislike the notion of debates and their influences on campaigns. In the recent New South Wales state election, Labor leader Michael Daley won the debate against Gladys Berejiklian—that win in the debate didn't do Daley any good at all, as he still lost the election. Of course, other factors came into play for Michael Daley, but the debate didn't influence the final election outcome. The debates in the 2016 campaign were all won by Bill Shorten, but he didn't win the election: maybe he should have but he didn't. Political debates are part of this American notion about playing to television—getting debates onto television, and it looks good, but then nobody watches them. In television ratings, the debate would have lost against all other televisions programs it was up against. And not as many people are watching broadcast television as they used to, especially younger people. Holding one debate; having six debates or twenty debates, probably doesn't mean that much, particularly in an electorate where almost three-in-four people have already decided who they will vote for.

EJ: It also relates to the level of trust people have in the political system. The public has such a low interest in politics, and they have a low level of trust in politicians, so they're unlikely to watch a political debate. But how do debates relate to the final election result? In the 2004 election campaign, Labor leader, Mark Latham, won all of the debates against John Howard. Kim Beazley won all the debates, also against John Howard, in 1998 and 2001, but in each of those cases, the winner of the debates didn't end up winning the election. Winning the debates is not as important as the media would like to think it might be.

DL: The two best political public speakers I've witnessed are former NSW Labor Premier, Bob Carr and John Howard—I didn't necessarily agree with either of them—but they were superb public speakers, especially John Howard. However, I don't think the debates mean very much at all and if Scott Morrison decided the debates are a waste of time and he wasn't going to do any more, I wouldn't blame him in the slightest.

EJ: It's coming up to the end of week three of this election campaign, and just two more weeks to follow. I disagree completely with the general media assessment: this has been quite an exciting campaign, and I wish they could find some more enthusiasm for it as well. May 18 is rapidly appearing on the horizon, and the excitement will continue.

DL: It will not be dull...

*

Music in this episode

Smoke On The Water, performed by Iron Horse
Rise (instrumental), Public Image Limited
Cosby Sweater, Hilltop Hoods

A Labor victory is in sight

6 May 2019

Eddy Jokovich

We're into the final two weeks of the 2019 federal election campaign, and two opinion polls released today still point towards a Labor victory. The monthly Ipsos shows a two-party preferred vote of 52 per cent to the Australian Labor Party, and 48 per cent to the Liberal–National Party.

While this is a slight improvement for the LNP when compared to the April figures, it would still result in a loss of eleven seats, for a total of eighty-three seats to the ALP, sixty-two to the LNP, and six independents, if a uniform swing occurred.

In addition to these eleven seats, there are two other Liberal-held seats that are expected to fall to the ALP—Reid in NSW, and Swan in Western Australia—and six other seats—Boothby, Sturt, La Trobe, Dawson, Bonner and Pearce—are in serious contention as Labor gains.

The Newspoll result is slightly different to Ipsos, and confirms the figures it published in its poll last week—ALP 51 per cent, to LNP 49 per cent in the two-party preferred vote. With a uniform swing, this would result in seventy-nine seats to the ALP, sixty-six to the LNP, with six independents.

Based on both of these opinion poll figures, the best-case scenario for the ALP is a win of around ninety seats, while a worst-case scenario is a slim margin of around three or four seats. Conversely, the best outcome for the LNP would be a narrow victory or a close 'save-the-furniture' loss, providing a springboard for the next election, due in 2022. But this doesn't seem likely.

An election victory for the LNP using either the Ipsos or Newspoll figures is close to impossible—the lowest ever two-party preferred vote to win an election is 49.02 per cent, achieved by John Howard in the 1998 election. The LNP needs to gain three seats just to achieve a one-seat majority and it's difficult to see where these seats can be gained. Aside from this difficult feat, the LNP also has to ensure it doesn't lose any of the seventy-three seats it currently holds. It's hard to see either of these critical factors being achieved.

Should this government be rewarded?

A more deserved election result is a punitive loss of around fifteen-to-twenty seats, which would provide the LNP with ample time to sort out their differences in opposition and develop a liberal philosophy that is more in tune with a modern Australia.

The LNP has not provided stability of government, or stability of policy outcomes, and the current collection of Liberal–National Party MPs is based more around division, political opportunism, inane nationalism, corruption and personal ambition, rather than working towards a more cohesive community.

A close loss, or even an unlikely victory, would be a reward to a government of low achievement and poor performance since it was first installed in September 2013. The LNP was offered a second chance in the 2016 election when it barely scraped through with a one-seat majority. Its response after that election was to meander without a clear agenda, and it then removed Malcolm Turnbull as prime minister in August 2018.

The electorate is usually patient and will re-elect governments, if they can see a worthwhile agenda for the future, but they rarely offer incompetent governments a third chance. Although the media has been generally supportive of Scott Morrison during this campaign, it's struggling to maintain its enthusiasm, and many journalists are now willing to call out the 'threadbare policy agenda' offered by LNP.

And the lack of a clear policy agenda is now a looming problem for the Morrison and the LNP. As former Prime Minister Paul

Keating remarked, "every now and then you have to flick the switch to vaudeville" during election campaigns, and offer nuanced and wide-ranging policies to different groups in the electorate.

So far, the LNP has campaigned strongly on two issues: the economy, and Labor leader Bill Shorten. But peel back these two layers, and there's not much else. The economy has actually spluttered over the past twelve months, and any gains over the past five years have gone through to corporate profits, rather than filtering through to increases in wages and salaries.

Consumer sentiment and retail confidence has suffered the biggest plunge in decades, gross national government debt has risen under this government from $257 billion to $532 billion, housing prices have plummeted nation-wide, especially in the Sydney and Melbourne markets, and the economy is in a per-capita recession.

The LNP keeps pushing the message that its economic management is far superior to Labor, but the evidence suggests otherwise.

The personal attacks on Bill Shorten are also starting to wear thin, as suggested during the two leaders' debates hosted by Channel 7/*The West Australian*, and Sky News. Shorten was selected as the winner in both debates by the respective studio audiences.

Labor continues to present itself as a viable alternative to this government, and Shorten's messages are resonating with the electorate. The preferred prime minister rating is not a substantial metric, only used to prop up Morrison's standing in the media against poor two-party-preferred opinion polls but, even so, the latest Ipsos poll shows there's not much difference between Morrison (preferred as prime minister by 45 per cent of the electorate) and Shorten (40 per cent).

There are not many other issues the LNP is able to campaign on during these final two weeks, and the message on the economic management and attacking Shorten now have limited credibility. They are not offering a great deal of confidence to the electorate in their abilities to produce competent government over the next three years, especially when compared with the large collection of policies on offer from Labor.

LNP needs a break from its past

The LNP governments of 2013–2019 attempted to revive the Howard years that ended in 2007, but with little success—the same brand of economic philosophy, the same brand of social conservatism and the same desire to exploit social divisions to reap political benefits.

It's a party that needs to make a clear break from the Howard era and decide whether it wants to be a modern liberal party offering a better link to community, or an archaic hard-right conservative party that holds irrelevant debates in small cloistered rooms, inspired by the free-market economist, F.A. Hayek and former British Prime Minister, Margaret Thatcher. Those days are well and truly over.

Labor enters the final fortnight with momentum, holding its campaign launch in Brisbane and announcing a raft of new policy initiatives in emergency health care, tax cuts for small business employing under-25s and over-55s, constitutional recognition for Aboriginal and Torres Strait Islander people, and a National Redress Agency to assist the delivery of compensation to child sexual abuse survivors.

There seems to be a mood for a change of government, and Labor has prosecuted their case for change, even if the electorate hasn't warmed to the idea of Bill Shorten as prime minister.

The LNP's campaign has dropped off, but there will be one last attempt to capture the attention of the electorate—their campaign launch is on Sunday, just six days before election day. If the Reserve Bank cuts interest rates at its Tuesday meeting, there's no doubt the LNP will push this as much possible—and why not? They've got very little else to run with.

But will it make a difference? There's not much more this government has to offer to the public and we're just waiting to see if the electorate will confirm this sentiment on May 18.

*

A tale of two eggs: Gillard and Morrison

10 May 2019

Eddy Jokovich

Five-letter word; to egg on. That was my first cryptic crossword clue many years ago and after staring and thinking about what the answer could possible mean, the *double-entendre* finally clicked, and I've been a fan of the cryptics ever since. And the answer? More on that later.

Eggs have been the protest missile of choice for political activists all around the world but other items have also been used, including a dildo, glitter, salad dressing, sandwiches, shoes, pies, flour, tomatoes, custard and purple powder, among many other items. But it was a single unbroken egg that became the focus of the federal election campaign this week.

The Prime Minister, Scott Morrison, was involved in an incident at a Country Women's Association event in Albury, when 24-year-old Amber Paige Holt rolled an egg on the top of Morrison's head. The egg wasn't "thrown" or "smashed" on his head, as claimed by many in the media, but rolled from the top of his head, onto the side of his head, and onto the ground, where it remained intact.

Morrison quickly saw a political opportunity and derided Holt as a "cowardly activist" and said he would "stand up to thuggery" and "militant unionists", even though there is no link at all between Holt and unions.

The incident overshadowed all other campaign events and captured the attention of the media for almost forty-eight hours, especially Morrison's attempt to create a link between the incident and unions—which would ultimately make a link with Labor leader, Bill Shorten—and, no doubt, an issue Morrison will continue to make a link with into the final week of the election campaign.

There's no suggestion that throwing eggs or other missiles at public figures should be an acceptable act, or something that should be encouraged, but how does this incident in Albury compare with others throughout Australia's political history?

There was the most recent 'egging' incident in March, when Will Connolly cracked an egg over Senator Fraser Anning's head; on this occasion, breaking the egg and setting up a chain of events where Connolly was punched in the head by Anning, and kicked and headlocked by Anning's supporters.

Eggs have been thrown at many senior politicians in the past, including Robert Menzies, Malcolm Fraser, John Hewson, Bob Hawke and Julia Gillard, but little was made of those incidents, and most of those political figures downplayed the events.

The most stark comparison with Morrison's over-the-top response is from 2010, when Enrico Von Felten, a man "angry with government policy affecting his business" threw an egg at Gillard, which narrowly missed her and ricocheted into a policewoman's leg instead.

The media brushed aside the incident, filing their new reports with puns about Gillard having 'egg-on-the-face' on refugee policy, and 'over-egging her Timor solution'. The Australian Federal Police seemed quite amused by it as well, downplaying the significance of the event. Gillard was asked by a reporter: "what about the egg?" to which she responded: "I'm fine, thank you very much", before adding; "the man thought I needed to have some scrambled eggs this morning for breakfast."

An angry man violently throws an egg at a female prime minister, albeit not hitting her, and it's laughed off in the media. But when a women casually rolls an egg innocuously over a man's head, it's almost a national emergency. What makes Scott Morrison so different?

Back in 2010, we never heard any outrage about Von Felten actions as a cowardly activist, or accusations of thuggery in the business community. Why was Morrison so keen to make a link between Amber Holt and "militant unionists", when no link exists?

Why was there so much confected outrage in the media about Morrison's incident, but almost a comical response to Gillard?

Morrison's outburst is reminiscent of Australia's most infamous egg-throwing incident in 1917, when Prime Minister Billy Hughes was campaigning in Queensland for a national plebiscite on war conscription. Hughes was a fierce proponent of the divisive issue of conscription, the issue splitting the community, and resulted in the expulsion of Hughes from the Labor Party.

While Hughes addressed an audience at the Warwick railway station, an egg thrown by anti-conscription activist Paddy Brosnan knocked off his hat. Hughes was outraged and reached into his coat for a revolver, but it had been left behind in his railway carriage. This enraged Hughes even further, who then ordered a local policeman to arrest Brosnan, but was told "you have no jurisdiction", as it was a Commonwealth matter.

Hughes remained outraged by this incident for some time and witnesses from that day insist if Hughes did indeed have the revolver in his coat pocket, he would have shot Brosnan dead. This incident became the catalyst for the formation of the Commonwealth Police, which later became the Australian Federal Police.

Should Morrison have made such a big fuss about an egg? What would have happened if he had a revolver in his coat?

Other politicians have brushed these incidents off for being the innocuous events they really are. In 1993, students were pelting Liberal leader John Hewson at a GST rally with apples, tomatoes, broccoli—and eggs. Hewson managed to catch one of the eggs and shouted out: "Those cricketers have nothing on me!"

Many other leaders have responded with good humour in the numerous egg-throwing incidents throughout political history and, if it was good enough for the media to laugh off the incident that happened to Gillard, it should be good enough for the media to also do this with Morrison.

Obviously, Morrison has considered he should grab every opportunity available to him, even if it is to equate an egg-rolling prank with a national security alert, and release all the hyperbole affiliated with militant unionism and environmental activism.

Today, he was in a bingo hall in the outer-Sydney town of Windsor, calling out numbers to a geriatric audience, and encouraged the media to make puns about his number call-outs and budget figures. If a prime minister wants to call out 'clicketty-click-sixty-six' in a bingo hall towards the end of an election campaign, that's their prerogative.

But it's not the image of a prime minister in a desperate ideological battle, trying to win over every single vote and slugging it out until 6pm on election day, when the ballot boxes are sealed and the vote counting commences.

It seemed more like a sign of resignation, to enjoy the ride for the next week, because the seat of his prime-ministership may come to an end soon. But it won't be a celebration: he's *toast*.

It's also the five-letter word solution to the cryptic clue: *To egg on*.

*

Who wins the 2019 election final countdown?

14 May 2019

Eddy Jokovich + David Lewis / Podcast

In this episode, we assessed the progress of the final stages of the election campaign; is it just an egg-throwing contest, or is there a lot more to it? And we made our final predictions and observations for the election result. Also in this episode, David Lewis brings you all the gossip from Hollywood.

Eddy Jokovich: It has been a strange fortnight in the federal election campaign; we've had rolling eggs make an appearance; the Prime Minister calling out bingo numbers in small regional towns; the Leader of the Opposition was in tears; and we've had the two official campaign launches as well. So far, there has been a role-reversal in this campaign: the Labor Opposition behaves more like a government; and the Liberal–National government behaves more like an opposition, and it's not by accident. Labor wants to present itself as the government-in-waiting, while the LNP wants to look low-frill and present itself as the people who don't want to make a 'song and dance' about themselves. However, elections are all about 'song and dance' and, as Paul Keating once said, politicians need to make the switch to vaudeville and entertain the public: the monkey and the organ grinder act hasn't made an appearance during this campaign but Scott Morrison and Bill Shorten have played to their relative strengths and tried their very best to extract every single vote from the electorate for their respective sides. Who has had the better campaign so far?

David Lewis: They've been interesting campaigns in terms of the lack of errors and performance: but the campaign is slightly leaning towards the Labor Party. They haven't run a brilliant campaign, but they've run a very capable campaign. There has been the right mix of focussing on the direction of the policies, focussing on some of the personalities; focusing on the strengths they bring, letting the government demonstrate their own weaknesses. The government hasn't had a great campaign, but sometimes the campaign appearance in the media masks what might actually be happening on the ground.

EJ: Both Morrison and Shorten have performed well but when assessing the overall campaigns, Labor does seem to have more substance than the Coalition's, which has been more dour and lacking in energy. The Liberal–National Party campaign launch over the weekend was more about the profile of Morrison and his wife Jenny: that might be sufficient for day-time television, or more like an evangelist revivalist meeting but this campaign is supposed to be about who forms government. It's obvious the Liberal Party is making this a contest between leaders, instead of ideas, but if it does end up being an election between the personalities of Morrison and Shorten, Morrison probably wins the election.

DL: This is an election where preferences are going to make a large difference, and the Liberal Party has realised this. Since the pre-poll booths opened a few weeks ago, there have been many Liberal Party campaigners distributing One Nation and United Australia Party pamphlets and how-to-vote cards, in an attempt to swing the preference flows to the Liberal Party, particularly in marginal seats. This election, contrary to expectations, isn't in the bag for Labor, and it's wrong to assume that it is. I'm hoping to be proved wrong about this, not because the Liberal Party has awful candidates—although, clearly, there are some awful candidates there, as there would be in all political parties—but, based on their performance over the past three years, the

Liberal Party doesn't deserve an election win: it needs to reform, it needs to restructure itself and move away from its more destructive tendencies. And that tends to not happen when a party is in government—why would it—and is best left to the time when they're in opposition.

EJ: We did see many of those destructive tendencies in 2018, when Morrison replaced Malcolm Turnbull as prime minister. And replacing prime ministers—two since 2013—has caused problems for the Liberal Party, where they haven't been able to talk about the past, in the same way Labor found it difficult to form their narrative after they removed Kevin Rudd in 2010: how can a party discuss the achievements of the past, if they've just removed the leader responsible for those achievements? At the Liberal–National Party campaign launch last weekend, there were no luminaries from the Liberal Party: we didn't see John Howard, or Tony Abbott, or Malcolm Turnbull—all former prime ministers. Scott Morrison is still presenting himself as the 'solo man', and that's fine if the party wants to run a campaign like that, but it's a very similar strategy to the Liberal campaign in the 2016 election, where it was all about Malcolm Turnbull. If a political party is unable to discuss the past and their history with the electorate, it's also hard to talk about the future. This has caused Scott Morrison and the Liberal–National Party to be hamstrung: lacking confidence about the past, means there won't be any confidence in the conversations about the future.

DL: One of the issues of the Liberal–National government is: what is their legacy? What could they point to as achievements in the past term of Parliament? Scott Morrison had that infamous saying, where he claimed: "we've delivered a Budget surplus next year", mixing his grammar and tenses in a way that certainly an advertising man shouldn't do. He struggled to talk about one major legacy: the economy is deteriorating; house prices are dropping. These issues in isolation might not necessarily be a bad thing—property is and should be a long-term investment, rather than based on immediate gains. The fall in house prices means housing becomes more affordable for first-home buyers, which is a good thing. However, this government has set up the economic narrative of never-ending growth as a virtue. Conversely, there are many people worried about falling property values—maintaining property values is another promise the Coalition hasn't delivered on. Australia's foreign relations are in a mess—although that's not the fault just of the government; there are so many issues going on internationally that are outside of their control, but there is a sense that you make your own luck in politics.

EJ: It does seem like a very long time ago, but Labor also had its campaign launch: one week before the Liberal–National Party launch. The Labor Party has released the costings of their policies program, and they are quite substantial, especially when compared with costings released by opposition parties in previous campaigns. Labor has also claimed they will have a $17 billion Budget surplus over the next four fiscal years, which doesn't seem credible: figures, costings and promises released during election campaigns are usually quite malleable when considering costings over the next twelve months, and many of these assumptions can change quite dramatically. But when considering costings over the next four years, there's an astronomical amount of issues that can affect those estimates: the world economy; climate change issues and drought affecting the domestic economy; consumer sentiment—these can all affect the delivery of a Budget surplus. And this, of course, doesn't take into account whether a Budget surplus is even required at this stage of the economic cycle. But economic factors are the serious part of an election campaign: on a lighter note, it's not a true election campaign unless something is thrown at a political leader and, last week, there was an egg-throwing incident. Scott Morrison was at a Country Women's Association meeting in the regional town of Albury and a protester, 24-year-old Amber Holt, rolled an egg off the Prime Minister's head. It's not good for anyone to throw an egg at a political leader but it seemed to be quite an innocuous incident. The last such incident was when an egg was thrown at Julia Gillard during the 2010 election campaign: Gillard laughed the incident off, and the media reported the incident with great humour, but this time around, Morrison has almost called a national emergency. Did Morrison make too much of an issue out of having an egg rolling down the side of his face?

DL: After the incident early this year where 17-year-old Will Connolly broke an egg on the back of Senator Fraser Anning's head, and the resulting outcry from that, you'd expect Scott Morrison would distance himself from that. Instead, the secret police raced in and they knocked over an old woman in their haste to arrest this 24-year-old woman. The media was very sure in reporting that she was tattooed and associated with The Greens—even though she is not. It was an act of insecurity: the Prime Minister just couldn't laugh off an egg, like Julia Gillard did—sure, escort the offending person out of the building, and give a police warning, but to charge her with common assault seemed to be an overreaction.

EJ: The first major egg-throwing incident occurred in 1917, and the prime minister at the time was Billy Hughes. The egg didn't actually hit Hughes, it missed and knocked off his hat. Hughes was so furious, he wanted to kill the culprit: he reached inside his pocket for a gun but the egg-thrower managed to run away. It was this incident that led to the formation of the Commonwealth Police, which was the precursor to the Australian Federal Police—a sign of how seriously Hughes regarded this incident. Most other prime ministers have dismissed these types of incidents: Robert Menzies, Bob Hawke, Julia Gillard. In the 1993 election campaign, the Leader of the Opposition at the time, John Hewson, managed to catch an egg that was thrown at him when he was on the stage at an outdoor rally—no mean feat. These are not major incidents—people shouldn't thrown objects at politicians, but when they do happen on this level, they should be played down. Scott Morrison did the opposite, he tried to make a national emergency out of this and it would have better just to let it flow.

DL: The British Prime Minister, Harold Wilson, had eggs thrown at him by Young Conservatives during the 1970 election campaign, and his reply was: "eggs must be cheap enough under Labor to throw about". That was a good response.

EJ: A politician needs to have the correct riposte for these incidents: in Gillard's case, her response was: "the man thought I needed to have some scrambled eggs this morning for breakfast". Morrison's incident wasn't a massive incident but, of course, he used it a political opportunity to rail against unionism, green activism, thuggery against the business community—even though Amber Holt's motivations had nothing to do with those issues: she wanted to highlight the government's mistreatment of asylum seekers on Manus Island and Nauru. But Morrison is not one to miss out on the political opportunity. On his trip to southern New South Wales, he ended up in Nowra at an RSL Club and started calling out bingo numbers. I'm not sure what type of audience these images of bingo halls are playing to, but Morrison went to two bingo halls on the same day. It made Scott Morrison look like a local council mayor instead of a prime minister, as if he hasn't got very much to say, except call out bingo numbers on the south coast of New South Wales.

DL: Morrison is not a substantial figure: he's not a deep intellect, he's not a sharp thinker. There's nothing wrong with bingo: many people enjoy the game, it's a great social day out. But Morrison's actions contrast with those of John Howard in 2007 and his response to appearing on *Rove Live!*—he refused to appear. Rove MacManus continuously invited him, and it finally came out that John Howard realised there were no votes for him to gain by appearing on the show. As a result, why would he waste his time campaigning on a television show in which those who are watching had made up their minds about the election, and probably weren't going to vote for him anyway, when he could be out winning votes in other areas? Kevin Rudd did appear on *Rove Live!* and he probably did swing a few wavering voters towards Labor. But I wouldn't have thought there would be too many votes doing the bingo halls of New South Wales. The media footage of Morrison at the Pentecostal Horizon church was also a very strange choice to make: again, it's not a criticism about attending church—Bill Shorten also went to church on the same day—but to allow the media in to record footage of the church service, probably cost him more votes, than it gained.

EJ: Morrison might have lost some votes by his Pentecostal church appearance, but surely he has the bingo vote sewn up.

*

Mothers make an appearance in the campaign

> Bill Shorten: My mum was a brilliant woman, she wasn't bitter. She worked here [Monash University] for thirty-five years. But I also know that if she had had other opportunities, she could have done anything. I can't make it right for my mum—and she wouldn't want me to. But my point is this: what motivates me, if you really want to know who Bill Shorten is, I can't make it right for my mum, but I can make it right for everyone else.

EJ: We did have an incident with the media last week, and it was about Bill Shorten and his mother, Anne Shorten. The *Daily Telegraph*, a News Corp publication from the Murdoch stable, decided it was best to do yet another media hatchet job on Shorten: this time, they decided to attack him for not providing as much information as possible about his mother, alluding to some type of cover up—although it wasn't clear what was supposedly being covered up—and it seemed to backfire on the Murdoch empire, and it also backfired on the Liberal–National Party.

DL: Mothers of politicians are off limits—it's that simple. I don't know who in the Liberal–National Party decided it was a good idea to attack Shorten's mother—and I'd be just as shocked and perplexed if someone attacked Morrison's mother too. Of course, if your mother is a prominent political figure or enters into a public debate, then she is open to the same level of scrutiny that any other public figure would have. But that's not the case of anyone in Parliament at the moment. The former Governor–General, Quentin Bryce is Shorten's mother-in-law, but she's no longer in the public eye. The decision of the Murdoch media was very strange, but we have to remember that News Corp will stoop to any low level to attack the Labor side of politics. Spouses of politicians are off limits, as are children, and other family members, unless there is some genuine matter of public interest. The story of Shorten's mother putting off her career to raise her children—essentially as a sole parent—and then going on to become a barrister and legal academic, is a story of success. But News Corp wanted to turn that into a bad news story and one littered with innuendo that something untoward was happening in the background.

EJ: The conservative media has form: after all, they are the ones that keep telling the electorate how unpopular Bill Shorten is and, if they run out of material on him, they'll make up spurious material about family members. The *Sydney Morning Herald* and *The Age*, formerly Fairfax publications, and now part of the Nine Group, were attacking Chloe Shorten for not being so 'accessible to the media'—whatever that means. Chloe Shorten's name is not on any ballot paper across Australia, nor is there a requirement for her to be directly accessible to the media in the same way as politicians would be, but the conservative media has decided any issue is fair game on the Labor side. In the meantime, Jenny Morrison, the spouse of Morrison, receives the glowing write-ups and puff-pieces on her favourite fashion items. It's a sickening double standard that we've come to expect from the media.

DL: It does reek of desperation from the conservative side of politics. Certainly, the media in Australia prefers Liberal governments, or non-Labor governments: that's well documented and effectively admitted by all the players involved, and there's a wide range of historical reasons for why this is the case. Occasionally, usually when the writing is on the wall and the Liberal–National Party is facing oblivion at the ballot box, they will sway the other way; after all, it's best to be on the winning side. The media hasn't quite embraced Bill Shorten, which is where the narrative of 'Bill-Shorten-is-so-unpopular' comes from. In reality, Shorten is unpopular among media owners; and it's more subtle and nuanced outside of that rather small bubble. The current Liberal–National government is far more in line with the thinking of big business, particularly how tax should be collected, who should pay, and how much tax should be collected, and who should receive the benefits of that tax once it has been collected. In the minds of the media magnates, Labor doesn't reflect that.

EJ: Virtually all media owners and barons are conservative supporters and will look at every opportunity to point out a flaw in the Labor Party, or their leadership. Shorten may have made a mistake when he announced he wasn't going to make a trip to New York to have lunch with Rupert Murdoch, and that could end being an expensive snub. Not that the Murdoch empire is any friend of the Labor Party but as soon as Shorten made that announcement, the attacks on him from News Corp went up a notch. How precious is Murdoch's ego? The conservative media has forced the issue of Shorten's perceived unpopularity ever since he became leader of the Labor Party in 2013 and one strategy he has used to counter this is to push forward his entire leadership team, to let the electorate know that a Labor government won't just be based around the leader, but the team behind him: it's not all about Shorten and when looking at the Labor leadership team and prospective ministry, there's quite a few talented MPs there. Compared to the Liberal Party campaign, it would be easy to think Scott Morrison is the only member of the government: very few people are taking the limelight away from him.

DL: The Labor strategy has been to knock on every possible door, and speak to as many people as possible: the town hall meetings have been successful, but it's just a question of whether this can reach the amount of people required to swing the election. Shorten's appearances on programs such as *Q&A* have impressed people and he has pushed forward the perception of being a chairman of the government, instead of a micromanaging CEO-style, where nothing ever gets done. We've had too much of the micromanager prime ministers: Kevin Rudd was notorious for it; Malcolm Turnbull as well. Tony Abbott tried to be a micromanager but, like most other things, couldn't do that very well, and Scott Morrison is possibly a micromanager that surpasses all the other previous prime ministers. The trouble with this is that a micromanager has to be good at everything and be multiskilled, but it also shows that there is not enough trust in the team that supports the prime minister. It's also a question of whether this ends up being an issue for the electorate, and whether they take any notice of it when casting their votes.

*

A look at the final countdown to the 2019 election

EJ: We're now into the final few days of the election campaign, and the final opinions polls are still pointing towards a Labor election victory, although the polls have been narrowing. But, as we know, it's not an election victory for any side until the polling booths close at 6pm on Saturday night and the Australian Electoral Commission commences the counting of the votes. The mainstream media is still pushing the idea of the campaign lacking inspiration and a process that we all have to endure, rather than enjoy. I've got a different perspective on this: this election is potentially a 'change' election and, as Paul Keating once said, when the government changes, Australia changes as well. The final week of a campaign also has potential for dramas and missteps, as we found out in the recent New South Wales election, where video recordings of racist comments made by Labor leader Michael Daley were released on the final Tuesday before election day: he never recovered from that, and had the wind blown out of the sails of his campaign. Are we likely to see last minute dramas in the final week of this federal campaign?

DL: There's always some dubious claim of some kind coming in from both sides—allusions of financial discretion or some kind of sexual indiscretion that may or may not have actually happened. The media tried to prompt comments from sacked workers criticising Shorten for their retrenchment, somehow blaming unions, instead of the employer. This was quite a bizarre spectacle and, as usual, there would be more to the story than the media puts forward. But virtually everything has been thrown at Shorten since 2013, and he's still there: he's outlasted two prime ministers, which is quite remarkable. There has been a surprising lack of scandal on the Labor side, and very few leaks against Shorten. It's hard to see what else could be thrown at Shorten by the media and the Liberal Party, because it's all happened: a Trade Unions Royal Commission; various inquiries into Shorten's management of union affairs from many years ago; union raids; police raids upon Labor Party headquarters—classic Stasi-style techniques. All of these acts uncovered no irregular or illegal activity by Shorten or his union at the time, except for the failure to produce a receipt in the correct format for campaign donations in 2007.

EJ: If a scandal doesn't exist, one can be invented. Every negative sentiment on Shorten has been pushed forward by the media, and that includes News Corp, Fairfax/Nine, the ABC and, to a lesser extent, *The Guardian Australia*, although that seems to have dropped off ever since Scott Morrison replaced Malcolm Turnbull in 2018. And it seems there are no other negative sentiments out there, except for repeating the same ones over again. If there was anything else about Shorten, it probably would have used against him in the 2016 election campaign. There was some speculation floating around that some big negative news items were to be published about Shorten in this final week, but we're not sure what that could be, or whether this will actually occur. But in the absence of a real story, one can be manufactured based on one small element of truth: of course, once the information is put out there, it sucks up the energy of the campaign and by the time any rebuttals are made, or the time it takes for the truth to catch up with the fabrication, it's far too late. If it manages to swing the election the other way, the damage has already been done.

DL: One other factor in this campaign is that 2.6 million electors have already voted, out of the 16.4 million people eligible to vote in this election: over 15 per cent have already made up their minds, and if a major news story comes out in this final week that could have influenced their vote, they can't change their mind: they've already cast their vote. For the first time, the pre-polling period will be three weeks and there are estimates that by the time the booths open at 8am on the election day on Saturday, between 35–40 per cent of the electorate—four million voters—will have already cast their vote: surely that affects the nature of the campaign and it's one area political parties will have to take into account in future elections.

*

EJ: The opinion polls and the betting markets are all pointing towards a Labor victory on Saturday: betting on elections is a boutique market and is completely unreliable, but it does mean something.

Opinion polling tends to be far more reliable than the betting markets but for both of these measurements, they are absolutely brilliant for predicting the past, but not so good for predicting the future: they are never going to be accurate predictors of electoral behaviour and sentiment—that's why we have elections, rather than ongoing opinions polls to determine who holds government. There will be a range of final opinion polls released this week: Galaxy, Morgan, Newspoll and Essential, and their reputations are on the line. Political parties usually know on the Thursday night before the election whether they are likely to win or lose the election—and that's through a combination of reports from candidates and campaign teams in each seat and internal party polling.

DL: Reports are suggesting the Liberal Party has conceded the seat of Warringah—Tony Abbott's seat—but put in a great amount of resources into Peter Dutton's seat in Dickson. The seat of Kooyong—Josh Frydenberg's seat—is also tight, but not as tight as the neighbouring seat of Chisholm. The independent Kerryn Phelps holds the seat of Wentworth in Sydney and should be able to hold that seat, but possibly not by as much as she won the seat in the 2018 by-election. These are seats the Liberals will need to win or retain. But, quite often, it's the seats that few people are watching that create the surprises—seats that are expected to fall, don't end up falling; or the seats expected to be retained by either party, end up being lost. Adam Blakester in New England is challenging Barnaby Joyce: it's hard to imagine it being lost by the National Party, but that could be a surprise seat to watch.

EJ: In the House of Representatives, there are 151 seats contested and it's easy to forget that in each of these seats is a mini-election based on local factors, local campaigning issues, and the relative merits between those candidates in those seats. There are always local issues that are missed by the national media; sometimes seats can be lost on a simple factor of respective positioning on the ballot paper, or the effectiveness of each candidate's how-to-vote card. And then there's the factor of how the national campaign of each political party is travelling, the performance of the leaders: there are so many factors that come into play in determining the winners and losers in each seat.

DL: It was the former Speaker in the United States Congress, Tip O'Neill, who said that all politics is local. There might be specific local issues within the boundaries of a seat that just need to occur in about six or seven seats across the country to swing the election for the Liberal–National Party: it could be something simple such as a series of pedestrian crossings that were delivered at the right time and at the right location; a critical building development that faced great public opposition and the local MP managed to veto the development application; a new mine; or it could be the announcement of a desperately needed hospital. There are many local issues that can either swing or hold an election and when there are 151 seats in play, it's not possible for any election analyst to stay on top of all the micro-details in each of those seats.

EJ: There are many developing issues and only the people close to the ground know what is really happening in those seats. There are community newspapers, community radio in each of those seats, and then there is social media: every candidate around Australia—or, at least, those expecting to win a reasonable amount of votes—have Facebook, Twitter and Instagram accounts. It's difficult to keep a track of the performances of all candidates. Aside from what may happen in the House of Representatives, there's also the Senate, which also promises to be a messy affair, resulting in Senators that are unlikely to be easy for either Labor or the LNP to deal with. If the Liberal–National Party wins this election, they haven't actually promised very much at all during this campaign, so their idea of a mandate and legislative program will be flexible—they'll be able to present whatever they want after the election. The Labor Party has a more specific agenda: their negative gearing amendments; the overhaul of the generous franking credits scheme—the scheme the media loves to talk about and misrepresent at every opportunity. If Labor wins the election, it might be very difficult for them to have any of their reforms and proposals passed by the Senate and, at the least, possibly have them watered down so much by the Senate, they become ineffective.

DL: Labor has used its time in opposition since 2013 well, in terms of rebuilding and restructuring, thinking and listening: compared to the Liberal–National Party during 2007–13, who ended up being totally unprepared for government after they won the 2013 election. Parties always need to have a period of reflection; a period of time out of government where they can reform themselves and clear out some of the deadwood. And this may be forced upon them by the electorate: Tony Abbott's seat has already been conceded; Peter Dutton's seat is precarious. Of course, we won't know until the Saturday night of the election but removing some of these older less representative members will help the Liberal Party bring in some new people and regenerate. There is a sense that Labor should be performing much better than it is and, because of this, we shouldn't be saying Labor will win a landslide victory—we shouldn't be even saying for certain Labor will win the election at all, as most people are claiming. It's certainly not impossible, nor is a Liberal–National victory but, living in New South Wales, we can see how an unpopular, inept and corrupt government can be returned to office, as was the case with the NSW Labor Party in early 2007.

EJ: Generally within federal politics, unexpected election results don't occur very often—the surprises are usually confined to the magnitude of the victory, instead of the victory itself, such as the 2004 and 2016 elections: in both of those elections, the Liberal Party was expected to win, but won by a massive margin in 2004, but only by one seat in 2016. The last genuinely unexpected result in federal politics was the 1993 election won by Labor, in a campaign dominated by the Liberal–National *Fightback!* package; but these types of results tend to occur more frequently in state politics: Bracks' Labor defeated Jeff Kennett in Victoria in 1999; Gallop's Labor defeated Richard Court in 2001 in Western Australia; Jay Wetherall's Labor managed to hold onto government in South Australia in 2014; Annastacia Palaszczuk in Queensland in 2015, defeating Campbell Newman's LNP. There are many unexpected election results as the state level, but not so much at the federal level.

DL: As I keep mentioning, the rules of politics have changed since around 2009–10. Tony Abbott shouldn't have won in a landslide at the 2013 election: that was a terrible campaign and destructive performance as Leader of the Opposition between 2009–13, yet Abbott wins the election by the biggest margin ever in Australia's electoral history. Malcolm Turnbull shouldn't have scraped back in by one seat in 2016: his campaign was also quite poor, losing fifteen seats for the Liberal–National Party, although he wasn't expected to perform so poorly. All the evidence that we have at hand points towards Labor picking up fifteen-to-twenty seats: the Liberal Party has performed poorly, there was a redistribution of seats in 2018 which means they've notionally lost seats even before this election campaign began; they've changed their leaders—twice—they've made all kinds of promises to all kinds of people, yet nothing seems to work. But the cynic in me wonders whether we're reverting to the pre-2010 rules of politics, or if we're still operating in the chaos of the past nine years. If we play according to the normal rules of politics, Labor wins this election. But if we play according to the rules of the chaos that we've had for almost a decade, it becomes a lot more unpredictable and it's more difficult to say that Labor will win this election and, in these circumstances, a Coalition victory seems more likely. And a minority Labor or Coalition government also can't be ruled out.

EJ: I'm going out on a limb—Labor should be confident of winning around fifteen seats but, of course, the proviso is that it depends on which political rules we play by: the normal rules of politics, or by chaos theory. There might be some last minute surprises that pop out of the box and create the result that no-one saw coming. Bill Shorten, indeed, might be the severely unpopular leader that no-one can vote for, and that drags Labor's vote down. The United Australia Party preference deals with the Liberal–National Party could create havoc in Queensland: if the LNP manages to hold or pick up seats in Queensland, that will be a fine effort, but there's other seats where it's likely to lose in Victoria, South Australia, and New South Wales. Mathematically, it will be difficult for the LNP to make a net gain of three seats to hold onto government: that's not to say that it can't be done, but it will be difficult. They've been behind in all opinion polls for almost three years: the polls don't mean everything, but they do mean something. If the Liberal–National Party does win the election on Saturday night, it will be one of the most remarkable election victories in Australian history.

DL: The Liberal–National Party hasn't done very much during this last term to deserve an election victory, but politics isn't about who deserves to win. The Senate vote will be unpredictable, as it usually is, with One Nation, the United Australia Party and other micro-parties guaranteed to provide for some unusual results. All indications in the House of Representatives are pointing towards a victory for the Labor Party, but indications and predictions are not results. This election is still up for grabs.

*

Music in this episode
Dayan Cowboy, The Boards Of Canada
The Final Countdown (cabaret version), Gunhild Carling
Cantaloupe Island, Herbie Hancock

The 2019 federal election wrap-up, politics for sale, and the new Parliament

7 June 2019

Eddy Jokovich + David Lewis / Podcast

In this episode, we analysed the 2019 federal election results; asked if Australian democracy is for sale and how much does it cost; and looked at the upcoming Parliament—what can we expect to see over the next three years? And in this episode, David Lewis is milliner to the stars.

Eddy Jokovich: The May election resulted in a yet another Liberal–National Coalition victory, their third in a row, and the result went against the flow of a generally anticipated Labor victory. The Coalition made a net gain of one additional seat, to land on seventy-seven, while the Labor Party lost one seat to land on sixty-eight seats; the other six seats going to minor parties and independents. There was a 1.2 per cent swing towards the government, and the final result was almost the reverse of most people's expectations. It was one of the most surprising election victories in Australian history, more surprising than Labor's victory in 1993, and ruining the reputation of all the major polling companies along the way. During the last parliamentary term, there had been leadership changes in both the Liberal and

National parties and, compared to the stability of the Labor Party, the Liberals were divided and unstable for the best part of three years, and had little to show in their policy agenda for the future. There was a stench of corruption and dysfunction that followed the Coalition everywhere yet, somehow, the electorate chose to have more of the same for the next three years. It is commonly said 'there is no such thing as an unwinnable election', and so it proved to be for the Coalition. What went right for the Coalition, where did it all go wrong for Labor?

David Lewis: We can look at the fear of change as a big motivator for the electorate. On a superficial level, we can look at all the changes that we've had in prime ministers in recent time, and the electorate just didn't want to see any more change at the top: since 2007, there have been six prime ministers: Rudd, Gillard, Rudd (again), Abbott, Turnbull and Morrison. Perhaps a change to Morrison in 2018 was also considered as a change of government, so why change if the government is still 'new'? In specific electorates, jobs were seen as a major issue and Labor didn't really address this issue in any real or substantive way. They also got stuck on details of key policy announcements, such as their franking credits scheme, which most people didn't understand. They also got stuck on defending Bill Shorten as 'a good bloke', and someone who is really likeable, when in fact, Shorten was not seen as a very likeable figure, or a very popular figure. The Liberal Party was able to hold key marginal seats, which were swinging seats, but had a Liberal Party bias: Scott Morrison visited Tasmania eight times, as well as spending a great deal of time in Queensland, and these states swung very strongly towards the LNP. There were other factors in the mainstream media: the Adani mine was widely reported as being the saviour for jobs in north and central Queensland—seen as a positive for the Liberal–National Party. There was a great deal of opposition to the mine, but the opponents had no real plan about what to do if the mine didn't proceed: there was some vague discussion about renewables and retraining, but nothing of great substance. There is now a feeling among the commentariat—and the Labor Party—that the time of the big-picture-detailed-policy campaign is over.

EJ: Elections are never based on just the one issue: there is always going to be a multitude of issues that affect the final outcome. And the collection of ideas, policies, imagery and 'feelings' each party puts out affects the result. Before the election, I predicted the Labor Party would comfortably win, and this was based on overall performance over the past three years, opinions polls all pointing to a Labor victory, betting markets, and general expectations that Labor would win. But, like many other people, I got that one wrong. You weren't so sanguine, and you expected the Liberal–National Party to be returned to government, on the back of preferences from independents, One Nation and the United Australia Party, in key marginal seats.

DL: I do get it right occasionally! Most of the evidence pointed to a swing to Labor of about 4–5 per cent, and the Liberal Party was in an organisational mess: not just federally, but in New South Wales as well. I've mentioned this before, but most of the political orthodoxy has changed over the past decade, largely due to the ascension of Tony Abbott as the Leader of the Opposition in 2009, and then on to become prime minister. Political parties on the right started to behave differently and unpredictably, and many of the political rules have changed, as has electorate behaviour and responses. And maybe that's one aspect that was misunderstood as far as predicting the election winner: the rules of politics have changed substantially, but the methods of assessing the value of politics—through opinion polling and media analysis—hasn't changed very much at all. If politics was still operating by the pre-2009 'rules', there was no way the Liberal Party would have won the election; there should have been a decisive electoral defeat for them, with an organisational restructure after they lost the election. But politics has changed, it has become more unpredictable, and the 2019 election provides an excellent case study of that.

EJ: Of course, hindsight is wonderful, and it is much easier to become an expert after the event. In retrospect, we can look at other factors as well for Labor: equivocation on mining, where they collected the worst of both worlds through indecision about supporting or sanctioning the Adani mine, and this meant their opponents could pick and choose which tactics to use to attack

Labor. The issue about mining jobs in Queensland, Western Australia and, to a lesser extent, northern Tasmania was a key factor for Labor. Even though there won't be many new jobs created through the Adani project—ultimately, there will only be around 100 ongoing positions—the lack of a clear outline of where Labor stood on Adani cost the party a number of seats in Queensland, and thwarted their quest to pick up additional seats in Melbourne, where closing the Adani mine was popular. Politically, it would have been better for Labor to at least make a clear decision, and it seems the correct decision would have been to say they were prepared to close the Adani proposal—those seats in Queensland would have been lost anyway, and they would have picked more seats in Melbourne, and possibly other capital-city seats around the country.

DL: There's also the factor of Labor expecting to win too much, and perhaps because of this, overlooking the smaller tactics the Liberal Party used. The Liberal Party seemed to have the attitude of 'nothing to lose'—except government, of course—and tried every political trick in the book. But even still, we also have to remember that the Labor Party lost the election through around 29,000 votes in just over eight seats, seats that are volatile and can change quickly. The seats won by independents is interesting as well: there are three right-leaning members, and three left-leaning, including Adam Bandt from the Greens. Essentially, it's only a one-seat majority for the Liberal–National Party.

EJ: A one-seat majority is not very much over the cycle of the three-year electoral term. All that's required is the death or resignation of one or two government MPs in marginal seats—or another constitutional issue going to the High Court—and there's always a chance those seats could be lost in subsequent by-elections, and then the government falls into a minority position. So it's a majority that's still wafer thin, and there's not much room for the Coalition to move.

DL: There are some interesting seat issues that may become problematic, and it may happen sooner than we think. The Melbourne seat of Chisholm—won by the Liberal Party—seems to have had its voters misled, with Liberal Party posters suggesting in Mandarin and mimicking official Australian Electoral Commission signage, that the only way to vote is to put the Liberal Party first. I'm sure members of the Chinese community would have been able to see through that but, perhaps reading signage in a second language, and coming from a political system that's different to Australia's, the messaging may have been strong enough to deceive enough voters to push the Liberal candidate, Gladys Liu, over the line. Of course, it's a case of whether these incidents end up in the High Court, and there's also the question of eligibility of some of the United Australia Party candidates—there is an argument suggesting the UAP didn't win any seats so it shouldn't matter, but their preferences were very helpful in getting the Liberal Party re-elected in many seats, so that's certainly something that should be looked at as well.

EJ: Bill Shorten has resigned as leader of the Labor Party but during his resignation speech, he said there were many vested interests acting against him and Labor: News Corp, Sky News, the real estate industry, the banking sectors. And of course, as soon as he made this claim, these vested interests all proceeded to attack him even further—left, right and centre—the *Sydney Morning Herald* and *The Age* attacked him as well. It's almost axiomatic—they spent a great deal of resources telling everyone how unpopular Bill Shorten is and now claim the election result as vindication of their position. And now the mainstream media is attacking Shorten for resigning from the leadership, even thought that's what leaders normally do in modern politics, if they're lost two consecutive elections and spent six years as the leader. It's what Labor leader Arthur Caldwell did many years ago in the 1960s; Kim Beazley did the same in 2001. Shorten resigned of his own accord; it's the obvious thing to do. But as soon as he did resign, the mainstream media claimed it was only a matter of time before he'd want to take back the leadership, he still had leadership ambitions, and he would continue to be a destabilising force in the Labor Party and whoever did become the new leader, they would be under constant pressure from Shorten. Shorten and Labor can just never get a break from the mainstream media.

DL: It's what the media do—they were always clamouring for Tony Abbott to return to the Liberal Party leadership after he was toppled by Malcolm Turnbull in 2015, and there was a group of Abbott supporters who were working towards that, destabilising Turnbull's position and claiming Abbott didn't really get 'a fair go'. But he did have two years as prime minister and his performance showed he just wasn't up to the job. But Abbott is now out of Parliament, having lost his seat to the independent, Zali Steggall, so it's all over for him, and he probably knows it. For Bill Shorten, there's always the media agenda against him. The ABC's Michael Rowland aired a photograph of Shorten putting out the garbage at his family home on the Sunday morning after the election, as if to humiliate him even further. Rowland claimed it was just to show the fine line between being the potential prime minister one day, and then just being another person in the street on the next day, and the brutality of politics. But to be fair to Shorten, there have been many worse people than him that have gone on to become prime minister.

EJ: History has shown that once a leader resigns from the leadership of the party, there's very little chance of coming back as the leader again. Kevin Rudd managed to do it, but he only did it after he spent the best part of three years undermining Julia Gillard and the Labor Party. John Howard came back after resigning the leadership of the Liberal Party, as did Andrew Peacock, with Howard then going on to become prime minister. Kim Beazley did return to the leadership in 2005 after Simon Crean resigned. There are those precedents, so Shorten returning to the position can never be entirely ruled out. It's unlikely though, but we can also never underestimate the right wing of the Labor Party and it's desire to cause trouble for their left wing—which is where the new Labor leader Anthony Albanese comes from.

DL: It's right for the Labor Party to keep Shorten in the shadow ministry—if he wants to—and it's likely he'll be the shadow minister for the National Disability Insurance Scheme. Labor has to honour its former leaders—with the exception of Mark Latham—as does the Liberal Party, and it's right for Shorten to stay on, even if it is as a mentor to other Labor MPs, in the same way Wayne Swan stayed in Parliament for an extra term, made a quiet transition and then quietly resigned. Malcolm Turnbull, of course, resigned immediately after he was toppled by Morrison in 2018 but why would he stay in Parliament after the way he was treated by the Liberal Party? It's going to be different for different politicians, and it depends on the circumstances. Whether Shorten remains in Parliament in support of the new Labor leader, or genuinely goes on fighting every day for the causes he believes in remains to be seen. Either way, it really doesn't matter.

*

The big target claims another victim

EJ: Many political commentators have been suggesting we're unlikely to see a political party enter an election campaign with a big-target strategy for a long time. The 2019 election loss for Labor is similar to what happened to the Coalition back in the 1993 election, when they released their *Fightback!* manifesto: that really was a big target. Labor's platform in 2019 wasn't anywhere near as comprehensive as *Fightback!* but there were enough targets for the Coalition to take aim, especially the proposal to reduce franking credits—which was misread and misunderstood by many people in the electorate—and their negative gearing policy, which was attacked by the partisan real estate industry and simplified to a very sharp political message by Josh Frydenberg. What are the ramifications for elections into the future? Will we see Labor crawl up into a ball and adopt a small-target campaign—which hasn't really worked for them in the past—and have even smaller policy details presented by the Liberal–National Party? The LNP didn't have much of a policy agenda at all, and this ended up being a very successful election strategy for them.

DL: There is an inherent imbalance in the political system in Australia: Labor has to be inspiring to the electorate, it has to provide good reasons to the electorate to vote for them, when compared to conservative governments. Labor can't just be 'more of the same'; they have to offer key differences. In 2007, the last time Labor won government from opposition, they had simple pithy slogans—Kevin '07—and a leader in Kevin Rudd who had solid electoral appeal. Sometimes, it's those big slogans that resonate with the electorate—Gough Whitlam's 'It's Time' slogan in 1972. This is in contrast with John Howard's 'Incentivation' slogan from 1987, which was a total turn off for the electorate. 'Kevin '07' was simple; it succeeded, but it was also backed up by key policies announcements. In 2019, the franking credits scheme was difficult to explain—Labor spokespeople had to go through the process of explaining how many shares someone would need to own to be able to receive $26,000 worth of franking credits; and then explain franking credits had been paid to people who have invested in certain companies, who pay their dividends back through credits that have already had tax paid on them—but is counted as separate income, yet is tax free. Well, by the time they would get to this point, they'd already lost their audience. Shorten did run a good campaign, but it lacked the 'snap and pop', and watching Labor ministers trying to explain the franking credits proposals was a good example of this. The Liberal Party doesn't need to be inspiring to the electorate: they're traditionally considered to be the party of the 'steady hand', and there for the 'forgotten people', that idea that was successfully cultivated by Robert Menzies in the 1940s. Whether this is fair or not is a different matter: politics is never played out according to which party deserves to win; it's about who succeeds in the game of politics, and the Liberal Party has won that game.

EJ: The Liberal Party probably doesn't need to create a new inspirational strategy for the next election: Labor did have 'Kevin 07' back in 2007, but didn't have anything like that for 2019. But whatever the case, Labor will have to make sure the election doesn't end up being a *Catch-22* for them.

*

Is Australian democracy for sale, and how much does it cost?

EJ: The billionaire owner of Mineralogy, mining tycoon Clive Palmer, spent almost $78 million on advertising for the United Australia

Party during the election campaign—not so much to win any seats, but to act like a stalking horse for the Coalition, picking up 450,000 primary votes across Australia, with 75 per cent of those preferences directed back to the Coalition. It wasn't possible to look at a screen, watch television, listen to radio or read a newspaper without coming across a United Australia Party advertisement campaigning against the Labor Party and Bill Shorten: it was brazen, it was audacious and it worked. There are currently no laws to stop anyone in Australia from advertising during political campaigns and elections, as long as it's authorised and amounts of spending and donations are declared, albeit, the information about this spending is embargoed until at least eight months after this election. Australian politics and election outcomes are being highly influenced by the asset rich class and business tycoons: this is becoming an increasing problem for Australian politics.

DL: And it has been a problem for some time. In 2010, Kevin Rudd retreated on his climate change policies after a massive negative advertising campaign promoted by the mining industries. The mining sector seems like it's a big employer of workers when driving through mining areas such as the Hunter Valley in New South Wales, but across Australia, it only makes up around 1 per cent of the entire workforce, and that's a number that's dropping, as automated mining becomes more prevalent in the industry. But it's an industry that still has a large and undue influence in Australian politics.

EJ: There was a large amount of attention during the election campaign on the Adani mine in Queensland—and not only during the campaign, but over the past two or three years. What is largely unknown to the electorate is another development application through Clive Palmer's company, Minerology—it's the Alpha–North Development Plan, almost double the size of Adani's Carmichael mine. And, if it's approved, it will produce over 33 per cent more coal than the Adani mine. Clive Palmer's intentions in the 2019 election didn't have much to do with winning seats or getting United Australia Party members into the Senate—it was all about making sure the Labor Party didn't get into office. But Palmer isn't altruistic enough that he'll just spend

$78 million to make sure Labor didn't win the election; he'd be looking at a trade off for his political work. The Adani mine was the mine receiving all the political attention, as well as the political heat, and there doesn't seem to be an economic case to support the Adani proposal going ahead. But it's Minerology's Alpha–North mine that will end up getting the approval—and Palmer's $78 million investment in what was essentially Liberal Party political advertising will offer a great return.

DL: Not once did Clive Palmer mention the Liberal Party in a negative way in any of the UAP advertising: it was all a hatchet job on how terrible the Labor government had been in the past, and how awful Bill Shorten would be if he ever became prime minister. Palmer would have been hoping to win at least one seat, or have at least one Senator, but he didn't even come close. To spend $78 million on advertising shows how much money can go into these campaigns across Australia, but he achieved what he wanted: to deny Labor a term in government, and probably get the approval for the Alpha–North mine.

EJ: The United Australia Party achieved 3.4 per cent of the primary vote across Australia and the party provided candidates in all 151 seats in the House of Representatives. The level of primary vote fluctuated between 2.8 to 4.5 per cent in every single seat, so we can say the $78 million spent on advertising was effective in picking up that level of primary votes. Around 75 per cent of these primary votes went back to the Liberal–National Party through preferences, so it definitely had influence in marginal seats, especially in Queensland and other mining areas—and that's just votes that went to the UAP: there's little doubt the negative Labor advertising would have directed other primary votes towards the LNP.

DL: We can see the UAP and Clive Palmer directly supported the Liberal–National Party, and there will be payback, but it doesn't take too many external factors for favours to be denied: if a politician or a political party can sniff the wind and detect changes in the political environment, they'll dump Clive Palmer like a hot potato, particularly in light of some of his more questionable dealings. One of his mining companies still owes his employees almost $7 million in worker entitlements, and owes the Australian Tax Office around $70 million. Of course, there are other companies that may still owe him vast amounts of money, but there are some interesting questions about where some of his revenue is coming from. There are also questions about the links between his company, Minerology, and the Liberal Party, the National Party, big farming companies, the banks, and the mining industry overall.

EJ: The Minerals Council of Australia is a very conservative organisation, with its board of directors comprising some very right-wing individuals. Back in 2009, the Council spent $122 million on a highly aggressive campaign against Labor's emission trading, mining tax and carbon pricing proposals, and kick started the moves by the Labor Party to depose Kevin Rudd as prime minister. There wasn't even an election campaign at that time, but the Minerals Council did their upmost to ensure all of these proposals became a major political issue. The emissions trading system was dumped, although the mining tax and carbon pricing proposals eventually were introduced by the Labor Party. But the ongoing campaigns implemented by the Minerals Council were so great that they helped remove the Labor government in 2013, and by 2014, both the mining tax and carbon pricing were also removed. Of course, in a democratic country, everyone and every business has the right to spend money on political campaigning in whichever they wish to, but $122 million to campaign on one issue? That's a large amount of money. The Minerals Council also managed to mobilise many of its workers to campaign against Labor, but they were pawns in the machine: most of these workers were retrenched after the mining boom ended in 2014, and their jobs have been largely replaced by automated machines: so much for loyalty. We can see how big business has a massive advantage over the left side of politics, and it's difficult to launch counter arguments if your side of politics doesn't have the same access to that level of funding. It's a vexed question, but for the other highly moneyed people in society—the likes of Gina Rinehart, Harry Triguboff, Frank Lowy, Kerry Stokes—they'd be looking at how the United Australia Party performed in the 2019 election and they'd be taking notes on how to influence elections in the future, with the support of the Liberal Party and other conservative parties.

DL: What is not understood very well is the products of mining belong to the Commonwealth of Australia, not the mining companies: the mining companies claim they do, but they don't, they just receive a licence to mine. From this point, the federal government has the right and the obligation to charge a good and fair levy for the privilege of mining companies being able to do this. It's actually irresponsible for governments to continue giving highly favourable and preferential treatment to some of these corporations, with little or no return to the public. They hold too much sway, too much power, and too much influence in Australian politics. The honest response to many workers in the mining industry is there will need to be a structural adjustment plan, where workers may need to retrain and move into other worker-viable industries. But the convenient lie has more currency, and when industries promote these advertising campaigns to protect their vested interests against the community interests, everyone else misses out.

EJ: The amounts of money spent by vested interests and industry groups is one issue in Australian politics: there are no limits on how much money can be spent on elections by individuals or corporations, and that's one area that will need to be looked at in the future, but it will be a question of who becomes responsible for this. The Australian Electoral Commission is responsible for the management of elections in Australia, but they're limited by the amount of resources available to them during election campaigns. There were a few incidents where electoral laws were breached—on eighty-seven occasions and most breaches were performed by the Liberal Party—in areas such as unauthorised advertisements, leaflets containing false messaging, signage in foreign languages that also contained incorrect information favourable to the Liberal–National Party. There was also some illegal text messaging, which contained further false information, some of it was litigious. The only action available to the Australian Electoral Commission in all of these circumstances is a 'cease and desist' order—and that's only if they can find out who's responsible for the messaging: by the time false or unauthorised material is removed, especially if it's been available for several weeks, it's just far too late—the messages are already in the public domain. Once these messages have been disseminated, it's not possible to unsee or undo that message, especially if it has already been distributed through digital and online media. But even with these peripheral issues, the Australian Electoral Commission is ill-equipped to deal with them, and it's hard to see how they could manage or regulate the amounts of money flowing into election campaigns.

DL: The more obvious solution is fully publicly-funded elections, and we're very close to that right now. The political parties or individuals that receive over 4 per cent of the primary vote not only have their electoral deposit refunded, but they also receive $2.77 per primary vote, which is designed to help fund their electoral costs, and support political campaign work in the future. It means the smaller parties—even that ones that we might vehemently disagree with—get to have a say within the political process, and this is the essence of democratic systems, even if this funding process is skewed towards the Liberal, National and Labor parties.

EJ: One other factor that was apparent during the election campaign was the increase in access to social media for the political parties and the style of social media campaigning. It was prevalent in the earlier New South Wales election, but federally, the major factors were the 'death taxes' and Bill Shorten memes appearing throughout Facebook and Instagram, on behalf of the Liberal Party. These were produced by a New Zealand agency, Topham Guerin—they're virtually unknown in Australia, but they're an agency with strong links with Australia's National Party and their job was to create and distribute anti-Labor social media material and digital advertising such as videos, animation and graphics, the most infamous graphic being 'The Bill Australia Can't Afford': that advertisement was absolutely everywhere online. The social media statistics were stark for the Labor Party: even through their aggregate of followers is substantially higher than the Coalition's, their viewer engagement was 30 per cent lower. The Coalition's social media and digital campaign work was quick and ultra-responsive, far superior to Labor's: it's clear they were the big winners in the 'info wars'.

DL: 'The Bill Australia Can't Afford' was one of those all-capturing meme messages, and it worked extremely well. Was it fair and was it accurate? Probably not, but it put enough doubt into people's minds and it helped to swing the election, although we can't be sure by how much. And in contemporary politics, the online factor can't be underestimated. Although it was still in its nascent form, it helped Kevin Rudd win the 2007 election. Twelve years down the track, the mainstream media and journalism is going through major changes and reforms. News Corp has just announced fifty journalists will be retrenched. Fairfax Media has been purchased by the Nine Group. Mainstream media is still highly influential in political matters, and that's still where most people receive their political news and information, but online media is increasingly becoming more influential.

EJ: The newspaper industry is travelling in a slow-moving death vortex, and has been dying for some time. The old advertising 'rivers of gold' have dried up, and it's now a question of how long print newspapers will be around for. But, to be sure, these are still the news and information behemoths and will be there in the future on some level, albeit in different forms. The future for traditional news outlets such as the *Daily Telegraph*, *Sydney Morning Herald* or *The Age* is to go purely online, with a weekly print version containing more long-form analytical material that has a longer shelf-life than yesterday's news. Whether there would be a public appetite for that type of printed publication is unknown, although *The Saturday Paper* is one independent news outlet that has bucked the trend. *The Australian* will perhaps disappear, once Rupert Murdoch also departs the scene, so we may be in for a major realignment in the news media industry.

DL: As always, the media played an influential part in the election and, as they usually do, they favoured the Liberal–National Party, especially the commercial mainstream media and, increasingly, the ABC. But that's a known quantity, we've come to expect this: Labor had so much material to work with on the incompetence of this government, but failed to make progress in this area. The

Howard government was competent; the Fraser government was competent; both of these governments had the look and feel of long-term, stable governments, but lost elections when they had outstayed their welcome and the electorate decided it was time for fresh faces in politics. But the Liberal–National governments since 2013 haven't been effective at all: they've had many leadership changes; they've been divided; they can't agree with each other. There have been questions about government corruption. The LNP member for the Queensland seat of Dawson, George Christensen, had spent 300 days in the previous year chasing a fiancée in Manila, claiming he could still do his parliamentary business from overseas on his iPad—which, on the surface, seems like outrageous behaviour by a Member of Parliament—yet Labor couldn't make political mileage out of this. Some of this, of course, was deflected by friends in the parochial media: for example, media management and story framing depicted Christensen as getting a hard time from outsiders in Sydney and Melbourne, and downplayed the idea of an absent MP spending most of their time overseas. It all seems incongruous, and the electorate of Dawson had the wool pulled over their eyes. Essentially, Labor didn't capitalise on many of these behaviours and poor government performance and didn't push these issues to the electorate as hard as they could have.

*

What to expect in politics over the next year

EJ: The counting is over and most of the seats in this election have been declared. The election writs will soon be returned, and that's when the next session of Parliament will commence. Before this election, we predicted a massive realignment of conservative politics in the wake of an expected defeat, but this didn't turn out to be the case. All of the Coalition ministers who emptied out their offices and shredded all the ministerial documents will have to fill up their bookcases again and develop what their agenda is going to be for the next three years. Labor has a new leadership team led by a new leader, Anthony Albanese, and they've already embarked on listening tours in Queensland, Western Australia and Tasmania—areas that swung strongly against Labor—to talk to the electorate and find out where they went wrong. The mainstream media has already upped the ante and relentlessly attacked Labor and its new team, and started talking up the prospects of former leader Bill Shorten creating havoc by wanting to return to the leadership, even though he voluntarily resigned from his leadership just a few days ago. If this is the way the media is going to behave in the future, it's going to be a very long three years before the next election.

DL: Albanese has commenced the process of media management: there has been some good reporting on him, although some media—from the predictable areas—have started to attack him. And this is where it gets hard for Labor: Albanese is new to the job and new leaders usually have some level of a honeymoon period, but currently, the media doesn't want to give any respite. That should change though, as Albanese is, at least, a lot more televisual in a way Bill Shorten wasn't. But it's still too early to tell.

EJ: Media management is a key factor within politics, and Shorten, as the previous leader, continuously receive poor support from the media, the media constantly telling the electorate how unpopular Shorten is. Labor decided the best way to circumvent this was to speak directly to the people through 'town hall meetings'. This is a common strategy in United States politics and, during the last election cycle, Shorten appeared at eighty town hall meetings across Australia. The upshot is that all-comers were invited to these meetings, not just the party faithful; and undecided voters, or those skeptical about Shorten as a leader, would be suitably impressed, walk away from these meetings and then talk to others in the community about their impressions. And, in most cases, this worked: Shorten is a far more dynamic speaker in these town hall meetings, and it seems like it is a natural forum for him, whereas many of these qualities didn't translate at all televisually. The only problem here is that even if a meeting attracts 200 people, eighty town hall meetings would attract around 16,000 people. That's still a large number of people, but there are around fifteen million people voting in elections across Australia, and it's a strategy that isn't reaching enough people. It's unclear if Albanese will continue with the town hall meeting strategy, although he will be embarking on a series of headland speeches over the next six months. Having the media on-side is desirable, doing regular town hall meetings or headland speeches is desirable too: but it seems a bit too old style now, and too Clinton-esque—which worked very well in US politics in 1992, but may have lost some relevance in 2019. Social media and digital marketing is the avenue that needs to be explored and pushed further, and that's an area Labor needs to concentrate on over the next three years.

DL: The events that don't seem to work are the leaders' debates and it's hard to recall a time where issues discussed during the televised debate have swung an election. Bill Shorten easily won the three debates he had with Scott Morrison. The Liberal Premier in New South Wales, Gladys Berejiklian, lost the debates she had with NSW Labor leader, Michael Daley. Yet, these didn't make any discernible differences in the federal or New South Wales elections. The town hall meetings are a good idea, where leaders can practice their lines or their policy ideas in a public forum. For Shorten, it was an effective strategy and most people came out of those meetings impressed and surprised with how well he performed under pressure, and took on people in the electorate who disagreed with him. But it's an effective strategy that can't reach enough people in electorate.

EJ: This might be because most people just want to have a break from politics, but there still isn't much scrutiny being placed on the government, and their multitudes of corruption, which we'd assume would normally be a goldmine for political journalists. Water mismanagement in the Murray–Darling Basin; vast amounts of money spent on water rights and non-existent water; there's the Minister, Stuart Robert, who had to resign from the ministry several years ago—he had to repay $37,000 to the taxpayer for overusing his home internet account—he's now the Minister for the National Disability Insurance Scheme. Sussan Ley, the member for Farrer: she was disgraced for rorting her travel allowance and also resigned: she's now back as the Minister for Environment. It's hard to see what a Coalition minister would need to do to be banned from the ministry, and clear examples of corruption and incompetence have resulted in promotions.

DL: And there are many others: Senator Arthur Sinodinos is said to be taking over from Joe Hockey as Australian Ambassador to the United States. Sinodinos had those issues recently with the Sydney Water Corporation, where he couldn't recall anything at the inquiry, but here he is being promoted as Ambassador, although it's fair to say he is a far more substantial figure than the current Ambassador, Joe Hockey. There's the error-prone and even more incompetent Angus Taylor, the gift that keeps on giving to Labor, but Labor keeps throwing away. Senator Michaelia Cash, who has ignored subpoenas from the Australia Federal Police over tipping off media about union raids. It's almost limitless.

EJ: Political events that occurred three or four years ago, even the highly nefarious events, tend to be forgotten by the electorate and especially forgotten by the media. And unless the electorate and the media are reminded about these events by the Labor Party, these matters disappear into the ether. Sinodinos had been a good performer for the Liberal Party over many years: caught up in scandals, couldn't remember anything about it, but now his memory has miraculously returned. It's hard to know what will happen with Angus Taylor: politics is a moving caravan, and the media usually loses interest about specific events and looks for the next area of excitement and political intrigue.

DL: Angus Taylor's misdemeanours have related to water management, and perhaps this might be an ongoing issue, as there are many areas in New South Wales that are running out of water. Tamworth is having water issues; so is Armidale; Dubbo is running out of water. Walgett has actually run out of water. These are substantial towns, yet all three areas are in seats that voted the Liberal–National Party back into office. Taylor isn't out of trouble yet, but there are always future events that can come into play. And with a 24-hour media news cycle to fill in, the media is always going to be on the look out for more stories on water mismanagement—whether or not they decide to run hard on these stories is a different matter.

EJ: In his first press conference as Labor leader, Albanese said he wanted to 'slow things down a bit', and he wasn't prepared to front up to media conferences just to make impromptu policy announcements; rather than fulfilling that 24/7 media cycle, he wanted to be more considerate about what the Labor Party has to offer the community and spend more time on policy development. One factor the media keeps bringing up: Shorten is from the right faction of the Labor Party and took the party to the left on many issues—some would argue he didn't go left enough. Albanese is from the left, historically, but seems to want to take the party to the right. This should create an interesting party dynamic, and will need to be managed carefully by Albanese and Labor. The call to spend more time developing nuanced and carefully crafted policy should be welcomed as well.

DL: That's the obvious way to go, except for the possibility of this all being lost in the flotsam and jetsam of the 24-hour news cycle. Albanese runs the risk of being lost in the flow of events but, to avoid this, has to manufacture some of kind of pithy slogan that he can run with and hold up the policies he wishes to formulate and promote. It's very hard to do.

EJ: If the Labor Party turns up to the next election as a small target with virtually no policy agenda, the electoral will ask: 'what's the point of voting Labor if you're not offering us anything different?' It's a fine balancing act: they have to offer substantial policy, but not enough for their opponents to be able to launch a major attack. We can look at the 1996 election campaign, where John Howard won the election comprehensively for the Coalition but offered virtually nothing substantial on policy matters, and certainly nothing resembling the *Fightback!* package from the preceding election. Can a small-target strategy work for the Labor Party? Conventional wisdom is that Labor needs to provide inspiration to the electorate but what has been forgotten is that in 2007, Kevin Rudd also offered very little during the election campaign. He closely mimicked the Liberal Party so much that it infuriated the media—as well as the Liberal Party. Rudd rode on the wave of climate change issues at that time, promoted the idea of the 'fiscal conservative', where he actually promised to spend less money than the Liberal Party, and even made a virtue out of this. The political adage is oppositions don't win elections; it's governments that lose them and it's also a case where oppositions shouldn't do anything at all to stand in the way of an electorate ready to throw out an incompetent government.

DL: But it's also the job of the opposition to force a government into a position where they lose. Labor failed this time around, but they didn't fail by too much. It was only a 1.2 per swing towards the government, which was probably around 5 per cent more than most people were expecting, but it doesn't really matter how large the swing is—the Coalition won the most seats, and that's all that matters.

EJ: Scott Morrison replicated John Howard's opening act from the 2004 election: he announced the election date by claiming: 'who do you trust on the economy?'. And, of course, this fed into the Liberal–National rhetoric of 'superior economic manager': it's rhetoric they've been running with for a long time, ever since Labor vacated the economic space after the 1996 election loss— Labor created the conditions for twenty-three years of stable economic growth after 1996, but decided not to take any credit for this. Labor decided not to talk about the economy anymore, one of the more bizarre decisions in modern politics. We can also look at Labor's management of the 2009 global financial crisis: the Treasurer Wayne Swan guided Australia away from the calamity that afflicted the rest of the world—Australia was one of only four developed countries to avoid recession during the GFC—but Swan failed to make political capital out of this feat: it's almost a case where Labor is too afraid to talk about their economic credibility. Labor vacates the economic space in politics; the Liberal Party fills in the void—they promote the idea of superior economic management, even though the facts don't support this myth. But the mythology of the Liberal Party and superior economic management will soon have a major test, with a possible recession just around the corner. Already, Australia is in a per capita recession—interest rates keep falling, and that's usually the sign of a sluggish economy. But, of course, when conservative governments are faced with economic problems that they've created and can't control, they'll trigger up peripheral issues such as religious freedom, terrorism, attacking unions, or creating other diversions to keep the electorate and the media occupied.

DL: It's a strategy that arrives straight from the American playbook, and the Americanisation of the far right: libertarianism promoted by the Koch brothers, Rupert Murdoch, and the whole gamut of billionaires who don't want to pay taxes; the notion that business shouldn't be constrained by government regulation. But it's a form of libertarianism that only benefits the wealth class; it's the form that promotes individual freedoms and rights, yet severely limiting and restricting them at the same time. The idea of 'the moral majority' or the lunacy of 'the quiet Australians'. Many freedoms are being restricted by social and cultural disadvantage and, increasingly, through the use of religion. In Australia, few people are concerned about religion, as long as it doesn't impede on other people's rights, or infringes the law, it's largely accepted. But Parliament is opened in each session with the 'Lord's Prayer', a ridiculous situation in a supposedly secular country. Certainly, additional religious freedom isn't required in Australia and the government will probably continue to use the issue as deflection when faced with economic problems.

EJ: Laws protecting religious freedoms are already in place. It's evident this continued debate about religious freedom—which somehow has become a topic of debate, and came out of nowhere—is going to appear as a smokescreen for other political problems. The issue of religious freedom will take up much energy and attention from the media, and in the electorate: in the background, workers' rights will be cut back; union influence will be diminished; wages will go down. This election result hasn't resolved anything: there are many serious economic issues facing the country, and all of these are worthy of attention. But the government will be doing their best to deflect from the bad news and promote all sorts of nonsense to the forefront.

*

Music in this episode
La Femme d'Argent, Air
Dreaming Of Me, Depeche Mode
The Hard Road, Hilltop Hoods

Surprise agendas, mandates and codes of conduct

3 July 2019

Eddy Jokovich + David Lewis / Podcast

In this episode, we looked at the agendas and mandates for this third term of Liberal–National government and the ministerial code of conduct: What's the point of having one if it's ignored by our political leaders? And also in this episode, David Lewis wore a Gucci backless evening gown in red sequins, with brogues by John Karandonis.

Eddy Jokovich: The third term of the Liberal–National government is underway, but it seems like it's a government reaching for an agenda it never took to an election campaign, and it's arguing it has a mandate to implement unaffordable tax cuts in the year 2025 and beyond. The Prime Minister, Scott Morrison, announced he wants to revisit industrial relations, cut red tape, scale back the rights of green groups that stand in the way of mining projects, and implement the legislation that not too many people want or care about—the Religious Discrimination Bill. There's always a debate about mandates and agendas just after an election, but we closely followed the recent campaign, and there wasn't much discussion about industrial relations, red tape, green tape—or any other colour of tape—and there certainly wasn't much of a debate about religious freedom in Australia. Is it critical for political parties to outline their agendas for the future during an election campaign, or should they just get on with governing after they've won the election. Have we lost that idea of what a political mandate is?

David Lewis: Many people expected the Liberal–Nationals to lose the election, the campaign was seen as an attempt to save as many seats as possible for them in the lower house, and still have some level of control in the Senate—there were a few people in the party who thought they could win by targeting particular seats, and that proved to be correct. But if most of the energy goes into saving seats rather than pushing forward an agenda, and then if that party wins government, it comes into government within much of an idea of what it wants to do, and without much of an idea of how to achieve anything. And if doesn't create an agenda, there are others outside of government that can provide that for them, such as the 100-point plan coming from the Institute of Public Affairs—the IPA has their 100 suggestions for running the country, but those are ideas that aren't terribly popular even among Liberal Party supporters: selling off Medicare; selling off the ABC; selling off SBS; cutting awards and wages. There's a great deal of selling off in these IPA ideas, there's a great deal of breaking down public institutions; and a great deal of removal. There's not much building or creating good things for the community. The religious discrimination bill does one of two things: it speaks to something that is genuinely important to the Prime Minister and it also allows old debates that have never been resolved for the Christian right wing of the Liberal Party, and it's partially a pushback against some of the policy advancements that have happened in recent times: the same-sex marriage plebiscite which was passed successfully in 2017; Section 18c of the *Racial Discrimination Act*, which is one area they've been trying to repeal ever since the right-wing commentator Andrew Bolt was found in breach of 18c by the Courts.

EJ: There might not have been an expectation the Liberal–National Party was going to win the election, according to the opinions polls and the commentariat, but politics is a psychological process and played through bluff, bluster and mind games, and every political party has to go into an election thinking that it can win that election, otherwise there's no point in turning up. And that's exactly what happened with Scott Morrison and the Liberals: they believed they would win, counter to all expectations, and they did end up winning the election. But when it comes to formulating an agenda, if a political party is so worried about trying to simply hold onto its seats, its political agenda recedes into the background. Perhaps it's an area that is overrated: the electorate usually forgets the details about what might have been promised during an election campaign, or where the origins of a policy idea came from. The much-maligned franking credits policy that caused so many problems for the Labor Party, was actually an idea first proposed by Joe Hockey when he was Treasurer, and then supported by Scott Morrison when he replaced Hockey in 2015. The franking credits scheme is a very generous policy and it does need to be scaled back. But Labor is the party that copped all of the flak for this scheme—they were the ones that also ran strongly on the policy to reduce negative gearing benefits during the election campaign, another policy initially discussed by the Liberal Party. Hypothetically, in two years time, Scott Morrison could introduce Labor's negative gearing policy in full, and the electorate would probably forget or ignore that he campaigned strongly against it during the 2019 election. But perhaps it's never a good idea for an opposition party to take big ideas into an election campaign: there were many policies the Labor Party introduced in government after they won office in 1983—Bob Hawke and Paul Keating deregulated the banking system, floated the Australian dollar, reduced tariffs, and sold-off public assets. They never took these policies to an election, and this process worked for them. Conversely, after he won the 2004 election, John Howard introduced the WorkChoices policy, a draconian anti-worker framework, without a word about it during that election campaign and three years later, he was thrown out of office.

DL: The general wisdom is that John Howard did the one thing politicians can't do to any Australian, and that's to threaten to take away their public holidays. He never actually claimed that this is what would occur under WorkChoices, but the Labor Opposition at the time was able to put enough doubt into peoples' minds that public holidays were under threat. Of course, there have been other issues left over from WorkChoices that have come to fruition: penalty rates for many industries were reduced on 1 July this year. This didn't feature very much at all during the election campaign and, perhaps, it's an issue Labor could have highlighted a lot more.

EJ: And following on the debates about political agendas is the discussion about what constitutes a "mandate". The Liberal–National Party has a one-seat majority in the current Parliament, a very slim margin. When Tony Abbott won government in 2013, he had a majority of thirty seats—so when it comes to majorities and authority over Parliament, Scott Morrison would certainly have a greater authority over the Liberal Party, but a one-seat majority doesn't provide any sort of ascendancy in Parliament. It's difficult to claim a mandate with a one-seat majority, especially when the Liberal Party didn't really bring much with it to the election campaign.

DL: Morrison can't take his majority of seats for granted, and no prime minister can, especially when there's only a margin of one seat—all it takes is a current Liberal or National Party member to resign or cross the floor on any kind of reason of general principle, or for ego and ambition, and all of a sudden, the Prime Minister is in a difficult or untenable situation. The Liberal–National Party doesn't handle minority government very well, and one aspect that makes the Gillard minority government between 2010–13 fascinating is she passed more legislation than most previous governments, and certainly the governments since that time. This government doesn't seem to be interested in breaking any such records; they're not sitting in Parliament for anywhere near the amount of time needed to debate legislation procedurally, and because of this, they don't have a legislative mandate.

EJ: Scott Morrison and the Liberal Party: they have been constantly saying they're very keen to look forward and forget about the past, but there have been two books that have been recently published as a reminder of the past. *Highway to Hell*, by Nikki

Savva and *Venom*, by David Crowe: insider journalists from News Corp, although Crowe recently shifted over to the *Sydney Morning Herald*—both books outline the background to how Scott Morrison did become prime minister back in August 2018. Morrison doesn't really want to talk about this time, simply referring this as the 'Canberra bubble', or dismissing the events as a history not too many people are interested in. But there have been a few very interesting observations to come out of these publications: former Minister for Justice, Michael Keenan, reveals that Scott Morrison is "an absolute arsehole". We should encourage honesty in politics, but could Keenan's observations have gone just a little bit too far and is he being too honest?

DL: Michael Keenan has resigned from Parliament, so he's free to say whatever he would like to. A prime minister doesn't reach the position by making friends, and many enemies are going to be made on the way. It's very clear Scott Morrison is a ruthless operator, and you don't become prime minister unless you are a ruthless operator. The difference between Morrison and John Howard, Bob Hawke, Paul Keating, Kevin Rudd—who were also very ruthless and highly ambitious—is the public, more or less, knew what they stood for. We are still a little bit unclear about what Scott Morrison stands for—perhaps aside from his religious discrimination agenda—but we don't quite know what the details are as yet.

EJ: This government wants to look forwards, but we'd like to look backwards, even if it is for a short time: Malcolm Turnbull replaced Tony Abbott in 2015; Scott Morrison replaced Turnbull in 2018. Both the Liberal and National parties were divided, they changed all of their leaders. They've been quite an incompetent government since 2013, they've created a poor national broadband network, the economy has been stumbling yet, somehow, they still managed to win the 2019 election: it's almost a case of being rewarded for all of their incompetence. For sure, Morrison will keep saying that nobody cares about this sordid history, and that it's all ancient history: and he's probably right; the election victory proved that to be the case. But the one big issue that could be the Achilles heel for the Liberal Party is complacency and the belief that the government has become electorally invincible. Looking far back into the past, complacency, invincibility and hubris have been the features of the final stages of long-term governments. For the Liberal Party, they imagined that the dismissal of Gough Whitlam in 1975 and issues surrounding that would keep Labor out of office forever. But they lost office to Bob Hawke in 1983. The final years of Labor in the 1990s had all the hallmarks of a tired government, and they thought they'd be in office forever as well after their surprise victory in 1993—they lost office in 1996. The same issue for the final term of the Howard government between 2004–07. All of these governments won elections they were expected to lose—perhaps not so much the Howard victory against Mark Latham's Labor in 2004—but afterwards, they felt invincible and felt that they could deal with whatever was thrown at them by the media and by the opposition, and this ultimately led to their respective downfalls: each of these governments were thrown out in landside losses at the next election they faced. Scott Morrison currently has good reason to feel invincible: he's just won the unwinnable election, after the majority of the media and the community expected him to lose. But the Liberals of 1983 and 2007, and the Labor government of 1996; these were competent and stable governments. In comparison, the Liberal–National government of today resembles a rabble: Morrison still leads a Liberal Party deeply divided and, perhaps, there's a feeling within the government that winning elections can't be too difficult: after all, they changed leaders, Treasurers, and deputies; they've virtually had no policies; national government debt has almost doubled since 2013, and they still find themselves in government. If doing nothing was such a successful strategy for the Liberal–National Party, can we expect to see more of the same over the next term of government?

DL: What the government does need to remember—and it's a significant point—they didn't so much win the election, as Bill Shorten and the Labor Party lost the election: there's a slight difference. The Liberal–National Party wasn't warmly embraced like John Howard in 1996, Kevin Rudd in 2007, or even Tony Abbott in 2013, after the Labor Party decided to throw government away. This is where overreach comes into effect. It's easy for a prime minister, psychologically, to think the majority of people must like them, except for a few. It's very easy for a politician to overrate their own success.

EJ: That level of complacency can be built through media support, and prime ministers will do their best to fan favourable media. It's not a surprise to suggest the mainstream media generally supports the Liberal Party and conservative governments: that's who their proprietors support, and their editorial is usually directed in that way. Their journalists usually behave like courtiers protecting the establishment, rather than acting like balanced reporters—it has always been that way in Australia— and nothing presents this better than Scott Morrison's return from the recent G20 meeting in Osaka: he was lauded by the mainstream media; *The West Australian*, owned by Liberal Party supporter, Kerry Stokes, gave Morrison a "10 out of 10" for his appearance, when all he really did was shake hands with murderous Saudi dictators and invited US President Donald Trump to Australia for a game of golf. The same for Tony Abbott at the Davos economic forum in 2014: he was a non-event there and gave the equivalent of a shop-keeper's economic address and was rewarded with glowing media reports when he returned to Australia. Julia Gillard, on the other hand, during her first international visit in 2010, was pilloried by the media for not having enough international and foreign affairs experience. But, of course, the Australian media holds different rules for women in politics. Perhaps with the wind in his sails, Morrison can be confident that he can do whatever he wants in this next term, and will escape scrutiny and receive all the favourable media reporting in the world.

DL: During her first international visits in 2010, Julia Gillard was invited to extra meetings and met a wide range of world leaders: the exposure for Tony Abbott and Scott Morrison was limited. That's neither here nor there though, there may have been a wide range of reasons why this occurred, and it could all be a case of timing. The point is that at exactly the same time in their prime ministerships, Gillard, Abbott and Morrison had the same level of international experience: close to zero. It's interesting to see two male Liberal prime ministers returning as heroes from their first international visit: it just goes to show what can be achieved with a soft press. When Wayne Swan received the prestigious Finance Minister of the Year award in 2011, there were many Australian media reports complaining about how it wasn't a real award and it didn't really mean very much in the world of finance. But when Minister for the Environment Greg Hunt received the inaugural 'Best Minister in The World' award—provided by the United Arab Emirates for supposedly reducing carbon emissions, even though they had increased dramatically—it was lauded by the Australian media as a great achievement for the government. In Australia, the mainstream media leans solidly to the right; independent media leans to the left. The ABC runs an impossible line, trying to be all things to everyone and doesn't succeed in that at all. Private organisations in a democratic system, of course, can have whatever opinions they like and pay for whatever opinions they can afford. But this is problematic in a society that needs to have a more open debate and discussion, especially on complex issues.

*

The ineffective ministerial code of conduct

EJ: In August 2018, soon after he became prime minister, Scott Morrison introduced a new set of Ministerial Standards. In this document, we have the usual information we'd expect to see—integrity, principles, fairness, accountability, responsibility and public interest—but it's like the Constitution of the former Soviet Union, which talked about protecting humans rights and dignity, while in the background, political prisoners were shipped off to Siberia, and people in provinces such as Chechnya were bombed and murdered by the Red Army. Essentially, a ministerial code of conduct doesn't mean anything because MPs and former ministers can bypass it quite easily. But there's one clear code that stipulates former ministers shouldn't take employment in an industry directly relating to their portfolio within eighteen months of leaving Parliament. Former Defence Minister, Christopher Pyne has taken up a consultancy with Ernst and Young, as part of their desire to expand their footprint in the defence industry. Pyne only left Parliament a few months ago and it seems it's a clear breach of the ministerial code of conduct, but he's still there acting as a consultant to EY.

DL: There's a bit of media trope floating about that suggests the ministerial code of conduct is way too strict and way too high for any human being to be able to meet, but that's not the case at all. It basically says: be honest; don't rort your entitlements; avoid conflicts of interest and, essentially, serve the Parliament of Australia and the Commonwealth of Australia—that approach can't be too difficult. There are some other technical issues, such as the so-called Minchin Protocol, where if a Member of Parliament makes the honest mistake on their parliamentary entitlements, they can quietly pay the money back and avoid having to resign. Mistakes can be easily made: the rules can be complex for what constitutes parliamentary business, MPs are busy people, and there is quite a bit of paperwork involved, but sometimes MPs do claim entitlements that they really shouldn't. And perhaps they could also set up a breaching system where an MP is allowed two breaches before they receive a sanction. But if the Minchin Protocol was applied equally across the board, we really wouldn't have a problem…

EJ: …and of course, it isn't: we did have that selective application of the Minchin Protocol for the former Speaker of the House, Peter Slipper…

DL: … and that was for $900 in taxi bills that the Liberals wouldn't allow him to pay back. Perhaps Slipper did do the wrong thing back in 2010. But other MPs have rorted their entitlements to a far greater level, applied the Minchin Protocol and simply paid the money back—no questions asked. The Protocol has to be absolutely 100 per cent consistent, otherwise it just becomes a political weapon.

EJ: John Howard was the first prime minister to implement a ministerial code of conduct, back in 1996. He did campaign on clean government, as he kept on pushing the idea that the Keating Labor government was 'corrupt' and 'dirty'. He introduced that code of conduct after he became prime minister in 1996 and lost seven ministers and secretaries over various aspects such as undeclared shareholdings and travel rorts, and that was within the first nine months of his prime ministership.

DL: Parliament has all kinds of issues now: for example, the asset holdings of Peter Dutton's wife. He made sure that everybody knew he had divested himself of the family trust, but it still belongs to his wife and this is a grey area of law. If they were to divorce—this is just a hypothetical—both of their incomes, holdings and assets would all be measured and divided according to the law. So there's still a matter of influence there.

EJ: The most important part about any code of conduct is to have consistency. Prior to 1996, any issue of perceived corruption or other ministerial malfeasance was a matter of opinion for the prime minister of the day and it was, essentially, whatever they could get away with politically. But there were tougher political standards back then: in 1982, Liberal Party ministers John Moore and Michael McKellar were forced to resign because they incorrectly filled out a customs form, stating they imported a black and white television set, when it was actually colour. There were other reasons Prime Minister Malcolm Fraser decided to act in this case: both of those ministers were not competent, but Fraser used the television incident as a reason to remove them. The Labor MP, Mick Young, was stood down for an incorrect customs declaration for a Paddington Bear he tried to bring into the country in 1984. He wasn't forced to resign, but was stood down while an investigation into the Paddington Bear took place and after the inquiry, Bob Hawke put him straight back into the ministry. These were relatively minor incidents and not too much to get carried away with, but that's how it was in the early 1980s, not so long ago: completing an incorrect customs form or bringing in an oversized teddy bear from an overseas trip could force an MP to lose their ministerial position. These days, it seems to be quite different. Christopher Pyne; he probably should resign from his contract with Ernst and Young as it's a clear breach of the ministerial code of conduct. The code clearly states a retiring minister shouldn't work in an area that directly relates to their portfolio for at least eighteen months after leaving Parliament. Supporters of the current inadequate system have pointed to the code just being that: it's not a piece of legislation or law, and it should really be up to the prime minister of the day to decide whether the code has been breached or not. There are other codes in a range of professions, of various gauges: auditors and company directors have a strict code of conduct; breaching them results in fines and jail terms. There is a code of conduct for journalists that we have to adhere to, although there's no sanction if that's broken, with the exception of defamation law. There is a building code in New South Wales: but after the problems we've seen in Sydney with the cracking of the Opal Towers and Mascot Towers, it seems that the building code is not being adhered to either. Journalists writing factually incorrect information; politicians behaving corruptly; buildings falling apart: what is the point of any of these codes of conduct if there's no way to make sure they're being adhered to?

DL: It shows the failure of self-regulation systems, and the failure of some of the market theories behind self-regulation. The rationale was, of course, businesses such as building companies would follow their own codes of conduct because if they didn't, they would fail and go out of business. It hasn't quite worked out that way. In the case of the Opal Towers, people bought those apartments in good faith, believing they had been built according to at least a basic building standard. We don't know why this has happened, but people bought apartments that were fundamentally flawed. In journalism: we could probably look at about twenty articles in today's so-called quality newspapers, and a similar number on television, and find that many of them have breached the journalists' code of conduct, but there will be little to no consequence for these breaches.

EJ: And that leads to other issues in media reporting and false news: once a viewer has read an article in a newspaper or watched a report on television that has been found to be untrue or misleading, it's not possible to 'unread' the article or 'unsee' what has just seen on a screen. Once certain information is out there in the public domain, it's very difficult to undo it. There's also the issue of the authority and veracity of the media. Despite suspicions, the public is generally trusting of what they view in mainstream newspapers and television reports, and that's why it's essential for them to contain information that is factually correct and backed up with a strong and enforceable code of conduct. In political matters, there still haven't been any developments on a national integrity commission, as promised by Scott Morrison in December 2018. He didn't really discuss this during the election campaign, and it has definitely been placed on the backburner, possibly never to appear again.

DL: An integrity commission isn't the same as a commission against corruption, because 'integrity' is fungible. It's a little bit like jazz music: everyone knows what it isn't. Whereas corruption is a lot easier to legislate against, it's easier to put down the parameters in full. But even on looser definitions of corrupt behaviour, it might be a case of many government ministers not being able to meet even a basic level of acceptable conduct, and quite possible, many opposition MPs and independents as well. And to be fair, most Members of Parliament do behave properly, work incredibly hard and do try their very best to work in the best interests of everyone, but we don't tend to hear too much about these MPs in the media.

EJ: Sometimes, there are developing issues in politics that don't need to wait for the creation of an integrity or corruption commission to apply further investigation. Senate inquiries and Estimates Committees can be very powerful, and perhaps there's a need for another inquiry just around the corner. The 'Watergate' issue concerning large amounts of water buybacks under the Murray–Darling Basin Plan first became prominent just before the federal election: it involved Minister for Energy, Angus Taylor, and the National MP, Barnaby Joyce. But the issue has permeated from federal politics into New South Wales state politics: it now involves the wife of Angus Taylor, his brother, his sister-in-law—who just happens to also be a minister in the New South Wales Government—and there's a wide range of allegations of misuse of water resources that needs to be cleared up. Angus Taylor should be fronting up somewhere to explain himself, but it's not clear whether it should be through a statement to Parliament, an appearance at a Senate inquiry, or some other public forum. 'Watergate' has dropped off from the media's interest but, in the absence of a national ICAC, there does need to be further investigation into the wholesale corruption in this area.

DL: There has been some good work in trying to expose the corruption in 'Watergate'. We are looking at some very serious real-world consequences of the drying up of the Murray–Darling Basin, and the mismanagement of water resources—and that's aside from the ongoing corruption that seems to keep appearing. There is a general lack of accountability, but it's the same names that keep coming up—Angus Taylor and Barnaby Joyce. Under a different media construct in Australia, we'd probably see more outrage and corruption being uncovered. However, 'Watergate' might just be one of those issues that is too big for politicians to be able to cover up: it's not like the rorting of the entitlements system which can easily be covered up by political staffers or pliant public servants; this issue is much bigger. It may keep bubbling along as an issue and keep getting worse, and it could be one of those issues that helps to bring the government down—that's how serious it is.

*

The new Labor leadership and rules of engagement

EJ: There's a few other issues of interest in New South Wales politics: Jodi McKay has been elected leader of the NSW Labor Party, through a formula of a 50 per cent vote from the NSW caucus, and 50 per cent from the rank-and-file members. It's the second time a Labor leader has been elected in this way—it takes some time to co-ordinate but it seems like it's a good way to select the leader of a political party. The British Conservative Party also has a membership vote for its leader—their MPs choose two candidates, and the membership makes a choice between these two candidates. Is it time for the Liberal Party to also follow this format?

DL: When the Australian Democrats had some relevance in Australian politics, the party would hold a vote from all membership: that didn't work so well as they sometimes had leaders who were voted in by their members, but Senators in Parliament couldn't work with that leader, or they were stuck with a leader who didn't perform very well. The British Conservative Party generally ends up with the least disliked candidate, and that explains the surprise selection of John Major in 1990, after Margaret Thatcher was forced to resign as prime minister. Theresa May: the same situation—the leader was meant to be someone else, but she was the least disliked candidate and the Conservatives ended up with a leader who most people could work with, rather than the person that most people would have wanted. And with the option of Boris Johnson, that might have been the best way of choosing their leader. Populist figures such as Johnson in Britain, or Donald Trump in the United States might seem appealing but, sometimes, it's better to have a safe pair of hands.

EJ: It does seem like a good practice to involve more people within the democratic process, although in Labor's case, it's a selection that involved direct party membership, rather than the general community: it's not like the US primaries, where in many states, registered voters can participate without being attached to a particular political party. Ever since Labor introduced meaningful rank-and-file engagement for choosing their leader, and ever since the Conservative Party introduced a similar process in Britain, membership of those respective parties has increased dramatically. The more people engaged within a political party and the more engagement from party membership, the better it is for the entire democratic system.

DL: There are merits in all of these options—a process where MPs nominate themselves for leadership and party members vote, or even if the existing MPs choose two MPs for the leadership and a membership ballot follows. But whatever the case is, it's essential to have member engagement in the process. It's always a balance of choosing a leader that will appeal to existing MPs, the party membership, and most important of all, who will appeal to the electorate. For Labor, leaders such as Simon Crean and Bill Shorten were well liked within the party but not so much outside the party. And there are the issues of the leadership selection rules for each party.

EJ: Changes in leadership rules are normally implemented through accidents of history. Kevin Rudd brought in rank-and-file leadership rules for the Labor Party in 2013, following on from the Labor coup that deposed him in 2010. Scott Morrison also brought in modified leadership rules for the Liberal Party after the series of challenges in August 2018, although these changes don't include a vote by general members of the Liberal Party. These are not pressing issues for the community and there's unlikely to be a groundswell of support to demand the leader of the Liberal Party be chosen by members. It's unlikely for the Liberal Party to take on this process, but it would be a good measure for them to adopt. But for a different MP who became leader of the Labor Party without a membership ballot—because of a lack of challengers—there are some issues that are developing. He has only been Labor leader for one month, but already there are complaints being made about Anthony Albanese for being a disappointment and not being a suitable leader—the criticisms are that he's not standing up on key issues and equivocating on passing the government's tax cuts package. As we've mentioned elsewhere, Albanese is from the left of the Labor Party, but the accusation is, he's taking the party to the right. Politics is a long haul, and it's another thirty-five months before the next federal election is due. Is this early criticism of Albanese just a normal part of putting a new leader under the microscope, and will it dissipate once Parliament reconvenes and more attention is placed back onto the government?

DL: Anthony Albanese is having a reverse honeymoon: usually, a new leader will be given a month or so to find their feet and any mistakes or perceptions of mistakes are considered to be a part of the leader getting a feel for the job and finding their own style of leadership. Albanese has disappointed the people who would normally considered to be his supporters, mainly because of his decision to consider all of the Coalition's proposed tax cuts for high-income earners. It's possible to see this consideration from a technical point of view: not standing in the way of tax cuts and then letting the government wear the decision if bad economic news comes out of this, and then taking the issue all the way to the next election. Conversely, he could behave like Tony Abbott did in opposition; to block everything in his path and just be a continual thorn in the side of the government. But we have to remember that Tony Abbott was a terrible prime minister, and never effectively made that transition from Leader of the Opposition. The leader of the Labor Party has to balance so many contradictory factions, so many contradictory members: there's the Shoppies Union, whose leadership is hard right, religious and conservative; then there's the CFMMEU, which is further to the left of other general unions. Then there's urban Labor and rural Labor; different state organisations, and the federal party. It's a difficult job of a leader of any party to manage, and especially so for a Labor leader.

EJ: Bill Shorten also had his problems when he first became leader in 2013. So did Brendan Nelson when he first became the Liberal Leader of the Opposition in 2007. Being the opposition leader after a party has just lost an election is probably the most thankless task in politics. At the time he became Labor leader, critics complained Shorten was not as good as Albanese, who was the rank-and-file choice in that 2013 leadership ballot, but Shorten ultimately won because he had enough support from the Labor Caucus. Shorten did stabilise the Labor Party after their crushing defeat at the 2013 election but, ultimately, he was not successful: he never became prime minister. Although they lost the 2016 and 2019 elections, the Labor Party is still within reach of government at the next election, with a margin of only eight seats: that's still a difficult task, but it's not insurmountable. Perhaps the early criticism of Albanese is the essence of becoming the Leader of the Opposition after a difficult election loss.

DL: Certainly, the 2019 election was a devastating result for the Labor Party, in the same way the 2007 election was a devastating result for the Liberal–National Party. But it's more difficult when a party is expecting to win an election and then it doesn't: Labor expected to win the 1969 election—they had to wait until 1972. The Liberals expected victory in 1993, but that didn't happen. These devastating election losses have a real impact on a political party.

EJ: It's always possible to regroup after a devastating election loss, and when it's least expected, a party can make a return to office after five or six years. There's always the obituaries about the political party when they have suffered a bad loss, but they do return: sometimes it takes longer than they expect; sometimes it's sooner. The Coalition was 'dead and buried' after the 2007 election yet, six years later, Tony Abbott leads them to the biggest landslide victory in Australian history. Kevin Rudd's landslide victory in 2007 occurred after a devastating Labor loss in 2004. There is the cliché that one week is a long time in politics, but three years in political terms: it's like going to the edge of the universe and then returning.

DL: It might be the case that this parliamentary term doesn't go the full distance, it might be a term that only last eighteen months, with a Liberal–National Party wanting to head off bad economic news in the 2020/21 financial period and seek a new term before the full effects of the economic downturn arrive. But there's still a long way to go—it has only been one month since the 2019 election, and so many more factors will come into play between now and the next election, whenever it is held.

*

Music in this episode
A Little Less Conversation (remix), Elvis Presley
Stranger In Moscow (remix), Tame Impala

Why democracy is broken

17 July 2019

David Lewis + Kim Wingerei / Podcast

Democracy is being held hostage by the adversarial nature of party politics, and the electorate deserves better. An upgrade for democracy is long overdue, but is the system actually broken and do we need a blueprint for change? Political systems need to function in a way that's more relevant and useful to people's lives, but what is the best way to achieve this? In this podcast, the author of *Why Democracy Is Broken: A Blueprint for Change* and editor of theindependents.org.au, Kim Wingerei, outlined why democracy is broken and the solutions we all need to consider for a better future.

David Lewis: On the surface, the political system in Australia seems to be working: even if we might disagree with the results, it works. A majority of people in a majority of seats get to choose the government of the day, and the winning political party choose the prime minister. Why does the system need to change?

Kim Wingerei: I don't think democracy is working as it was originally intended—and maybe it never has. But that shouldn't stop us from continuing to improve it. I think we live in a plutocracy, not a democracy: the political parties have, over the past 100 to 200 years, really usurped control over the entire democratic process. At elections, we elect party delegates—it seems we don't actually vote representatives in the way democracy was originally intended to work and in many ways, that is the core of the problem: we have a political class which runs government, and political representation of the people is an illusion that we are provided with every three or four years when we go to the election polls. In between those elections, the public has no influence, we have no impact: all the electorate really does is 'go with the flow', or complain. And most people will just go with the flow, I recognise that.

DL: Who do you think is to blame for this situation?

KW: We are probably all to blame for this predicament. It's very easy to say—as many of my contemporaries do—that it's all just too hard; it's just what the politicians do down in Canberra, or wherever it might be; whatever decisions are made don't impact upon them. People don't seem to care too much, and that is a big part of the problem. In Australia, we tend to pat ourselves on the back: that we have compulsory voting, and we have over 90 per cent of eligible voters that actually vote in elections. I originally came from Norway, where there's no compulsory voting, but around 80 per cent of the eligible voters cast a vote on election day, partially because, in my opinion, there is actual engagement by the community. And then, if we look at the other end of the extreme in the United States where, at best, 35 to 40 per cent of the electorate actually votes. In a way, we're all to blame—in as much as we need to be engaged to make the system more effective. Is engagement the solution? It's a part of the solution. But is the system itself to blame? It's not just what I refer to as 'the plutocracy' but also the fact that there's such a cosy relationship between economic power and political power, and that's been around for a very long time. Unions have influence on democracies; big business has influence and, above all, the media has undue influence over the political process. There are some reforms that might end up being like the low-hanging fruit to start addressing these influences because, if anything, this is the biggest part of the problem: that relationship between the political and the powerful.

DL: And the media is a part of this problem?

KW: Yes, in my opinion, it certainly is—and that's one reason behind the creation of theindependents.org.au, a website that promotes independent media which, loosely defined, at the moment is anything that is not Murdoch, Fairfax/Nine, or Seven–West Media.

DL: Looking at reforms to democracy, the French Revolution that you dedicate a section to in *Why Democracy Is Broken*, lead to 'The Terror'. Does this bode well for any democratic reform, or was the French Revolution a one-off historical event?

KW: The French Revolution was anything but a 'one-off': that is what history has really shown, and that's a really scary prospect. Our generation—in the Western world—has lived in peace pretty much all of our lives. In comparison, my parent's generation lived through the Occupation during the Second World War. Major upheavals: the French Revolution is an example; the Arab Spring in the early 2010s is another example. History is littered with examples like that, that show how change is such a hard process to implement, and most of the times, there is violence, there is the revolution, which ends up being pacified and then something else arrives after that; which is really what took place in France. The second revolution in France is the one that actually led to democratic systems being put into place in that country; the first revolution resulted in the Terror, led by Napoleon. I'm not for a moment advocating that a violent revolution is the way it should be: I'm simply pointing out that has been the way that it has been in the past. Is there a way around this? There were some signs during the Arab Spring where there was a greater engagement by the people than we've ever seen in the world: we can look to India in 1947 for how it managed to implement a democracy of sorts, breaking away from their colonial powers, so there are examples throughout world history where, more or less, it can happen peacefully. But, even in India: Pakistan and Bangladesh would disagree that the transition was particularly peaceful. I hope the facilities that we have in this day and age of engagement, including social media and general communications, will eventually allow us to start making the changes that I strongly believe we need to make. The other factor is the faith I have in the younger generations: we're seeing it at the moment through activism on the environment. They are seeing the world in a different way to our current political leaders, and are currently able to act upon that. That's my Utopian hope.

DL: One of the other issues you highlighted in your book—and it's been one of those issues that bubbles around Australian political discussion—is the 'bill of rights'. Given the issues of what the American bill of rights can deliver, for example, gun ownership and what that all means for the community, or concepts such as freedom of speech which, of course, keeps rearing its head in Australia: can we actually construct a bill of rights in Australia that will remain relatively consistent for over a century or more, and which rights do you think should be enshrined in a bill of rights?

KW: When I published *Why Democracy Is Broken*, I researched the different types of bills of rights in various constitutions from around the world: none of them are perfect, but I arrived at the conclusion that the UN Declaration of Human Rights from 1948 is as close as we can get to a bill of rights that is all-encompassing but, of course, that Declaration does need updating: for instance, its doesn't deal sufficiently with gender issues, and it certainly doesn't deal at all with sexual orientation as part of the rights that need to be protected, but as a construct and as a starting point, that is about as good as it gets.

DL: How would you propose the changes to the system would be implemented?

KW: That comes back to our original discussion and the debate about 'do we need a revolution'. Sometimes, it's possible to get into despair when writing about these issues and voicing opinions about them. The biggest fear for humankind is not death: our biggest fear is change. And that holds humanity back, and it has always held humanity back: our fear of change. We're afraid of the unknown, and this permeates through the human condition. And the fear of change also comes from that human need 'to belong'. There's a tipping point that usually arrives in a society that looks for change, where that need for change becomes overwhelming. We can look at what occurred in the Soviet Union in the 1980s from the eyes of Mikhail Gorbachev and the others that made that change happen, but they only made that change happen because they understood that the people of the Soviet Union would no longer accept the status quo. I come back also to the Arab Spring, which has mainly petered out into just a series of new dictatorships in those countries, but that groundswell at least started in those areas. I can see some signs of that groundswell in Australia, but we just have to keep talking about change and I think the platforms that we have to keep the discussions going—for all the hate-speech and all of the flaws of Facebook, of Twitter and Instagram, it does provide the public with ubiquitous platforms they haven't had before. The change has to come from us; from the people. There is no other way, and it's not going to come from the powers-that-be, until the powers-that-be understand change has to happen.

DL: One of the ideas you argue for is to diminish or demolish the states and territories of the Commonwealth of Australia. Why would it be better to reduce this level of government, rather than diminish the federal level or even local councils?

KW: This isn't an essential part of the changes that need to take place in Australia, but it does make up a large part: I've always held that view about the states and territories in Australia, and their different jurisdictions, but I'm also not exactly sure where and how that line should be drawn. We have too much overlap between the different levels of government, and there are too many people involved in governing this country. Australia has more politicians per capita than any other Western nation, or any other true democracy in the world. For example, when I moved from Victoria to Queensland: why on earth do I need to obtain a new driver's license? Also, as someone who has managed small businesses in both of those two states; the differences in regulation that seem to be, from my experiences, completely unnecessary. Our legal system that requires a criminal to be extradited from one state to another: it just seems to be ridiculous. There are many examples that could be addressed. And also, by the way you've framed your question: perhaps it is the federal government that needs to stop intervening in state and territory issues. I'm a strong advocate for the notion of 'think global, act local' and strengthening local councils in so many ways is very important.

But the most important reform is to get engagement from the electorate, because engagement is all about community: to have communities stronger and more unified is also a major part of that reform picture.

DL: Have you had support for these ideas either from people in power or the general public?

KW: Because I'm pushing that idea of Australia existing as a plutocracy and the problems of the major political parties, the way that they control our democracy, there have been positive responses from some of the independent candidates and MPs that look at Canberra and Parliament through a different prism. But this process of engagement is more of a long-term approach, pushing forward the passion of the changes that need to be implemented. It's a matter of getting these ideas out there, I realise that it's a slow process, but it needs to start somewhere. The subtitle of *Why Democracy Is Broken* is 'a blueprint for change' and I deliberately focussed on the changes that are needed to start the debate. Because that's what we need to do: we need to start the debate about some very fundamental changes that need to happen in Australia.

*

The divisive Scott Morrison

2 August 2019

Eddy Jokovich

Whose side are you on? In an instant, it's both an aggressive and divisive question, demanding a choice between the favourable and the unfavourable, the good and the bad. Whose side? Your side or mine? Black or white? Haves or have nots? Rich or poor? Hard working or lazy? Left or right?

In sporting terms, it's the most base form of tribalism: Arsenal or Hotspur? Collingwood or Carlton? Cronulla or Canterbury? Wanderers or Sydney FC? Perhaps in sport and athletic pursuits, it might be acceptable to choose sides, although we should never forget that in its extreme forms, it leads to events such as the Heysel Stadium disaster, when thirty-nine football fans were killed and 600 were injured during a wave of extreme football hooliganism and violence.

That's sport: but politics and societies are supposed to be different. Of course, communities tend to form into social classes and 'sides', although it's essential in good functioning democracies for political leaders to ensure that all sides and class structures in a community work towards common goals.

Life is more complicated than sport when it comes to choosing sides, but politics rarely deals with the complexities of life and so it came to be this week when the Prime Minister, Scott Morrison, reduced the role of the citizen in Australia to one simple choice: whose side are you on?

It's not a unifying question, it promotes division through the corollary: if you're not on our side, whose side are you on? It's simpleton's language, but this is the trope that will be used by Morrison and Liberal Party until the next federal election, due in 2022.

In the absence of any realistic political agenda for the next three years, Morrison is using that old conservative ruse of appearing to seek unity within the community, while doing everything possible to create divisions and prise open the fractures that appear across every minor fault line.

The history of this goes back to his first media conference after he became prime minister in August 2018, when Morrison asked the question: "Whose side am I on?". To which he answered: "We're on your side. I'm on the side of the Australian people".

He even went so far to attach an Australian flag lapel pin to his suit to remind himself "every single day" whose side he was on.

But there are only a select few Morrison is siding with and, generally, it's not too many members within the Australian community.

So whose side is he on?

Morrison is on the side of high-income earners in the over $200,000 bracket—less than 1 per cent of the community—because, according to Morrison, "hard working people deserve a tax cut", and he's on the side of those claiming franking credit tax refunds, even when they haven't paid any tax in the first instance—a policy which now costs the Budget $6 billion per year.

He's also on the side of religious zealots, who claim they haven't enough freedom to practice their religious beliefs, including the right to discriminate against other people based on these personal religious beliefs. These are the same zealots who have demanded a Religious Discrimination Act, and it's a piece of legislation Morrison is likely to give to them.

He's on the side of climate change denialism and on the side of the large mining companies that consistently donate to the Liberal Party coffers to ensure key policy decisions aren't implemented to affect their business models.

And closer to home, he's on the side of the Minister for Energy, Angus Taylor, who is rapidly becoming embroiled in allegations of corruption and scandals relating to properties and assets he and his family have direct interests in.

He's also on the side of Liberal backbencher, Craig Kelly, who wants the family home to be included as part of the pension assets test.

He's on the side of Liberal-National MP, George Christensen, who spent $1,600 to travel to the Great Barrier Reef to meet with the right-wing *enfant terrible* celebrity racist, Lauren Southern, whose infamy includes distributing 'Allah is gay' flyers, provoking migrant communities in Canada, Britain and Australia, and promoting the Great Replacement conspiracy theory.

It's obvious he's on the side of the likes of Raheem Kassam, the former editor of the 'fake news' website, *Breitbart*, and the supporter of Holocaust denialism, Matt Gaetz. Both are appearing at the Conservative Political Action Conference in Sydney, and Morrison claims their appearance relates to freedom of speech issues and Liberal MPs and backbenchers who wish to participate do have a right to hear their repugnant sexist viewpoints and philosophies.

He's on the side of the banking industry, voting twenty-six times against the creation of the Royal Commission into Misconduct in the Banking, Superannuation and Financial Services Industry, an inquiry which uncovered a wide range of theft, illegalities and unethical banking practices across many Australian financial institutions, including stealing funds from people who have died and the inadvertent funding of terrorist organisations.

He's on the side of Liberal MPs Sussan Ley and Stuart Robert, who were forced to resign for ministerial impropriety during the era of the Turnbull government, but have been brought back into Cabinet since the 2019 election victory in May.

These are the sides Scott Morrison has chosen and once sides are chosen, it means there's a wide range of sides that miss out. And which sides are they?

He's most definitely not on the side of recipients of Newstart, asking this week: "are we increasing Newstart, well the answer is no, we are not" and claiming the calls to increase the Newstart allowance by $75 per week were simply a matter of "unfunded empathy".

To emphasise that this definitely is not their chosen side, the Morrison government messaged the newsroom of Channel 7 with details of how 78 per cent of Newstart recipients had their payments suspended at least once—without providing the reasons for why this might have occurred—which Channel 7's *Sunrise* program duly reported as "many dole bludgers are trying to take advantage of the welfare system".

Morrison then proceeded to end this week's Question Time session by suggesting he would bring in legislation to implement drug tests on Newstart and Youth Allowance recipients, and would resurrect a plan from 2017 to test sewerage to find traces of drug usage among these target groups.

He's not on the side of Indigenous Australians, dismissing a referendum to include Indigenous references within the Constitution and already vetoing the 'voice to parliament', erroneously claiming it would "create a third chamber of parliament".

He's not on the side of low-income employees or those who are seeking a wage rise, consistently ruling out a rise in the minimum wage while he was Treasurer, and denying there was actually an issue.

He's not on the side of asylum seekers or refugees, implementing a secret and harsh regime on Manus Island and Nauru while he was Minister for Immigration, and now seeking to repeal the asylum seeker medical evacuation legislation, which allows for medically unwell asylum seekers on those islands to be treated on mainland Australia.

And he's not on the side of those who seek cohesion and solutions for how to unify the community. Like Liberal Party prime ministers that have preceded him—Robert Menzies, John Howard and Tony Abbott—Morrison seeks to create divisions within the community, and nothing has been more apparent than the question he revisited this week, calling for the Australian community to take sides.

There were eighty-four references to "on your side" in Parliament this week. There were also sixteen 'Dorothy Dixers' which asked the Prime Minister and assorted government ministers: "whose side are you on" over a wide range of issues, including digital platforms, child exploitation, energy, roads, drought, taxes, education and childcare.

And, of course, the correct answer was always: "we're on the side of Australians".

It's insane, it's inane, it's childish and demeaning to the parliamentarians that have to act out this charade, and even more demeaning to the Australian public. The entire Liberal–National Party backbench was laughing maniacally like a cackle of drunken hyenas when Morrison and Treasurer Josh Frydenberg were taunting Labor with their 'whose-side-are-you-on' antics. It was embarrassing to watch, but this is what parliamentary Question Time has come to with the Liberals in power. No accountability and all about theatrics and political spin.

"Whose side on you on" is typical conservative political marketing: appearing to be a unifying force for the better, but replete with a sinister divisive undertone.

It's similar to John Howard's "For All of Us" message from the 1996 election campaign which, taken to the next level down, signals the subliminal message that it's for all of "us" (the white mainstream Anglo-sphere of the Australian community), but not "them" (the migrants, the Aborigines, the Bohemians, asylum seekers, unionists, the people who depend on welfare, the sick, and defenceless).

Morrison's mantra of "whose side are you on" holds similar racist and exclusive overtones, as well as the lower-level subliminal subtext of "we're on your side, but not theirs". The Liberal–National Party is brilliant at being able to exploit these areas of political messaging, and will use these tactics to provide smokescreens to cover their poor performance in government, which has been evident since they got back into office in September 2013.

It's facile but expect to hear more of it over the next three years.

*

Unfunded empathy, choosing sides, diversionary nuclear and s44 solutions

6 August 2019

Eddy Jokovich + David Lewis / Podcast

In this episode, we looked at the new political concept of 'unfunded empathy', tried to establish whose side we're on, because we do need to choose, and asked the question about nuclear energy: is it something that we really need? And David Lewis appears as Defence Against the Dark Arts Teacher at the Hogwarts School of Witchcraft and Wizardry.

Eddy Jokovich: The political landscape after the May election is becoming clearer and all sides of politics are starting to work out what their strategies are going to be over the next three years of the political cycle. Key battlelines and talking points are being pushed forward, there are new characters in new positions within the government and the Labor Opposition, and it's taking a while to get used to the new voices and new players in this new round of politics. The Prime Minister, Scott Morrison—he's not one of these new faces—but he has introduced new terminology to the political lexicon: the concept of "unfunded empathy". Morrison was all smiles during the election campaign, saying "yes" to everything and "*ni hao*" to anyone who looked remotely Chinese; drinking beer, shearing sheep and calling out all the winning numbers in bingo halls. But now the election has been won, he's turned to attack mode, and dismissed all the concerns of those who wanted to raise the levels of the Newstart allowance—unemployment benefit—claiming this type of increased government support is "unfunded empathy".

David Lewis: Unemployment is rising and more job seekers are going to become reliant on the Newstart allowance. To demonise people as "dole bludgers" becomes very dangerous politically, even among people who are doing quite well—they will know people receiving Newstart who aren't the clichéd "dole bludger" or rorting the system for their small sum of $245 per week.

EJ: The Newstart allowance hasn't been raised in real terms since 1994. There have been calls across a broad coalition of business groups, the Australian Council of Social Services, Labor MPs, Liberal MPs and Greens MPs: this call to raise Newstart by $75 per week comes from across the entire political spectrum. Economists have calculated this increase would cost the federal Budget $3 billion each year, and this compares with the $6 billion of the Budget that goes out in franking credits tax refunds. Of course, franking credits was a big issue in the federal election, but surely a compromise would be to scale back some of the obscene generosity of the franking credits scheme by $3 billion per year, so at least those wealthy people aren't losing out entirely, and using the proceeds to fund a $75 per week increase for Newstart recipients? Everyone will be a winner.

DL: Franking credits is the issue that just won't go away. It's only anecdotal, but there were some suggestions that after the election in May, some pensioners went to Centrelink to ask about their franking credits refunds, even though they didn't own any shares. There was a lack of knowledge about this scheme, and an even greater misunderstanding about how it operates. But once people started to gain a clearer understanding of the franking credits scheme, it became less popular for the government, and now that it has become a problem, they'd just prefer the whole issue to go away. In the context of an unfair system which gives benefits to a wealthy class at the expense of the unemployed—especially with a tightening job market and faltering economy—it's probably an issue that won't go away. Spending an additional $3 billion on Newstart does sound like a large sum of money but, as a comparison, defence spending alone is around $35 billion per year. In terms of a percentage of the overall government Budget, it's about half a per cent, but it taps into a philosophical question about who deserves to receive government money and who doesn't.

EJ: Initially, it was hard to see the reasons behind the government's recalcitrance—aside from the obvious ideological factor—because for a while it looked like it was actually going to raise Newstart, following on from the groundswell of support from so many different sectors of the community, including business: even Barnaby Joyce jumped onto this bandwagon. But we didn't take into account the main reason the government is avoiding any new spending at all is that this will affect their predicted $7 billion Budget surplus for the 2019/20 financial year. And their entire economic narrative in the future is based on keeping this small surplus. Of course, we won't know if there has been a surplus for the 2019/20 fiscal year until September 2020; that's when Treasury releases the actual figures that occurred during in this financial year. There was speculation the government was going to consider raising Newstart, but only on the condition that all recipients would be forced onto the controversial Indue welfare card, a payments card that dictates how welfare recipients can spend their money. Indue is a card that's currently being trialled around Australia, but it's managed by a private company which has strong links with the Liberal and National parties. In the end, Newstart wasn't increased, but the plan to manage all welfare payments through Indue is still an open option for this government.

DL: The Indue welfare card is a terrible idea. If welfare recipients are happy to have their payments quarantined, that's fine: but it shouldn't be a compulsory system for all people on welfare. Indue doesn't allow payments for alcohol or gambling and, for people wanting to break a cycle of addiction, having your income restricted can be a good thing. But people are adults:

what if you wish to celebrate a birthday and want to take a six-pack of beer to share with other people? The Indue card can only be used at specific businesses, and can't be used at opp shops and second hand shops—these are services which exist to help people on lower incomes to cheaply buy necessities, such as clothing, but that option is now removed. The card can be only used at approved supermarkets—what if lower prices are available at non-approved supermarkets? Indue has assets currently worth around $415 million, and its value will increase exponentially if its card is adopted on a massive scale across Australia. And, of course, this brings us back to the links to the Liberal and National parties, and Barnaby Joyce. He was the main supporter within the government of an increase in the Newstart allowance, but how much of his suddenly-found empathy for the poor actually has to do with increasing the value of the Indue company, which is owned partly by the mining magnate Andrew Forrest, and of great indirect benefit to the National Party?

EJ: Barnaby Joyce is a Nationals MP. The Indue company has very strong connections with the Liberal Party and the National Party. Larry Anthony was a former National Party MP and minister during the time of the Howard government between 1996–2004, and was a founding director of the Indue company as well. He did resign from Indue in 2013 but his trust company, Illalangi Pty Ltd, holds a substantial number of shares in Indue. We've got this preposterous situation of the possibility of massive amounts of government welfare funding being managed by a private company, with links to the political parties which will make the decisions about this program. For each card Indue issued in the trial program, the company is paid $4,000 by the government and up to $10,000 for certain types of cards; then there would be ongoing management costs into the future. For major financial institutions such as the Commonwealth Bank, ANZ, or Westpac: they would go broke if it cost them this much to manage banking accounts for their customers. Indue is a private company, linked to a political party; it's managing and controlling welfare money; and it's controlling who is the supplier of goods and services to welfare recipients. Something's not quite right here.

DL: Something is rotten in the state of the Commonwealth of Australia, as Hamlet would have said, had he been alive today. This is a case of a privatised government service, which should remain as a government service. Policing, major infrastructure, health, education and now welfare. Privatising these areas has always cost the taxpayer more than it would have under public control, and under this type of ideological pursuit, it's more about unravelling public money into private hands as quickly and efficiently as possible. And with welfare, it will be taken into private hands, while kicking the poorer in society at the same time.

EJ: The public needs to be suspicious about the Indue card scheme, and more information about the scheme needs to be released to the Australian public. The scheme has been trialled in the Northern Territory, the Kimberley region of Western Australia, the Goldfields, Ceduna in South Australia and Wide Bay in Queensland, and there are mixed reports about the success of the trials. But the Indue card itself was more of a background issue compared to the calls to raise Newstart and we had an interesting development between the government and the mainstream media on this issue which put an end to the debate. The community support to raise Newstart by $75 per week seemed insurmountable, but the government's media information unit provided data directly to the Seven Media Group, claiming 78 per cent of all Newstart recipients had been breached as least once. There was no background information provided, the figures were misleading and designed to mislead, and this media 'tip-off' resulted in the headline news on the *Sunrise* program the following morning: "New figures have been released showing just how many dole bludgers are trying to take advantage of the welfare system". It was a media message that ran for two days on Channel 7 News and was also taken up our other media outlets. Then Scott Morrison made the announcement that the Newstart rate would not be increased, the Minister for Employment Michaelia Cash amplified the message in the media, and that was the end of the matter.

DL: There was a backlash to these reports and Channel 7 took the unusual step in making a very profound apology about them, through the news reporter Natalie Barr. She seems like a nice enough person, but that was probably a part of trying to soften the backlash against Channel 7. Any serious journalist would have looked at the figures provided to them by government carefully, and scrutinised them. Many recipients of Newstart are breached and have their payments cancelled for quite innocuous reasons: some have been breached for missing a meeting with Centrelink; some were hospitalised at the time; some had actually been at a job interview. Others recorded the wrong date for their meetings with Centrelink; in some cases, Centrelink had actually recorded the wrong date. There are many genuine reasons, yet these people are breached, and recorded as a statistic by the government. While this act fed into the pre-existing beliefs many conservative voters hold, it became very apparent that the 'dole bludger' narrative pushed forward by the media wasn't going to take hold in the electorate, especially with the ongoing Robodebt fiasco hovering in the background, where many welfare recipients received debt collection letters from Centrelink, when in fact, they didn't owe any money at all. Trust in government agencies is at an all-time low, and labelling welfare recipients in a negative way doesn't work in the same way it has in the past.

EJ: That 'dole bludger' headline is still out there in the media, it still exists through the internet, and it provided the perfect cover for Morrison to announce his inaction on raising the levels of Newstart. It was almost as if he was saying: 'see, I told you these people are no good; they're unworthy of our support'. That cascaded into the next level for the Prime Minister where he said he was not going to be swayed by "unfunded empathy". Morrison presented himself as a smiley happy figure during the last election campaign but, now that it's all over, he's reverted to a hard-nut character that won't give anything away. Could this hardness and a total lack of empathy create problems in the future for Morrison, or it just a matter of releasing negative headlines to friends in the media to wash away these problems as they appear?

DL: Morrison is clearly playing to his base supporters, and his actions will have resonance with some voters. And this approach is consistent with the prevailing view of Morrison and his supporters: The Lord will provide to you, and if the Lord isn't providing, then you've done something wrong. Morrison also said people "work hard, the more they earn, the more they keep of what they earn", through generous and possibly unaffordable tax cuts for the well off. It's this relationship of 'working hard', and earning money that becomes a problem: for people that have worked on a farm, mustered sheep, worked on a building site or cleaned bathrooms—I've done all of those jobs—it's hard work, but not very well paid. How do we place a value on these jobs, just because they're not remunerated very well? Morrison's comments play to that segment of society that equates 'hard work' with 'high income', and to the aspirational class that highlights these notions above everything else.

*

We're all being forced to make a choice. So whose side are you really on?

EJ: In August 2018, on the day Scott Morrison became prime minister, he started talking about whose side people are on and this is what he had to say:

> Scott Morrison: There's been a lot of talk this week about whose side people are on and what Josh [Frydenberg] and I are here to tell you, as the new generation of Liberal leadership, is we're on your side; that's what matters. We're on your side.

EJ: That was just after a bruising leadership contest within the Liberal Party, and Morrison's question about whose side he was on seemed to be more about positioning his persona within the electorate. But over the past week, "whose side are you on" has resurfaced as a question to the Australian public, not as a seemingly innocuous question, but as an aggressive and divisive demand to choose a side and, as a corollary of this—'if you're not on our side, you must be against us'. It's a little bit of George W. Bush...

> George W. Bush: ...Either you're with us or you're with the terrorists...

EJ: ...a reminder of John Howard's "For All of Us" slogan from the 1996 election campaign, and it's the typical conservative mantra to seek division within the electorate. The role of the national leader is to seek unity within the community and work towards common goals. But Scott Morrison seems to be doing the opposite—he's asking the Australian public to choose a side. Life is not like a game of football where you get to choose between football teams, it's a lot more complicated.

DL: British Prime Minister Margaret Thatcher used the slogan 'one of us'; that's probably where this type of sloganeering commenced. 'Whose side are you on' is a threatening idea too, because if you're not with us, you must be against us. And a corollary is: those who are the 'other' are bad people by definition, they're 'different'; it's a very simplistic and divisive way of looking at the world. And in the world of politics, the various strands of influence are complex. The Australian Senate, for example, is a place where this is displayed the most, where diametrically opposed parties will work constructively together, to hammer out compromises. Sowing the seeds of division makes politics easier to manage for the governing party, but it can become very dangerous, very quickly. I'm seeing a slight resurgence of low-grade racism in schools, issues which I haven't seen for a number of years. In the community, people are talking about 'political correctness going mad' in slightly greater numbers and wanting to reduce the protections covered by the *Racial Discrimination Act*.

EJ: "Whose side are you on?" is a very loaded question. It's a combination of all those conservative leaders from the past: Thatcher, Ronald Reagan, George W. Bush, John Howard in various forms. These are questions loaded with subtext and exclusive interplays: it's for "all of us", but not for them or the "others". It's not for the people that have a worldview that is diametrically opposite to our own perspectives. On the surface, it sounds innocuous, but it's a brilliant example of the politics of division. And it's obvious the Liberal Party is positioning itself with this element of sloganeering over the next two or three years in the lead up to the next federal election. In the most recent session of Parliament, there were eighty-four references to "on your side" and the question of "whose side are you on?" featured in sixteen 'Dorothy Dixer' questions to the Prime Minister and other government ministers. This is a framing exercise, and it's a very obvious tactic—it's very exclusive and, depending on which way the question is answered, it neatly places people into clear political groupings.

DL: With this political approach, there is much looking back at 'the good old days', the ones that in reality, never really existed. Scott Morrison would be looking at how John Howard won four consecutive elections, and he'd be trying to invoke the spirit of Howard, politically. It's very tribal, it's very divisive, it's almost like a new brand of sectarianism. In sporting terms, it's one thing to be a supporter of the Cronulla Sharks in rugby league, it's another to be a supporter of the Roosters, and those divisions are taken in the spirit of sport, except for when violence erupts, which fortunately doesn't happen very often in Australia. But when this type of tribalism extends into governments, politics and social acceptability, it becomes divisive and difficult for communities to manage.

EJ: Scott Morrison is the number one ticket holder for the Cronulla Sharks, and that's fine: if he wants to support the Sharks instead of the Eastern Suburbs, that's his business—the Cronulla Sharks is his local team in rugby league. But politically, if the question is "whose side are you on?", we need to look at the answer for this and Morrison seemed to be on the side of high-income earners. He pushed through a massive tax cut for people earning over $200,000 per year, which, incidentally, makes up less than 1 per cent of the community. This fed into his prosperity narrative of all those hardworking people on high incomes deserving a tax break—as if no one else in the world works hard except for those people on high incomes. He's also on the side of high-income people receiving franking tax credit refunds, even when they haven't paid tax in the first place. He's on the side of those religious leaders that want to have the right to discriminate against other people, based on their own personal religious beliefs. He is on the side of Angus Taylor and all of those MPs that have seemingly engaged in corrupt behaviour in the Murray–Darling River system. He is on the side of bankers and wealthy miners. This is whose side Morrison is on, and it seems to be a very exclusive and prosperous section of Australia.

DL: To be a successful populist leader in the style of John Howard, this process of exclusiveness can't be overt; it has to be subtle. Howard became very good at knowing which sectors of the electorate needed to be included, which ones he could exclude, to extract maximum political benefit: it's cynical, but it worked for him. He learned some very harsh lessons in the 1980s: he appeared on national radio and television in 1988 saying Asian immigration needed to be cut, suffered a backlash from the media and the community, particularly within his own electorate. He never repeated that mistake again. Morrison is too obvious with his divisive practices, and it could sow the seeds for his own undoing.

EJ: Again, we're in the realm of the smokescreen, and this government has a habit of creating them. When a government hasn't got very much of an agenda, these superficial elements are created to give the impression of busy-ness. This goes back to not just the time when Scott Morrison became prime minister in 2018, but when Malcolm Turnbull became prime minister before him in 2015. At that time, Turnbull didn't have any big picture policy agenda, aside from large tax cuts for higher-income earners and corporate tax reductions, but pushed forward with the image of innovation and a high-tech Australia, ironic considering the disaster of the creation of the national broadband network. And this goes to the heart of not just the Liberal Party, but conservative governments around the world: their main purpose is to hold onto government to keep their opponents out, and not do very much with government once they've got it, except engage in crony-capitalism, and tax cuts for the rich. The Morrison government is just a continuation of this: there doesn't seem to be any overall agenda for this government and, three months since its election victory, it's meandering and trying to find a meaning for its own existence. And that's why the issues of 'whose side are you one', or niche issues such as religious discrimination, keep appearing, the issues that don't make any material difference to people's lives. The government sends up flares into the sky to grab the attention of the electorate, which are usually quite insignificant issues. But once all the smoke subsides, there's not actually very much substance behind them.

DL: The other factor to consider is, all of these diversions and smokescreens are being created to deflect blame from an impending economic recession—which many economists are suggesting. Studies are suggesting there are not many new jobs being created, and a walk though the CBD areas of Sydney and Melbourne, or nearly every other shopping centre around Australia, will show many shops are closing, or already closed. The 'for lease' sign is the most common signage seen in the Australian retail sector. The economy is tanking and government policy has to be the cause of that: it has the wrong policy settings and is quickly being found out. In these times of trouble for the government, what better way to hide from these problems than to find a scapegoat, and let that scapegoat define itself through the media. 'You're either with us, or against us'; it's a classic conservative government tactic, and it usually works.

*

A nuclear error but there won't be any fear

EJ: There have been a few other political issues capturing our attention recently, and we can't be too sure if the government is seriously considering these issues, or whether they've been drawn out of a hat to create a political diversion. Nuclear power: there's to be yet another review called by government; this time by the Minister for Energy, Angus Taylor. There have been many reviews and feasibility studies of nuclear energy in Australia; five serious attempts to create nuclear power stations in Australia between 1952 and 2007 but, each time, they've reached the same conclusion—it's an unviable industry and unrealistic. If nuclear power was ever to be developed in Australia, that time would have been in the 1950s, but that time has passed—not only is it economically unviable, but it's politically unviable: which seaside coastal town is going to the first to welcome a nuclear power plant in its backyard?

DL: With all the allegations surrounding him, Angus Taylor is probably not the best person to be putting forward any ideas at the moment, but it's clearly a push for nuclear power at a time when renewables are increasing—after all, it's the mining industry that wants nuclear power. There are a number of key factors: most of the areas proposed for nuclear power plants are on Indigenous land. Nuclear power is not very efficient: it appears to be more efficient than coal, but when taking into account all the water resources that are used up by nuclear extraction and cooling of nuclear plants, it's not terribly efficient. It's also not safe either—it might be 99 per cent safe, but if anything goes wrong, it tends to go horribly wrong, and history has shown that to be the case. The Chernobyl incident in 1986 was an outlier, but there have been many other smaller nuclear incidents.

EJ: The big three nuclear events over the past sixty years have been the Three Mile Island incident in the United States, Chernobyl in the former Soviet Union and, more recently, Fukushima in Japan. But there have been around 100 smaller incidents since 1957, ranging from small fires that have occurred outside the perimeter of nuclear power stations, to a wide range of other incidents, including fires within the nuclear reactors, damaged tile rods, leakage of contaminated nuclearised water and problems with disposal of nuclear waste. It's not a very safe industry but, aside from that, essentially for the government, this process of reviewing nuclear energy is a diversion and a large smokescreen: it has very little to do with the desire to create a nuclear energy industry in Australia because it's unlikely to ever happen. The last federal review was performed in 2006 and that was only thirteen years ago and there's not very much that has changed in the industry since that time. There was also a recent state government inquiry in South Australia, which mainly enquired about repositioning South Australia as a dumping zone for international nuclear waste—which I'm sure wouldn't be too great for the tourism industry. Every one of these government reviews has arrived at the same conclusions: nuclear power is not a viable industry in Australia and with this review due at the end of 2019, it will probably arrive at the same conclusions. But, it's not about finding new conclusions; it's a diversion to deflect from the other issues for the government and for the Minister for Energy. It's just a question of how long can this call for an inquiry deflect the media attention away from the embattled Taylor and the problems he's currently facing.

DL: Nuclear power is in the similar predicament to the Adani mine: it will be difficult to raise the funding for it, and it will be difficult to maintain. There is more of a future in renewables energy, and nuclear, with all of the costs, environmental, geographic and political difficulties, is becoming an outdated source of energy generation. But for the immediate future, this review is a diversion for this government, and this is a government that is hiding something.

*

Section 44 and the language of election cheating

EJ: There has been a Court challenge to the result in the Victoria seat of Kooyong at the last election, and the winning candidate, Treasurer Josh Frydenberg. It's a complaint lodged by one of the losing candidates, independent Oliver Yates, and it's a complaint about the types of signage used in the campaign which, according to Yates, was designed to mislead and deceive voters from the Mandarin-speaking community in that seat. The signage used the same purple colour used by the Australian Electoral Commission, placed strategically next to an official AEC sign, and mentioned in Mandarin: "Correct voting method, on the green paper ballot, put a '1' next to the Liberal Party candidate". This is clearly an attempt to cheat.

DL: It will probably come down to the subtlety of language, and which team brings in the right expert witness along to the High Court. The Mandarin signage was also used in the neighbouring seat of Chisholm; it also has a large Chinese community, and is also a seat won by the Liberal Party—their winning candidate was Gladys Liu—and is also the subject of a separate High

Court challenge. Certainly the signage in Mandarin was an attempt to game the system, and definitely an attempt to cheat, but will the Courts see it in the same way? It will be interesting to how this case proceeds, but the more worrying aspect for Frydenberg is yet another case against him, which is on his eligibility to actually sit in Parliament under section 44 of the Australian Constitution, based on his access to Hungarian and Israeli citizenship.

EJ: The legislation supporting the Australian Electoral Commission is weak and how the Court interprets this legislation will be fascinating: how can the case prove how many Mandarin-speaking people in the seats of Kooyong and Chisholm would have been swayed by reading these posters? There's quite a large level of unpredictability with the law here, because there haven't been too many Court cases that have been clear-cut in the past, and none that have overturned an election result based on AEC legislation. The section 44 issue for Frydenberg will be far more fascinating, as there were those recent interpretations from the High Court in 2017, where the judges made 'black letter' legal judgements, strictly applied the Constitution and annulled the election of several parliamentarians. The make-up of the High Court is exactly the same as it was two years ago, and it's difficult to see why they would make a different interpretation of section 44 in 2019.

DL: Frydenberg's section 44 case is more complex than the preceding High Court cases in 2017. He claimed his mother was stateless when she arrived in Australia, although there is a document in the public domain that clearly states she was a Hungarian citizen, and he is also claiming that any dispute about his citizenship, or his mother's citizenship, is anti-Semitic and an attack on the Holocaust. But it isn't an issue about anti-Semitism or the Holocaust, it's a legal question of whether Josh Frydenberg is a qualified citizen of the Parliament of Australia. Nobody would think that he's a secret agent promoting the Hungarian influence within Parliament; it's clearly an issue of law as it stands at the moment. It's obvious section 44 needs to be reformed and there are quite a few anomalies in there, but this case is about the law: that's why we have a Constitution, otherwise it becomes a worthless document. Hungary is a benign country from Australia's perspective, although it was only thirty years ago that it was a country on the other side of the 'Iron Curtain'. Imagine the outcry if his case related to Russian or Chinese citizenship—countries that can be hostile to Australia's interests. It's never clear cut: the China–Australia relationship fluctuates from wary friendship, to a terse tension, depending on whatever might be happening in the South China Sea or in Hong Kong. The United States was considered somewhat of a hostile nation to Australian interests 110 years ago, when the Great White Fleet visited Sydney Harbour in 1908, although that hostility towards the United States originated from Britain. Relationships between countries can change over time, and it's increasingly important for Parliament to comprise citizens that hold allegiance to Australia, rather than other countries.

EJ: Generally, there would be an expectation that a sitting member of the Parliament of Australia would need to be a citizen of Australia. But based on so many people in the Australian community coming from so many different countries that have different citizenship rules and regulations, it's essential that section 44 be amended: the issue here is that the only way section 44 can be amended is via a referendum and only eight of forty-four referenda questions have been passed since Federation in 1901. One solution to the section 44 citizenship issue would be to make a constitutional amendment where once a candidate is successfully elected to Parliament, they could have thirty days to clear up their citizenship credentials and renounce other claims to citizenship of another country, and the successful candidate couldn't sit in Parliament until they could prove this had been achieved. It's an anomaly within the Constitution—not an important issue, but perhaps it would be best to collate a number of other anomalies in the Constitution, taking into account it was written between 1898 and 1900, and hold a referendum on each question at the one time.

DL: One of the exemplary people in relinquishing citizenship was the former Labor Senator, Sam Dastyari, who had to go all the way to the United Nations to revoke his Iranian citizenship, at the cost of $20,000 in legal fees in Australia and Iran. Section 44 is creating problems for Jewish members of the Australian Parliament, because every Jewish person is eligible for Israeli citizenship, even if they don't want it. But it is an area that hasn't been tested in law and we'll soon find out what the outcome is. Section 44 does need to be reformed, as it's going to become an increasing problem into the future, as more people from diverse backgrounds enter Parliament, and the proposal to enable newly-elected Members of Parliament a period of time to get their citizenship matters in order could resolve this ongoing issue.

*

Music in this episode
Which Side Are You On, B. Dolan
Dirty Air, Two Door Cinema Club
Limousine, Jack River

Going the nuclear option

14 August 2019

Eddy Jokovich

Sometimes, it's difficult to know whether governments are genuinely interested in the agendas they push forward, or whether there are issues played out in the background resulting in other ulterior motivations. And, as part of this process, covering up some of their misadventures and mismanagement of political issues.

And so it is with the Australian Government's announcement to hold an inquiry into nuclear energy in Australia. It's the first federal report to review nuclear energy since 2006 and, as the announcement is coming from the embattled Minister for Energy, Angus Taylor, it's difficult to think of the review as anything other than a deceptive move to deflect from the many issues causing problems for the Morrison government.

There have been many reviews into nuclear energy in Australia, and five attempts, of varying degrees over the past seventy years, to install nuclear power stations. The first plan was announced in 1952 by South Australian Premier, Thomas Playford, for the Spencer Gulf region between Port Augusta and Whyalla.

The second plan was announced in 1969 in the Jervis Bay area but after strong opposition from the local population and union bans on the site, the federal government withdrew from the project in 1971.

In 1977, the Western Australian Government announced plans to construct a nuclear reactor on the northern outskirts of Perth but, again, anti-nuclear demonstrations forced the Court government to eventually back down.

The Portland area in Victoria was also the proposed site for a nuclear power station, first in 1980 and subsequently in 2007. Spencer Gulf also re-appeared as a proposed site in 2007, but these proposals were also dropped in late 2008.

While there are many technical and environmental problems with the installation and management of nuclear power stations—as well as opposition from local communities—the primary reason why all five proposals have been discarded, or lapsed, is economic: nuclear energy is not a viable industry in Australia. It never has been and, in all likelihood, never will be.

Every review prepared by Australian or state governments since 1952 has arrived with the same conclusions. If a nuclear industry was ever to be developed in Australia, that time would have been in the 1950s but the opportunity for this has passed.

And, politically, which seaside coastal town across Australia is going to be the first to welcome a nuclear power plant in its backyard?

Looking at where the push for nuclear energy is coming from, it's essentially the conservative friends and benefactors of the Liberal and National parties. It's a push coming from the Minerals Council of Australia and through its ability to spend large amounts of finance and resources to lobby Parliament. And given the widespread understanding the nuclear industry is highly unviable, they'd be looking at a large public subsidy in the unlikely event the industry was ever established. These are the ones that have a clear interest in developing nuclear as an alternative energy source, at a time when renewables are providing an economic threat to the mining industry and conventional forms of energy generation.

There are many other challenges with nuclear energy: many of the twenty locations identified by nuclear lobbyists in Australia are on Indigenous lands. While nuclear energy is more efficient than coal-powered energy, it's still not as efficient as renewable energy. And while proponents of nuclear energy claim the industry is 99.9 per cent safe, it's the 0.1 per cent of incidents that create the long-term environmental damage, and when incidents do occur, they go horribly wrong.

The three big nuclear catastrophes over the past sixty years have been the Three Mile Island incident in the United States in 1979; Chernobyl in the former Soviet Union in 1986 and, more recently, Fukushima in Japan in 2011. These incidents caused widespread environmental damage, and in the case of Chernobyl and Fukushima, the impact is still being felt over large geographic areas that are still housing large populations.

Given what we already know about the poor prospects of nuclear energy in Australia and, looking at other countries such as Germany that are decommissioning nuclear power stations and moving towards 100 per cent renewable energy, why has the Australian Government decided to commission yet another report into nuclear energy in Australia? The last major report, the *Review of Uranium Mining Processing and Nuclear Energy in Australia*, was commissioned only thirteen years ago.

The South Australian Government also held the Nuclear Fuel Cycle Royal Commission in 2015 to establish the credibility of nuclear storage in the state. It found that while there may be some prospects of a viable nuclear storage industry in Australia, the generation of nuclear power was likely to be unprofitable, as was the processing of uranium.

What has changed in the industry since the time of these last reviews? Certainly, governments need to be aware and keep pace with developments in the field of energy generation—especially this government, which currently has no national energy policy. But there haven't any large scale changes in the nuclear power industry internationally, and with many countries decommissioning nuclear power plants, it makes no sense now, for Australia to start considering nuclear energy.

This review will be carried out by the House Standing Committee on the Environment and Energy, and is due to complete its report by the end of 2019. While there have been some developments with small modular reactors, it's hard to see what this new review will find that hasn't already been found by previous reviews—essentially, that nuclear power is economically, politically and environmentally unviable.

But finding out what is already known is not the issue in this case. It's a classic diversionary strategy a government keeps up its sleeve to gloss over political problems and, in this case, it has worked—most of the media has been preoccupied with the issue of nuclear power over the past week, and the caravan has now moved onto other issues.

And it has definitely kept the attention away from the embattled federal Minister for Energy, Angus Taylor. Which might have been the purpose all along.

*

Cracks appearing in the Morrison government

18 August 2019

Eddy Jokovich

The political landscape continues to take shape, with all sides of politics providing a clearer idea of the types of strategies and policies they'll be developing in the future as they navigate a pathway towards the next election, due in 2022. It's still taking time to become used to the flavour of this new Parliament, and assess the quality of the new faces appearing in the Liberal–National government and Labor Opposition.

The Prime Minister, Scott Morrison, is not one of these new faces: he's been in the most prominent political position in this country since August 2018 and it's a face and voice that needs no introduction. But he has introduced new terminology into political lexicon: the concept of 'unfunded empathy'.

During the May 2019 federal election, the Prime Minister was very convivial, saying virtually 'yes' to everything—swilling beer, shearing sheep, and calling out all the winning numbers in rural bingo halls. But that was the election campaign: negativity about your own political intentions has no place on the campaign hustings, and with the election won, it's time to get back to the reality of governing. But is the Prime Minister and his cabinet team up to the task? Not if you're a recipient of Newstart, live in the Pacific Islands, or a supporter of the GetUp! group.

There was a broad chorus of support across the political spectrum to raise the Newstart allowance by $75 per week, up from $245 per week: Liberal, National, Labor, Greens; the business community; the Australian Council of Social Services. It's rare to have such a unilateral consensus of support for the unemployed—usually, they're on the receiving end of negative reports in the mainstream media, and deemed to be unworthy of any further support from government, irrespective of how severe the employment market might be.

But such a raise for Newstart was not on the agenda for the Prime Minister, immediately ruling out any possibility of an increase and claiming the government wasn't in the business of "unfunded empathy". Political narratives can sometimes hinge on key phrases uttered by a prime minister: John Howard was hamstrung by his notion of 'core promises' and 'non-core promises' to justify breaching important election campaign pledges (not that it hindered him too much—he was prime minister for another ten years after that). Will a few loose words about "unfunded empathy" create any issues for Scott Morrison?

Unemployment is starting to rise, which means there will be more Newstart recipients in the near future. And this also means more people—including those who are employed and are doing relatively well—will know either a friend or a family member on Newstart. Demonising these people, even if it an old favourite punching bag of the mainstream media is fraught with problems.

Contrary to the negative perceptions perpetrated by conservative media interests, there are very few people that actually 'rort the system' to obtain the Newstart allowance of $245 per week. In real terms, the Newstart allowance hasn't increased since 1994, twenty-five years ago. Over the same period, salaries for Members of Parliament have increased by 88 per cent; wages for most workers have increased by 44 per cent; and corporate remunerations for directors have increased ten-fold.

If Newstart was to increase by $75 per week, the cost to the annual Budget would be close to $3 billion dollars, an amount that compares quite favourably to the current franking credits refund system—

where shareholders receive a tax rebate, even if the tax hasn't been paid in the first instance—which costs around $6 billion per year.

But whether there is merit in increasing the Newstart allowance—and the evidence suggests there is—there is little chance of the government budging on any new spending up until July 2020. Morrison has staked the credibility of the government on the back of the promised $7 billion surplus for the 2019/20 fiscal year, and will do anything to avoid another deficit over the final ten months of this financial year.

If deflecting the calls to raise Newstart was considered an easy task for Morrison—with the support of a string of reports on mainstream media, which denigrated Newstart recipients and erroneously announced 78 per cent breached their obligations—there won't be as much luck dealing with a sinking economy and predictions of an economic recession over the next twelve months.

While some analysts are suggesting there is a 20–30 per cent chance of an economic recession, the Governor of the Reserve Bank of Australia had suggested there is a 100 per cent chance of recession, it was just a question of when.

While it's not a figure commonly used within economic circles, the Australian economy is currently in a per capita recession, after two consecutive quarters of negative growth between July and December 2018—0.1 and 0.2 per cent—and indications from the retail sector suggest the next round of reporting will show a further deterioration.

Annual growth figures are currently at 1.8 per cent, well below the expectations of the Reserve Bank.

How will the government explain these figures if their electoral credibility is based on the perceptions of superior economic management? During the recent election campaign, both Morrison and the Treasurer, Josh Frydenberg, suggested the Labor Party had created so many economic problems during their reign between 2007–13, that it's taking such a long period to correct these problems. Again, a compliant media can help with the government's attempt to push forward this message, but it's coming up to six years since Labor left office.

At what point does a government take on responsibility for economic management, and stop blaming its predecessors for their woes? Although they will continue to push this argument, attributing fault with a long-gone government only has a certain shelf-life, and other credible reasons will need to be found.

Other problems are starting to develop for this government and, while it's still early in this new term, it's starting to form patterns that were consistent with the early days of the Abbott government in 2014. While it might not register with the Australian electorate, Morrison's appearance at the recent Pacific Islands Forum was a disaster. Australia refused to agree to a communiqué until all references to coal (except for one); global warming and net zero emissions by 2050, were removed.

The Prime Minister of Fiji, Frank Bainimarama, accused Australia of being "insulting and condescending" towards other Pacific countries, and suggesting Morrison's negotiating style was confronting and heavy-handed, forcing other countries to accede to Australia's perspectives and wishes.

Generally, Pacific Island leaders can make political mileage by grandstanding and making attacks on Australian governments for not doing enough in the region but, in the context of expanding Chinese interests in the Pacific, Morrison's actions have been foolish. It's almost a repeat of the 2015 Pacific Islands Forum, when Prime Minister Tony Abbott, again, removed references to coal and rising sea temperatures, and dismissed the concerns of government leaders in the region.

On his return to Australia, Morrison addressed the South Australia Liberal state council, outlining his concerns about the activist group, GetUp!, suggesting he would launch another inquiry inspecting the links between GetUp! and the Labor Party—even though three previous inquiries by the Australian Electoral Commission have confirmed the independence of the organisation.

Again, this is a reflection of the antics of Tony Abbott in 2014, when he launched the Australian Charities and Not-for-profits Commission to restrict the actions of non-government organisations that were deemed to act against the interests of the Liberal–National government.

Essentially, electors vote in governments for the provision of economic security and the wellbeing of the Australia community. Targeting groups, such as GetUp!, in ideological pursuits and gamesmanship on the periphery of political activity, are a sign of a government obsessed with personal party interests rather than the community's interests. While this type of obsession didn't end the Liberal–National Party's time in government, it did end the Tony Abbott time as prime minister.

It has been just over three months since the Liberal–National Party won the 2019 election, but the Morrison government is quickly becoming rudderless and moving towards an empty cul-de-sac of ideologically-driven pursuits. It might be entertaining for the conservative base of the party, and provide for opportunities to divert attention away from the critical issues facing the economy, but it's no way to manage effective government.

*

Indue and the small matter of political corruption

28 August 2019

Eddy Jokovich

Would it ever be acceptable to appoint billionaires James Packer and Gerry Harvey to review social programs on behalf of government? Or Meriton property tycoon Harry Triguboff? The owner of the Seven Group, Kerry Stokes? Should we appoint Gina Rinehart to sit on the board of the Fair Work Commission?

These are Australia's wealthiest individuals and they certainly know a great deal about creating empires, making fortunes, and using their resources and privilege to ensure they remain in these privileged positions, complete with financial and political influence. But would we ever trust them to generate ideas for how governments should manage social welfare and payments systems?

In 2008, Harvey Norman chairman Gerry Harvey said welfare was for "no hopers", and giving money to homeless people was just a "waste", suggesting the money for this sector of society was "helping a whole heap of no-hopers to survive for no good reason… they are just a drag on the whole community".

In 2012, Gina Rinehart bemoaned the level of high salaries in the mining industry and compared Australian workers with west African labourers, who were "willing to work for less than $2 per day", as well as demanding government should lower the minimum wage, and force welfare recipients to "spend less time drinking or smoking and socialising, and more time working".

In 1984, her father, mining magnate Lang Hancock, suggested one solution to the 'Aboriginal problem' would be to "dope the water up so that they were sterile and would breed themselves out in the future, and that would solve the problem".

As we can see, there are good reasons why the wealthy class has traditionally been kept away from the management of government employment and welfare programs—they have no experience in government or welfare work, little commitment to public service and community wellbeing, no experience in sociology or behavioural science, their ideas are typically self-serving to their own financial interests and present an extreme conservative right-wing ideology.

Putting aside the fact the amount provided in corporate welfare in the form of government grants, loans, tax breaks, subsidies, graft and payola far exceeds social welfare payments, the best these entrepreneurs can do for the community is continue in their quest to create wealth and employment opportunities, even if they do reduce their tax liabilities to immoral extremes and the amounts of personal wealth they accumulate are obscene.

They're entitled to their opinions but shouldn't be proffering ideas directly to government for how to apportion taxpayer funds in the interest of the public, because they rarely consider the public interest. That's why we have elected representatives and a skilled public service to implement these critical community services, as well as take responsibility for the decisions they make.

Andrew Forrest enters the field

Taking this into account, it was perplexing in 2013 when the newly-elected Abbott government appointed the head of Fortescue Metals Group, Andrew Forrest, to review Indigenous employment and training programs. Forrest was briefly Australia's richest person—in 2008, with a net worth of $12.7 billion—but has no experience or expertise at all in welfare programs.

Like many others in his cohort—and anybody else in the community—he brings ideas and opinions to the table, but these are ineffective, harsh and demeaning to the people they are meant to support. And in many cases, these ideas are only provided to create more opportunities for the wealthy class.

Forrest's report, presented to government in 2014, holds the view that government payments to unemployed people, carers, people with disabilities and single parents should be quarantined, and introduced the idea of the 'Healthy Welfare Card', later to be known as the BasicsCard. The report, *Creating Parity*, is essentially a long opinion piece, epitomising the thoughts of Andrew Forrest, and typical of the 'robber-baron' corporate cowboy mentality that suggests his way is the only way to address welfare issues.

It's a report replete with all the positive attributes of a BasicsCard, but ignored the negative impact of many other income management schemes from around the world.

Even more curious is while *Creating Parity* consistently refers to National Australia Bank, Commonwealth Bank of Australia, Westpac and ANZ—surely the best providers to implement and manage such income management schemes—there is no mention of Indue, the company Forrest and other benefactors were involved with at the time, and the company that ultimately ended up managing the trial programs, which were rolled out from March 2016 onwards in Kununurra, Wyndham, Kalgoorlie, Ceduna, Tennant Creek and Bundaberg.

Of course, governments should be open to new ideas to address identified social problems but, essentially, Forrest has cynically sought money-making opportunities that will benefit friends of the Liberal and National parties, and syphon public monies into private hands.

Indue and conservative politics

The Indue company has existed in some form for fifty years but more recently, has developed a range of tentacles that reach out to a range of political players, primarily within the conservative domain. The most prominent of these is the former National Party MP and current Federal President, Larry Anthony.

During the time of the Howard government, Anthony was the Minister for Children and Youth Affairs, and after losing his seat at the 2004 federal election, became a director of ABC Learning, the corporatised childcare provider that attracted a wide range of

Liberal Party operatives and MPs, including Peter Dutton, Paul Neville, Sally Ann Atkinson and Mal Brough.

Through the 50 per cent childcare subsidy provided by the federal government, ABC Learning reached a market capitalisation of $2.5 billion, before it collapsed in 2010, leaving many children without access to early childhood services and childcare. This was an absolute disaster of policy, and a failure of government to adequately oversee funding of an essential social and educational service. The 570 services managed by ABC Learning when it collapsed were subsequently taken over by the not-for-profit provider, GoodStart.

Countless millions of public funds that should have been invested into early childhood education, were wasted and diverted through to the share market, speculators and private hands, including former MPs.

The experience of ABC Learning exists as a reminder to government that essential social services and welfare, when coupled with the private sector, are a poisonous well, and opening up these services attracts a wide range of opportunists, grifters, shysters and corporate criminals.

But it seems the mistakes from the past are on track to be repeated with Indue and the cashless welfare card system, and some of the players behind the ABC Learning disaster are set to re-appear. If there is largesse to be found and delivered from the government to the private sector, just like National MP Barnaby Joyce, Larry Anthony is never too far away. Anthony was the deputy chairman of Indue up until 2013 but his trust company, Illalangi, still owns substantial shares in Indue.

Public money transferred to private hands

During the welfare card trials, Indue has received between $4,000 to $10,000 for each participant in the trial, even though the Newstart allowance is less than $14,000 per year. Certainly, there are start-up costs involved in servicing this type of program, but up to $10,000 for a private company to manage an account only worth up to $14,000 annually raises questions of whether the Indue company is the most cost-effective option for this scheme. It also raises the question of why Indue was chosen in the first instance, especially when the expertise and experience provided by the National

Australia Bank, Commonwealth Bank, Westpac or ANZ would have been far superior.

Up to June 2018, the amount received by Indue was at least $8.8 million and, reportedly, up to $21.9 million as at August 2019. If the roll-out of the cashless welfare card is extended on a widespread basis—as many Liberal and National MPs are now calling for—the value of the Indue company, and the shares held by Anthony and other Liberal and National party operatives will increase exponentially.

Who else will benefit from the expansion of Indue? Just like the expansion of ABC Learning in the early 2000s, Indue has become a magnet for insiders wanting to cash in on government largesse.

How much money is Indue donating to Liberal and National party branches around Australia?

Why was Barnaby Joyce so vociferous in his support for raising the Newstart allowance by $75 per week? Joyce has been in Parliament since 2005 and has never once made a call to increase any form of welfare payment. Why the sudden interest?

Was the trade-off for increasing the Newstart allowance—if it were to ever happen—a large roll-out of the Indue card to all welfare recipients, which would have resulted in ongoing benefit to the Liberal and National parties?

Where does Andrew Forrest fit in with all of this? Like all the other moneyed interests in the world, Forrest goes to wherever the money rolls. What are the links—more than likely to be well-hidden behind a trail of trust accounts and subsidiaries—with the Liberal Party and the National Party?

The many problems of the Indue card

There are many problems with the cashless welfare card. Senate inquiries from 2015, 2017 and 2018, have all shown that in the trial regions, there has been no change in crime rates (in some areas such as Kununurra and Wyndham, there was actually an increase in crime statistics, as well as an increase in self-harm and suicide).

The Minister for Social Services at the time, Dan Tehan, claimed the "cashless debit card is making a real difference in the communities where it operates", even through the Australian National Audit Office found the trials and outcomes were not adequately monitored and, because of this, ANAO could not evaluate whether the trials were either effective in their desired social outcomes, or whether the relationship with Indue provided the taxpayer with value for money.

Despite this lack of effective data, and lack of transparency in the relationships between Indue and the Liberal and National parties, the cashless welfare card trials have been extended until the end of June 2020.

There are many fundamental flaws with the cashless welfare card trials, as recent Senate inquiries have shown. And the people promoting the trials—such as Andrew Forrest—should be nowhere the decision-making processes for how governments should spend and manage welfare monies.

Australia is on the verge of instigating a wholesale transfer of its welfare system towards a private company that has no interest in the wellbeing of welfare recipients, and sets up a wide range of opportunities for corruption and a very thin line between government, private corporations and political parties. And, just like the experience of ABC Learning just over a decade ago, it's another social and political disaster in the making which the public will be forced to bail out.

*

Economic disaster, compassionate conservatives, and do we need to talk about Albo?

12 September 2019

Eddy Jokovich + David Lewis / Podcast

In this episode, we looked at the Australian economy and asked the question: Is it on the edge of the abyss or just taking a short holiday? We were quite bemused by the 'compassionate conservative', because it does seem to be an impossible combination of ideas; and is the Labor Party in the doldrums or just waiting for the right opportunity to reveal itself? And in this episode, David Lewis appeared as parliamentary procedure advisor to Boris Johnson.

Eddy Jokovich: There seems to be a broad consensus that the Australian economy is on the nose—the markets are flat, and we're currently in a per capita recession, as well as a retail recession. Economic growth in the past two quarters has been incredibly poor—the June 2019 quarter showed a GDP growth of just 0.4 per cent and the growth of 1.4 per cent over the past twelve months has been the worst annual figure since 2001: that's not to say that the economy won't improve, but the conditions are set for the worst economic performance in a generation. The Treasurer, Josh Frydenberg, has deflected from these poor figures by focussing on the first current account surplus in forty-four years—the current account is a figure that does need to be managed but it doesn't have a direct influence over the overall state of the economy—and he continues to blame Labor for this poor economic performance, as well as sheeting the responsibility onto the Reserve Bank. The Reserve Bank does have an important role within the Australian economy, but it's the government that develops and implements monetary policies, and based on the evidence, the policies of this government haven't worked. Labor hasn't been in office since 2013—and that's over six years ago—how long can the government keep apportioning blame to others before the penny drops for the electorate and they realise the government is not taking responsibility for any of its actions?

David Lewis: It is incredible that after two terms in government, as well as having three different prime ministers, the Liberal Party is still blaming Labor. If the government didn't have such a soft press, they'd be in a far greater level of political trouble. Looking at economic figures historically, Labor has consistently performed better in most key economic indicators. Former Labor Treasurer, Wayne Swan performed much better than his predecessors and much, much better than his successors in Treasury. What wasn't really comprehended by many people in the electorate is just how bad the global financial crisis in 2008 was internationally, and Australia came through that period with very little impact on the local economy: that doesn't happen by accident. Australia did not go into a recession—only four developed countries in the world avoided a recession: Australia, Israel, Poland and South Korea. On close inspection of the economic data, it's hard to lay the blame for economic problems of today at the feet of the Labor Party, although politically, that's what the Liberal Party will try and do. And running surpluses isn't a sign of good economic management: national economies are complicated. The Menzies government actually had an entire decade of deficits during the 1960s, primarily to fund infrastructure, and if governments can afford debt and manage it well, running Budget deficits is not a real problem. But what

Economic disaster, compassionate conservatives, and do we need to talk about Albo?

governments do with finances is important and there has been very little recent spending on substantial items that benefit the wider community. The spending from this government has tended to go into the pockets of the few and not spread around to many people. Josh Frydenberg also has to be very careful that he doesn't lose the favour of the media, which could happen at any time if the economy starts to tank.

EJ: Having the media on side is very important for a politician but the most important factor politically is being onside with the electorate. Frydenberg claimed Australia is in a "sea of tranquility" compared to the mess of Brexit—any country would be at the moment—but he also trumpeted the news about employment growth of 2.6 per cent over the past year, even though the number of jobs in the economy has naturally increased through a combination of population growth, demographic changes, immigration and stagnant wages—the figure doesn't really mean very much in isolation. Politicians are in the business of highlighting the good news and deflecting the bad: Frydenberg is making flourishing references to the moon; he's drawing on figures that are either misleading or not relevant to the overall economic performance. Spinning the figures, bluff and bluster can only get you so far: the economic reality always catches up with the rhetoric, and when the reality does catch up for the electorate, the ramifications can be quite vicious for a politician, especially when unemployment starts to bite.

DL: Governments can hide the reasons behind low interest rates, and they can also hide the reasons behind a poorly performing Australian dollar. But they can't hide unemployment: it's currently just above 5 per cent and those Bureau of Statistics figures are based on the total number of people in the workforce, irrespective of how many hours they've worked. The figure doesn't account for underemployment, and it doesn't account for people who have given up looking: some economists, such as Michael West, are suggesting real unemployment is much higher than the published figures. And then there are other factors which are affecting the economy, such as the tightening credit market. It does get to a stage where figures can't continue to hide the economic realities for many people in the community. There is that old adage that the recession doesn't commence until the wealthy class start to feel the pinch, and it seems like we may be on the verge of that happening and, of course, there are flow-on effects, where middle management staff are retrenched, senior retail jobs go, jobs related to trade go. But a government that has great form in blaming others is not going to be in a hurry to stop this habit, so when the economy does start to falter badly, they'll look for other factors to blame, such as global trade issues.

EJ: There's only a certain amount of times governments can spin the figures and a certain amount of times they can keep paraphrasing the good figures and deflecting the bad. If the government is going to blame international conditions, and the economies of trading partners, statistically, the figures don't support this. The current GDP figure is slipping, in comparison with the rest of the world—admittedly, GDP is not the only economic indicator of how an economy is performing—but Australia's economy is now ranked twenty-third in the OECD group, comprising thirty-six different countries. This is Australia's worst ranking since 2003. Spin and manipulation of the figures can take a Treasurer and the government only so far, and it's a question of how quickly the reality will catch up with the rhetoric.

DL: The Liberal–National Party was lucky to win the last election: that's not to take away from their campaigning efforts, but they did spend a substantial amount of the campaign telling the electorate how good they were at economic management. But if the economy starts to falter and slide into recession, that negates the narrative of 'good economic management' and their luck will run out very quickly. In terms of experience, I don't think Josh Frydenberg was quite ready for such a senior position in government, and he's not surrounded by people very well suited to their roles either. He hasn't excelled in any of his previous portfolios and the position of Treasurer involves a fine balancing act of a broad range of competing interests. But the ideological issues the government wants to push within the economy will probably be its undoing as well. They've implemented massive tax cuts; reduction of penalty rates; more benefits to companies and corporations; they've pushed policies that lower wages; a maniacal pursuit of a Budget surplus, without consideration of the overall economy. These are the main components of their neoliberal agenda, an agenda the government commenced back in 2013 when they were first elected, and telling the electorate that these were important reforms that had to be implemented to stimulate the economy. But, so far, it seems these policies are on the verge of crashing the economy: there's that famous quote by the banker Baron Rothschild, where he said: 'the time to buy is when there's blood in the streets', where the wealthy can make large profits when prices crash, buy up assets at bargain prices, and then sell them when their value increases. These are the vested interests the Liberal Party caters for, and these are policies that are advantageous to a select few.

EJ: It is a perfect example of ideological considerations drowning out all other factors. The first austerity budget in 2014, delivered by then Treasurer, Joe Hockey, almost knocked the economy off its axis, and was a classic case of neoliberal orthodoxy doing the exact opposite of the intended consequences, as outlined by the government. The government talks in a big way about how new policies, such as the decision to cut penalty rates would lead to higher levels of employment, but this hasn't occurred. And when their policies fail, they're quick to blame others for their mistakes. The Reserve Bank—and also many other leading economists—did point out to the government time and time and again, that other policies had to be implemented to stimulate the economy, and their actions were leading to contractions in the economy, and all three Liberal Treasurers since 2013—Joe Hockey, Scott Morrison, and now Josh Frydenberg—have not listened to expert advice.

DL: For politicians, it's easy to blame the Reserve Bank; it's easy to blame everyone else. And, of course, no government is going to come and say economic circumstances are terrible. Paul Keating admitted to a recession back in 1990 and justified that by saying the Australian economy had fundamental issues that had to be addressed, and followed on from what he'd said a few years before, that an unsophisticated Australian economy could lead it towards a "banana republic". Those comments caused him immense political problems for many years, and has led to governments being less forthright about economic circumstances: and it's difficult to imagine a government talking about a poor economy and not knowing what to do about it. But for the Liberal Party today, they've guided an economy that's not in good shape and, to make matters worse, they've ignored most of the solutions that have been posited.

*

The compassionate conservative

EJ: In 1977, the American historian Douglas Wead published *The Compassionate Touch*, a book which looked at poverty levels in the Indian city of Kolkatta, and how governments at the time tackled endemic poverty, usually through a process of harsh measures and servitude to religious community institutions created by the Catholic nun, Mother Theresa. Several years later, Wead's ideas started to permeate the halls of American conservatism, with the belief that welfare provided by the state was destroying peoples lives and the free market was the best solution for poor and disadvantaged people—even though Fredrik Hayek, the doyen of free market philosophy, disputed this idea. The term "compassionate conservative" was then used by the Reagan administration in the early 1980s as one of its guiding principles on social policy. But "compassionate conservatism" is a dressed-up term for far-right wing ideologues that despise any form of state support for people in need, it diminishes the rights of people, and tries to achieve its goals by implementing practices that are not in the public interest and mainly benefit the private sector. George W. Bush also labelled himself as a "compassionate conservative" in the 2000 presidential election, but it's a term we've never really heard in Australia—until now.

DL: Adopting the idea of the compassionate conservative is an extension of the American model of how to be a nationalist and a patriot: politicians wearing the Australian flag on their coat lapel, or placing the right hand over their heart when the national flag goes up, and looked at with complete amusement by the people around them—which is what happened with Liberal MP Tim Wilson at this year's ANZAC Day commemoration. It starts off with the use of American phrases, going all the way to loosening Australia's gun laws, according to the wishes of the US National Rifle Association. Most people in the Australian community would have agreed with John Howard's decision to tighten gun laws after the Port Arthur shootings in 1996: now there's a group of people within the Liberal Party that want to soften those laws. There's a great deal of Americanisation of language and culture in Australia, but the adoption of 'compassionate conservative' is different: conservatives in Australia hate hip-hop music in the same way their predecessors hated rock 'n' roll, or movies they don't approve of. They just don't want other people to experience anything they consider to be unfavourable. And then this notion of 'compassionate conservative': certainly, most people favour compassion and from a conservative perspective, it might be public policy issues such as retraining or involvement in volunteer work for people receiving unemployment benefits. These policies are problematic, but we can accept them for what they are within the conservative field. But the notion of 'compassionate conservative' is quite radical, and it's more than just wanting people to maintain a sense of dignity; it's a veneer for something else that is quite disturbing.

EJ: It's a classic political marketing tool: 'compassion' is a term usually associated with the progressive side of politics, and conservatives have added the term to their own side to make particularly harsh and regressive policies sound more palatable and appealing to the public. It's a simple tactic, but it's highly misleading. But the 'compassionate conservative' is far more acceptable to the electorate than 'compassionate fascism', which would be a more accurate way of describing these policies.

DL: There are other unpalatable policies of the 'compassionate conservative': the Indue welfare card dictating certain products deemed to be undesirable by the government can't be purchased; random drug testing for social service recipients, another favourite policy measure conservative governments are always trying to introduce. In response, many people in the electorate have been suggesting if these drug testing policies are ever introduced, why not introduce them for parliamentarians and for journalists too: many of the media organisations that have been pushing these agendas have rampant drug cultures themselves, and Parliament probably has as well. These policies show a contempt for poor and underprivileged classes, but this government is hiding their contempt behind a veneer of compassion when, in fact, it's all quite nasty.

EJ: These measures are testing grounds for what could be applied to all recipients of any form of government assistance, and it's a question of where would it end: would drug testing eventually apply to everyone in the community? These programs have sinister overtones and intentions, and it's strongly related to the puritan and quite often hypocritical religious beliefs held by many current Liberal Party MPs, as well as related to typical neoliberal policies. This version of the Indue card and the idea of drug testing for social security recipients had its genesis in the intervention into Indigenous communities back in 2007— implemented in the dying days of the Howard government, but continued by the first Rudd government—but it has been taken to another level recently. At an Australian Council of Social Services meeting in 2015, Scott Morrison said "welfare must become a good deal for private investors, we have to make it a good deal for the returns to be there, to attract the level of capital". Again, this is another example of neoliberal ideology: it's a reframing of the provision of social capital, and it's an idea that transfers responsibilities from government over to private interests.

DL: Margaret Thatcher's "there's no such thing as society, people must look after themselves first" comment from the 1980s. It's that idea that the gatekeepers help, but they help at a cost, because the only good business is a profitable business, and the only way to run anything at all is at a profit, and taken away from government hands. In New South Wales, there has been the disaster of privatised roads, privatisation of hospitals, of privatised education. None of them worked effectively, and it's also true in Victoria and other states too: so many pointless roads that have taken years to build, so many educational providers closing down, with profits going into private hands, and any losses absorbed by government. This is an ineffective model that was introduced during the Nick Greiner years in New South Wales, which is now heading up to thirty years. For Morrison to say the provision of welfare has to be profitable for private providers was a terrible thing to say, and is a complete misunderstanding of the point of everything in society.

EJ: It gets back to what Ronald Reagan said in his inaugural presidential address in 1981: "government is not the solution to our problem, government is the problem". It's this idea that the state doesn't provide properly, so it's up to the private sector to fund these processes, when in fact all this does is transfer government funds to private benefactors and supporters of the government. The public has been inculcated with this belief that the private sector is more efficient, despite all the evidence suggesting this method does not work in other countries; so almost forty years after these ideas were first implemented and now, in 2019, when many economists have suggested we're at an end of a failed neoliberal experiment, Australia is still having its go. The Indue card trials are operating in five different locations around Australia, and on the verge of being implemented nationally: drug testing for social security recipients is also being trialled. If these programs are passed by the Senate, there will be a range of private companies managing drug tests on behalf of government, and most of these pathology companies will probably have strong links with the Liberal Party. There's a raft of issues that arise from this: privacy concerns, storage and integrity of tests, appeals processes. And then there's the profit incentive, where private companies will be chasing down social security recipients to cut strands of their hair, or take blood samples, to earn a profit.

DL: The types of problems that will arise from drug testing and implementation of the Indue card have already been witnessed under the government's Robodebt regime, where many people have been issued with debt notifications, claiming they owe the government thousands of dollars. The rank hypocrisy of the Prime Minister publicly stating suicide is a major issue in Australia, when some of those suicides have been from people receiving a debt notice from Centrelink: they didn't know how they incurred the debts, why they incurred the debts, and with no obvious way of being able to challenge these debts. In many of those cases, people were forced to pay those debts, even though they didn't have the means of paying those debts and the debt didn't exist in the first place.

EJ: Once these insidious programs are introduced, it's very difficult to remove or undo them, and incoming governments of a different persuasion maintain the convenience of these draconian policies. For example, government employment services were essentially outsourced through the Centrelink system by the Howard government, but the Labor governments between 2007–13 left the system intact, because to revert to a previous or different type of employment support service would have cost an exorbitant amount of money. And that's why these harsh measures should be resisted as much as possible: once they are in place, they are difficult to retract, so difficult to remove.

*

Labor Party missing in action and hibernating

EJ: Anthony Albanese has been leader of the Labor Party for just over three months, but there's a consensus forming that he has been lacklustre, travelling too closely to the Liberal– National government on key policy matters and not providing enough inspiration to the left of the Labor Party's rank-and-file membership—which is where Albanese actually comes from— and many from this part of the party are calling for him to be replaced. Under Albanese, Labor waved through all aspects of the Coalition's tax package, including the third tranche for high income earners; welcomed back the coal industry with a vengeance in Queensland and Newcastle, and made favourable noises about the government's proposal for their religious discrimination legislation. More recently, the shadow education minister, Tanya Plibersek, has welcomed increased funding levels for private school education, even though before the last election, she called it an "educational slush fund". There's speculation Labor has written-off 2019 politically—they currently have an election review underway, trying to find out where they went wrong in the 2019 federal election—and they seem to be in a holding pattern until this review is released. As we found out during the 2019 election in May, the electorate has a short-term memory and whatever is happening in politics now will barely be remembered at the time of the next election, due at some point before 2022. The Labor Party seems keen to reinvent itself, but it seems like it's a reinvention in the image of the Liberal–National government. Is Labor selling its soul or is this the type of pragmatism needed to plan a return to government?

DL: It's difficult being in opposition and it doesn't matter which party it is: it's always tough. And losing the 2019 election was a terrible blow to Labor Party members in an election they were expected to win. It was different to losing the 2013 election, where they were expected to lose, or the 2016 election, when Malcolm Turnbull managed to hold on to government by one seat, another election Labor was expected to lose: at least they came close. The 2019 election was a comprehensive loss and, ostensibly, they had run a better campaign against a government that was scandal ridden; lacking competence; and tired after six years in office. Yet Labor still lost. The factors for this loss can't all be blamed upon the electorate's dislike or mistrust of Bill Shorten, whether this was justified or not, there were a wide range of issues, and the Labor Party review will probably cover those. It probably wouldn't have helped in New South Wales, where Labor had the issue of $100,000 Chinese cash donations coming up at ICAC hearings, even though the NSW Liberal Party had ten Members of Parliament having to stand down because of corrupt political behaviour. The media could have focussed on those issues instead, but that's not where the narrative went. Right now, the Labor Party is in a state of shock over the result, and finding out what went wrong will be a good thing for them: whether they come to the right conclusions is another matter though. These reviews usually sheet the blame around to everyone else, except for whoever's talking at the time: let's hope Labor's review doesn't come to that and is more open about where they went wrong.

EJ: It's difficult for a new opposition leader just after their party has lost an election, and most of them never lead their party back into office: Bill Shorten, Brendan Nelson, Kim Beazley, Andrew Peacock, Billy Snedden—they all became Leader of the Opposition just after their party lost an election, or lost government, and none of them made the step to prime minister. That doesn't mean that it's impossible, but it is difficult: there's the task of regrouping and the thankless process of trying to win back government over the next three years, managing and dealing with impatient and ambitious colleagues, who always feel they can manage the party more effectively. Of course, members of a political party are always devastated when their party loses an election. Members of Parliament are especially devastated when their party loses an election, because they know there's a massive difference between being in government and being in opposition: there's a lack of resources; there's virtually no focus on an opposition, unless they make mistakes or are given the blame for issues they weren't responsible for in the first place. Oppositions want to get back into government as soon as possible, so it's understandable they'll try everything they can to achieve that goal. But is it wise for the Labor Party to mimic whatever the Liberal–National government is doing and simply copy most of their policies?

DL: The phrase Anthony Albanese is best remembered for is "I like fighting Tories, that's what I do", but perhaps that has been placed aside for the time being. For a political party after an election loss, consolidation is good, as is a period of reflection: developing great policy is also good. But I suspect these are not the solutions the Labor Party will look to: they'll probably go back to a small target strategy and probably lose the next election because of this. Traditionally, the progressive side of politics has to inspire the electorate; conservatives just have to demonstrate they're a "steady pair of hands". This might not be politically fair, but it seems to be the political reality in Australia. The Labor campaigns of 1972, 1983, 2007: these were all inspiring campaigns with ambitious leaders, and that's the approach Labor leadership has to take on. Albanese has to hit the ground running, start fighting more for an ambitious agenda, even if it is on the issues that don't matter too much at the moment, while the party consolidates and determines where they're going next: specifics about decisions made in 2019 will probably be forgotten at the time of the next election in 2022.

EJ: And perhaps that's the biggest issue for Labor's supporter base at the moment; that the leadership team isn't hitting the ground running. There might be reasons for the lack of energy at this stage, but it's hard to see what those reasons are. Politics is ultimately based around mathematics and, of course, it's the party that wins the most seats that wins government. On the surface, it might seem obvious and politically sensible for Labor to embrace the coal communities in Queensland and Western Australia: many coal communities swung strongly against Labor in those states, where they only hold eleven seats out of a total of forty-six seats. But there is a limit to how pragmatic a party can actually be to gain extra seats, and how closely Labor can try to mimic the actions of the government. In the field of marketing, businesses offering identical products—such as petrol, electricity or telephony—achieve product differentiation and points of difference through slick advertising. It's not clear if politics can work in this same way, but Labor seems to be going down the path of positioning itself as a replica of the Liberal–National Party, hoping to differentiate itself to the electorate through personality marketing and media management. Essentially, this is what the Labor Party tried to achieve under Kim Beazley in opposition between 1996–2001, but ultimately failed, especially on border security and asylum seeker policy. And this is the risk for Labor and Albanese not differentiating on key policy issues that matter to the electorate. If harsh right-wing policies are deemed to be important by the electorate, they'll vote for the party that will deliver this, rather than the party that pretends to believe those policies. There's no magic solution here and the next election is still three years away but it doesn't seem to be quite clicking for the Labor Party at the moment.

DL: It seems that whatever Albanese does right now, he just can't win. It's very difficult for any opposition to have the media airtime or newspaper columns written about it. And for a Labor Opposition leader, it's difficult managing the internal dynamics:

there are six states and two territories to balance, and each of those have different factions of varying influence; there is the wide range of trade unions, each with their own state and national branches, and the process of trying to get as many people on your side as possible, a support that can easily dissipate. Hopefully, Albanese can surround himself with a better team than those assembled for Julia Gillard or Kevin Rudd, both of whom were brought down by much lesser people. Many of the people that were involved at that time, as well as all the egos, have been removed. There might be longer-term plans in play here by Albanese and his team, but we don't know what they are at this stage.

EJ: At the last election, the major polling companies had an absolute disaster and, because of this, most of them haven't put out any polls at all—now three months since the last election—Newspoll has been the only polling company to have the courage to come out and publish: two since the last election, and it's pretty much the same result as the election result. The Liberal–National Party is on 51 per cent; the Labor Party is on 49 per cent in the two-party preferred voting pattern. However, there's not much trust in political polling at the moment and its difficult to see how they can change their methodology to retrieve the situation for themselves, so perhaps there's not much point in publishing anything at all. Labor has just had an incredibly bad election result, made worse by the large expectation that they were going to win. It's probably going through the process of making it as easy as possible for itself for the rest of this year, assess their election loss review, and establish a new mode of thinking for 2020 and beyond.

*

Music in this episode
Confessions of a Window Cleaner, Ed Kuepper
Sugar (instrumental), Robin Schulz

Mr Morrison goes to Washington, the mystery of QAnon and celebrity politics

19 October 2019

Eddy Jokovich + David Lewis / Podcast

In this episode, Mr Morrison went to Washington, and we discussed the merits of a US State Dinner; the surprising influences on the government coming from a far-right QAnon adherent; and should celebrities be hired to promote government programs? And in this episode, David Lewis is the reserve water boy for the Australian Rugby League.

Eddy Jokovich: Scott Morrison has been to Washington and back. He's the first Australian prime minister to visit an American president since John Howard's visit in 2006, and he's just the second foreign leader to have a State Dinner with US President, Donald Trump, following on from French President Emmanuel Macron in 2018. State Dinners are grand formal events for the *bon vivants* of both countries: fine wine and find food are always on offer, but they are also events that are held to highlight the special relationship between these two countries, even if it does offer the opportunity for mutual admiration:

> Donald Trump: I would say a man of titanium, you know, titanium is much tougher than steel.
>
> **Scott Morrison (blushing):** Heh, heh!
>
> DT: He's a man of titanium, believe me! I have to deal with this guy: he's not easy.
>
> **SM (coyly):** Eh hah hah hah!
>
> DT: You might think he's a nice guy, okay, he's a man of real, real strength and a great guy!

EJ: The media reported the success of Morrison's US visit and, as far as solidifying the relationship between the Australia and the United States, the visit was a success, even if it did put China offside. But the event as a personal success for Morrison, as it was solidly reported in the media?: I'm not so sure about that. In the current international political climate, it's not such a good idea to saddle up too closely to Donald Trump. But that's exactly what Morrison did: supporting the US trade war against China, and offering support for Australian military presence in the Persian Gulf. It's hard to see how Morrison could have become any closer to Donald Trump and he might be getting too close for his own good.

David Lewis: Foreign relations is difficult. Nobody doubts the aim in this case, which is to balance the strong relationship Australia has with the United States, without getting too close to Donald Trump who, domestically, is in a great deal of trouble: he is likely to be impeached, there's a chance he will be removed brutally from office, and there's even a slight chance he will go to jail. Cozying up to Donald Trump, the person, rather than the President of the United States, is a very courageous decision in the '*Yes, Minister*' sense. Annoying your biggest trading partner [China] in order to become closer to the United States is a very dangerous idea. We can criticise the Chinese government; they're not a perfect organisation by any means, but trade is very important to Australia. Good relations are very important: we can be political friends with the bigger powers and still criticise them when we have to. But Morrison getting personally close to Trump seems to be another agenda that is perhaps beyond what we can see.

EJ: If Australia did simply trade with all the countries that had exactly the same or similar political systems to itself, Australia wouldn't trade with too many countries, and that would be a disaster for the local economy. Most countries can differentiate between political issues and economic issues—Australia does have a trade surplus with China of $26 billion and 40 per cent of Australia's exports do go to China. It's the reverse with America: Australia has a $22 billion trade deficit with the United States: economically speaking, it's quite unwise for Morrison to start lecturing and criticising China, supporting the US trade war from a podium in Washington and sharing that stage with Donald Trump.

DL: He unnecessarily created a great deal of friction with Australia's most important trading partner and for no good reason, with no positive outcome for Australia. It was a very bizarre trip: it was not a success, as a personal success for the Prime Minister, or in terms of furthering Australian interests, and Australia came out of this US meeting far worse than it should have. The Prime Minister then attended what essentially became a re-election rally for Donald Trump in Ohio, and one of the rules of foreign affairs is that political leaders shouldn't become involved in the domestic partisan politics of another country, especially when they are in that country. World leaders do get together and, in their private moments, will discuss internal politics, or the issues that are facing both countries. And the political rally was a part of media opportunity with Australian businessman Anthony Pratt, who had just opened a cardboard box factory in the United States. Should the public in Australia be pleased with this? It seems to be a successful venture created by Pratt, but perhaps a better message for Morrison would have been to open up a factory in Australia, rather than the US.

EJ: US State Dinners, of course, they're always going to be a political event: guests don't just turn up to these events because they're hungry, or feel like having a good feed. Ever since he became prime minister, Scott Morrison has been making a big issue about being 'on the side' of the Australian people. But he's on the side of a very exclusive group of Australians: on his guest list at the US State Dinner, he had Gina Rinehart, Lachlan Murdoch,

Anthony Pratt, Andrew Forrest, Kerry Stokes: a wide range of business leaders from media, petrochemical, finance and pharmaceutical companies. These people don't seem to be your everyday Australians that Morrison claims to be on the side of.

DL: It was very odd collection of people to have at a State Dinner: not many were elected officials or appointed senior public servants; they were all on the side of big money. And it's peculiar to see pharmaceutical representatives appearing with government leaders: many in this industry want to see an American-styled system introduced in Australia, in the hope of linking up health care to the wealthy and keeping it away from low-income people. The other industries represented: coal mining is dying as an industry and, according to some market analysts, it's an industry that only has around twenty years before it becomes a stranded asset. The coal industry, of course, isn't going to end next week, but it won't be financially viable in the future. Lachlan Murdoch from News Corp: another dying industry—print media and the old broadcast media. Channel 9, Channel 10 and Channel 7 aren't going to disappear overnight but they're not going to bounce back to the levels of their halcyon days. News Corp is slowly dying; Fairfax has been sold off and its parent company, Nine Network, isn't travelling so well. And then there's the dinner appearance of Greg Norman, a golfer who has been retired for a long time. Surely there were more representative sportspeople that could have attended, who at least are still playing: the captain of the Test cricket team; the captain of the league team; AFL players, as well as the captains of the women's versions of those teams. The guest list seemed symbolic of an Australia of the past, not of the future.

EJ: For all of the debate about who attended the US State Dinner, there was great conjecture about one person who was not there: Brian Houston. Houston is the founder of the Pentecostal Hillsong Church in Australia, of which Scott Morrison is a member now, albeit with the Horizon Church in Sutherland. It has been reported Scott Morrison wanted Houston at the official US dinner and lobbied hard. The White House, of course, had other ideas, and with good reason. In 2014, Houston admitted to a failure to alert police about allegations his father had sexually abused nine boys in Australia and New Zealand during the 1980s, abuses that occurred within the Hillsong Church. The White House must have decided it was a bridge too far to have someone of this calibre at a State Dinner, although in the current political circumstances and allegations surrounding Jeffrey Epstein and his links with Trump, someone like Houston would be more than welcomed. Scott Morrison has neither confirmed or denied he wanted Brian Houston at the US State Dinner, and despite persistent questions from the media, he avoided the issue by claiming he's either already addressed the question or claiming the issue is not relevant to the public. It's a simple question, and he could have answered it quite simply. But because Morrison deflected the question, he showed he had something to hide: and I think he did. A previous prime minister, Tony Abbott, had quite a strong ideological blind spot, and this caused him great political damage. Is Morrison in a similar position to Abbott: does he have a political blind spot when it comes to religious matters and relationships that he has within the Pentecostal church?

DL: Australia is a secular nation: we have no official religion. There are still a few overhangs, such as the prayer to open Parliament, which is a ridiculous anachronism. It's perfectly appropriate for Members of Parliament to hold their own religious or spiritual beliefs, if that's what they'd like to do. But no one faith in Australia should be favoured over any other faith: secularism works the best in a democratic system. To have Brian Houston—a head of a church and regarded as a spiritual advisor to Morrison—attending the US State Dinner was going to be inappropriate anyway, and given all the allegations that have been made about him, it would have been political suicide and political stupidity to even suggest that he goes along. And NSW Police has confirmed the investigation into these allegations and Houston's failure to act is still an open investigation. Brian Houston may be the finest man alive who made a lapse in judgment; it does happen. But it was a terrible lapse in judgment by Houston. To be fair: how many people could actually turn their father into the police, regardless of what they've done? But we should be fair the other way: these were heinous acts committed by his father, Frank Houston. This was an issue which presented an ethical challenge, and he failed miserably.

EJ: Putting this religious factor in Australia and the relationship with politics into context: at the most recent Australian census in 2016, only 1 per cent of the Australian population identified as Pentecostal, 10 per cent claimed to be atheist, and 30 per cent were of no religion whatsoever. Almost 70 per cent of the population is not part of a church or frequent a regular religious service, so any attempt to bridge that gap between religion and the state is going to result in political failure. It's probably best for the Prime Minister to get back to the issues that are more relevant to the Australian community.

*

The external conservative influences on the Australian government and how this is affecting their ability to follow an agenda

EJ: Ever since Scott Morrison became prime minister, there has been a wide range of throw-away lines about the Australian Government being influenced by far-right politics and replicating the tendencies of fascist regimes—it's easy to think this—this government does lock up asylum seekers; downplays human rights; it's obsessed with national security; despises unions and protects corporate interests; it has a cosy relationship with the media, and whether or not it has engaged in electoral fraud is currently being decided by the High Court. But recent events have thrown up a series of questions about what is influencing Morrison and the direction of his government, and I was surprised to hear that within the Prime Minister's inner circle is something worse than fascism—an adherent of the QAnon far-right conspiracy theory. Prime ministers do need to mix with a wide range of people but would we expect a QAnon fanatic to be one of them?

DL: Many people of Pentecostal faith—I don't know if it's a majority or a significant vocal minority—are very much purveyors of conspiracy theories from the slightly loopy Bilderberg Group trying to impose capitalism on the world, to the completely insane, such as the conspiracy that the world is run by alien lizard people. I don't want to taint people of faith, or taint all members of any particular faith. Conspiracy theories, of course, have existed forever: secret societies; Freemasons; the Illuminati from the eighteenth century all may have had massive influence, or perceived influence on society, always pertaining to the idea of controlling the world. In modern times, we've seen the Protocols of the Elders of Zion, which was a fake document published in 1919 which has been used to justify all kinds of horrible acts. The Area 51 Roswell incident in 1947 claimed a UFO had landed on earth and that was documented quite entertainingly in the television series, *The X Files*. The notion of secret societies and aliens and shadowy groups running the world are ridiculous: the President of the World Bank suggested that if the World Bank really was a secret cabal managing the world, given its current state, we should be bloody ashamed of ourselves. Given Scott Morrison's faith, certainly he would have been exposed to some of these odd conspiracy theories, even if only indirectly through other members of his church: again, I'm not suggesting all members of his church follow these conspiracies, agree with them, or even acknowledge them. But some certainly do: there has been much literature that has been published, widely available through the internet.

EJ: It has been described as 'unhinged, evidence free, deranged and insane'. QAnon is a theory that believes in a secret plot against Donald Trump and the existence of an international network of Satan-worshipping pedophiles controlling the world, including all the politicians and the media. And, according to QAnon, Donald Trump is the one who is going to put an end to all of this control. It's a recent theory, and it commenced in the secure and secretive 4chan network during 2016, just in time for the US presidential election campaign. It also spread a wide range of rumours about the Democrat candidate, Hillary Clinton, including the bizarre allegation that she was part of a child sex ring at the Comet Ping Pong pizza restaurant in Washington DC. Just because someone is close to a prime minister or is a lifelong friend doesn't necessarily mean that person ends up influencing policy outcomes or benefits personally, even though that does seem to be the way this Liberal government operates. Generally, it's good for a prime minister to have some left-field influences and a wide range of different types of people to consult with. Former Prime Minister Paul Keating had a few Bohemians within his close circle of friends, and just because a person becomes the prime minister, it doesn't mean that they have to give up their friendship groups. But influences coming through QAnon and conspiracy theories: it this a serious issue and does it highlight the poor judgment of the Prime Minister, or is it just a case of bad appearances?

DL: It's not a good look. According to *Guardian Australia*, the Twitter account where the QAnon material was posted to, BurnedSpy34, has been identified as Tim Stewart. Stewart claims he has never spoken about any of these QAnon conspiracies to the Prime Minister, and just pointed out that they both get on very well with each other, he keeps his beliefs to himself. But the Prime Minister would have to be aware of these theories, and it's hard to imagine any previous prime ministers giving these theories any credence whatsoever. At the very least, the existence of someone subscribing to such theories within the Prime Minister's inner circle would appear to set up a security issue for the government.

EJ: Tim Stewart's wife works full-time as a personal assistant at Kirribilli House and Stewart has been taking photographs from within Kirribilli House and publishing them through his Twitter account, interspersed with his messages about how he believes the Australian Government is committing treason and the Christchurch massacre in New Zealand earlier this year didn't actually take place: it was supposedly a grand conspiracy to remove guns from people. This seems to be a big news story and, for political journalists, there would be a public expectation the story would be developed until the media got to the heart of the issue. The story appeared in *Guardian Australia* just once— the Prime Minister requested privacy, and we don't know what else went on behind the scenes to make this happen. No other mainstream media has published the story since, and this seems to be the end of the matter.

DL: For those journalists in the press gallery, access is important. But the role of the journalist is not just about writing good news stories for the government of the day. It's a matter of reporting the news as it is—good and bad—and letting the audience decide for themselves, depending on their views: cutting welfare spending might be considered appropriate by some people; adding to welfare might be considered desirable by others. But when the government acts in a manner that is sketchy, dodgy and corrupt, journalists should be able to report on that as well. The relationships between political journalists and government has always been fraught. Since at least the time of the Lyons government of 1932 through to 1939, the press gallery has been treated very well with drinks at the prime minister's office, social nights, the Midwinter Ball. It's not unreasonable for journalists to try and present themselves in the best possible light they can, and making themselves available for opportunities to get access to information and news direct from government ministers and the prime minister. It's a two-way process and it has been this way with every single government, with the possible exception of the Keating government, where Paul Keating treated the press gallery with absolute contempt mostly, and many of them loved him for it.

EJ: The position of prime minister is the most important position in the country. And when a prime minister asks for privacy, generally, the media should respect that, depending on what the issue is. But privacy seems to always be respected by the media for conservative prime ministers, rarely for Labor prime ministers. The media was always digging around for details about Paul Keating's personal life; the entrails of Julia Gillard's personal life were paraded for all to see. But whatever is the personal domain of John Howard, Tony Abbott and now Scott Morrison, it always seems to be off limits for the media. Morrison's relationship with Tim Stewart and QAnon might be a side issue, and the Prime Minister wants to get the focus back onto his government. The problem here is this government has not got very much of an agenda for the future, and when a government is lacking an agenda, that's when it goes off on ideological tangents and can be easily influenced by fringe dwellers such as Tim Stewart. The amount of sitting days in Parliament during 2019 has been below average, but when Parliament does sit, there's not that much to talk about. Scott Morrison has also cancelled the Council of Australian Government's meeting in December, claiming there won't be enough of an agenda for the states and territory leaders to discuss, and there's no point in meeting. Certainly, if there's no agenda, there is no point in meeting but the question has to be put: why isn't there an agenda? There are always important issues for heads of government around Australia to discuss. And the government has just embarked on an inquiry into interest rates, which essentially is another populist and puerile bank-bashing exercise. I've always assumed the task of government is an all consuming, difficult and intellectually-challenging process. But this doesn't seem to be the case for this Morrison government: this government just isn't busy enough.

DL: One of the big criticisms of the Gillard government between 2010–13 was that it lacked 'the narrative'. No one in the media ever outlined what a 'narrative' was or what is meant by 'the narrative' but it was an issue they could keep hammering Julia Gillard and the Labor government on. It's a struggle to see what this Liberal–National government wants to achieve, except to be in government and 'keep Labor out'. There's not much parliamentary debate: the low amount of sitting days in 2010 is disgraceful, it really is. Local members do need to spend time back with their constituents and deal with the many issues that do arise in their seats, all of which can be very time consuming. It's almost a case where the government doesn't want to set the agenda, and that their agenda is actually holding that power of government, and using it a way that is not in the public interest, such as the Robodebt fiasco. Having less sitting days of Parliament allows this government to avoid scrutiny, and that is a big issue for democracy.

EJ: If a government hasn't much of an agenda or a narrative, that creates a vacuum, and there's a wide range of lobby groups and individuals out there wanting to fill in that vacuum. The Institute of Public Affairs: that's definitely one of the group's filling the void. There's a strong relationship between the IPA and the Liberal Party, and the Liberal Party has quite a few IPA members sitting on the federal government benches. And whenever there's an opportunity, the IPA will push their right-wing brand of extreme libertarianism within this government. And that leads to a situation when all the rent seekers, the spivs, the donors and all the other hangers-on attached to the Liberal Party try to enforce their knowledge, philosophies and wisdom upon the government.

DL: The IPA is a highly problematic organisation: it seems to be occupied with the wealthy older people who are very happy with lower taxes and more money in their pocket, or the younger people who don't seem to be able to obtain meaningful work outside the IPA. It's the old 'trickle-down' supply side economics: their philosophy is all about lower taxes, less government, leaving industry without any regulations because apparently they have the public interest at heart—when we know they haven't. Or the extreme libertarianism, where they want to be able to infringe certain laws or treat other people badly, without having other people telling them that they can't do that. And we can always go back to the *Racial Discrimination Act*: they want section 18c repealed, mainly because Andrew Bolt was found to be a racist by those laws. The fact that Bolt was found objectively by the Courts to be acting as a racist at the time doesn't seem to occur to the IPA. And they've never clearly outlined what is it that they want to say, that they can't currently say under section 18c. They've never articulated this—either they know 18c of the *Racial Discrimination Act* is not really an issue of note, or there must be something they want to be able to say they know is pretty horrible.

*

EJ: There are many ongoing minor issues for the government, and it's always the accumulation of these smaller issues in politics that can create the much larger problems—there was Morrison's China-bashing while he was in the US; the Brian Houston non-attendance at the US State Dinner; there was the fiasco with the 'rugby diplomacy' in Fiji, where Scott Morrison was trying to be 'everyman', swilling tins of beer and running barefooted onto the rugby field. Not much criticism of these issues to report here in the mainstream media. And just as a comparison, when Julia Gillard lost her shoe in India in 2012, it was scandalous front-page news at the time, as if to suggest she was so incompetent, she couldn't even save her footwear. It seems like this government can pretty much do as it pleases without much of a backlash in the media, and it has been like this ever since the election in May this year. But looking at the political and media landscape, what are the issues that will put a dent in this government in the future?

DL: The Labor Party isn't providing much opposition to the government at the moment; they're still waiting for their election review post-mortem, which is due in November. So a weak opposition and a compliant media is not going to make much impact. But what will put a dent in the reputation of this government is an economic downturn and cost of living issues. We also have to take into account this government only won the May election by one seat, and it was only a matter of a few busloads of votes in a few seats that got them over the line, based on a clear analysis of the numbers from the election. One interest point was provided by ABC election analyst, Antony Green, that the Coalition was strongly supported during the pre-poll period, but the Labor Party won the most votes on election day: it wasn't enough for Labor to win the overall election though.

EJ: The 2019 federal election achieved the highest level of pre-polling votes in history—41 per cent of all votes were cast in the three-week pre-poll period before the day of the election. In the pre-poll period across Australia, 54 per cent voted for the Coalition in two-party preferred voting, but on election day, the vote for Labor was 50.7 per cent and 49.3 per cent for the Coalition. Unfortunately for the Labor Party, it's not just about the vote on election day; it's the total of all the votes, including the pre-poll votes. The Labor Party will be reassessing their pre-polling strategies for the next election and, with almost half of all votes cast before election day, this period is becoming a critical part of the overall election campaign.

DL: Labor had a good policy structure and they didn't lose the election on policies alone, although they did allow peripheral issues such as franking credits to be magnified by their opponents. The popularity of Bill Shorten was made into a major issue as well, but that's the nature of politics: it's rarely about fairness.

EJ: That might be the case, but for some people, politics is more than fair, and it's all a matter of being in the right place at the right time, especially for certain television personalities:

> Scott Cam: If you had have slowed and done it properly and improvised, it would have been sweet.
> *The Block* contestant: If I had to check everything that every other tradesman did, we wouldn't be finishing...
> SC: You gotta be joking me mate!
> TB: It's not my job!
> SC: These boys have built this structure and they had to knock down the old one: are you kidding me? And you're saying that because this is out a hundred mil, it's no good. I mean, you've gotta improvise around that situation from an 1850s building. That is the end of the story! As if I'm going to pay your bill, I'm not paying nothing mate! You get the job done, and get it done right. (Scott Cam storms off the building site)

EJ: Australia has a new ambassador, but it's not the normal type of ambassador we'd expect to see. The new ambassador is the television celebrity from the home renovation reality show, *The Block*, Scott Cam, and it's now his job to promote national careers in the trades. Exactly what he will be doing is very unclear, and Scott Morrison and Minister for Vocational Education, Senator Michaelia Cash, have refused to reveal how much this position will cost, claiming the arrangement is 'commercial-in-confidence', but market estimates suggest the cost will be in the order of $500,000 for two years of ambassadorial work. And that's nice work, if you can get it.

DL: Governments will occasionally hire television and media celebrities to promote political agendas or government programs, but it rarely ends well. The popular science commentator, Karl Kruszelnicki, appeared in a government advertising campaign to promote an intergenerational report about what Australia would look like in forty years time, believing it to be bipartisan, but suffered a backlash because the report made no mention at all about climate change, and flowed straight into the current government's agenda of inaction. That appearance damaged Kruszelnicki's credibility and lowered his profile, even though he backed away from the report. There's no issue in using celebrities to promote government programs; governments of all persuasions have been doing this for some time. But it is an area fraught with problems, usually for the celebrity.

EJ: Aside from the secrecy surrounding the contract, the question in Scott Cam's case and this notion of a national brand ambassador for trades: what is the government program that he's meant to be promoting? It doesn't seem to exist. This is also the context of the Liberal–National government removing $3 billion from vocational education and national apprenticeships over the past six years since 2013: state and territory TAFEs have been decimated and most government funding for trades education and apprenticeships usually favours private providers. It seems that Scott Cam will be promoting the value of high school students moving into trades if it's relevant for them, rather than making unrealistic attempts to enter university, and that's a good thing. But many high schools are already promoting this process and already have their own mechanisms in place. It's hard to see which federal government programs Scott Cam will be supporting because this government has been doing its best to remove trades as an option for many high students.

DL: The decision to appoint Scott Cam as brand ambassador for trades is a decision made by a marketing person, and Scott Morrison does like to see himself as a 'marketing man'. But it's a decision that also invites great ridicule, outside of whether there might be any merits behind the idea. The satirical comedy, *Utopia*, actually contained a sketch earlier this year where they suggested employing Scott Cam as a brand ambassador to solve a certain political problem—so the real-life decision to appoint Scott Cam suggests this government's propensity for replicating television comedies, without realising that it's a parody. And this type of process of politics-imitating-art has happened before: Malcolm Turnbull used the 'continuity and change' slogan in the lead-up to the 2016 election campaign, a slogan lifted straight from the American HBO satirical series, *Veep*. And now we have government policy lifted from an episode of *Utopia*. We should just hope government policy doesn't start to replicate other political satire such as *Yes, Minister* or *In The Thick of It*, because politics would then start to become seriously embarrassing.

*

Music in this episode
Demise of a Nation, Greg Dombrowski
Madam Medusa, UB40

Divided Opinions: Eddy Jokovich + David Lewis

Another nail in the coffin for democracy

29 October 2019

Eddy Jokovich

In January 2019, Scott Morrison announced environmental legislation to protect native species was one of his government's top priorities, and said "we already introduced and passed legislation through the Senate actually dealing with that very issue, we've been taking action on that". A minor problem though: no such legislation existed, nor was there any legislative schedule to remotely support this claim. Morrison just lied.

It was the middle of the holiday season; perhaps too many senior journalists were still soaking up the sun at their beach retreats but, nevertheless, this factually incorrect claim should have been questioned by the media and corrected, either by the Prime Minister, or the media themselves.

As it turned out, the only media outlet to run the story disputing Morrison's claim was *The Guardian Australia*, in a report from Paul Karp, although the story did briefly reappear on *Ten News* in a news report from Elfy Scott, one week before the federal election in May.

In hindsight, Morrison's statement in mid-January was a test run in an election year: could he get away with a complete lie, and what would be the repercussions? As it turned out, there were absolutely no repercussions at all.

Manipulation by politicians, of course, is nothing new and in an election year, truth is a commodity stretched and compressed in every permutation possible, with desperate politicians of all persuasions attempting to extract every possible opportunity and advantage over their opponents.

But outright lying?

This year, the Australian body politic crossed the same Rubicon traversed by Donald Trump in the United States, and now by Boris Johnson in Britain. Agreed facts no longer matter: politicians can now tell any story they wish to and knowingly lie. They know the media is too weak and lacks the intellectual capacity to understand they're being lied to, and when they're caught out, they know the public is largely disinterested and not too concerned about a political system that delivers so much trickery and chicanery to them.

Better economic managers?

This is why we have the erstwhile belief pushed by the Liberal Party, and supported by the media, that they are the far superior economic manager, even though this isn't supported by critical analysis of all key elements of government finances.

In terms of spending as a percentage of gross domestic product; economic growth; management of deficits and surpluses in comparison to the world economy; Labor has been the better economic manager since the early 1970s. This is clearly outlined by John Menadue in 'The myth that the Liberals are better economic managers?', published at *johnmenadue.com.au*. There isn't a significant difference but, in normal circumstances, the analysis would be at least enough to neutralise the argument about which side of politics provides better economic management.

Politically, it's understandable why this public perception exists. The Liberals have pushed the 'better-economic-manager' mantra since 1996—who could forget 'Beazley's $10 billion black hole'—and Labor failed to adequately defend its economic legacy. The national economy is complex with reams of statistics detailing government finances but each statistic read in isolation is meaningless. Which is why the government focuses on the most easily explained statistic— which is also the least meaningful—the Budget surplus.

The Liberal Party has also successfully convinced large sections of the community that managing a national economy is similar to running a household budget—it's not—and the pursuit of a Budget surplus is a noble ideal and the only economic value worth pursuing.

Forgotten within this debate is the fact that under Robert Menzies, Coalition governments ran massive deficits between 1958–59 and 1966–67 of up to 3.3 per cent of GDP, under the narrative of "nation-building deficits".

Deficits and surpluses are neither good nor bad, but do need to be relevant and relative to the state of the economy, and just right now doesn't seem to be the best time to produce a Budget surplus.

What will be the government's narrative when the economy grinds to a halt in 2020, largely because of this pursuit of a Budget surplus?

Also heard within the halls of Parliament last week were the calls of 'paying down Labor's debt', as well as Scott Morrison claiming "net government debt is falling". Again, there is a problem with this claim: net government debt is not falling; it's increasing, and based on current trajectories, net government debt will continue to rise. The figure was $209 billion (13 per cent of GDP) when the Liberal–National Party formed government in 2013, and now sits at $373 billion (19 per cent of GDP). And Morrison should be aware of this—the figures were actually tabled in Parliament by Treasurer Josh Frydenberg, just five weeks ago.

Now, there is a possibility by the time actual figures are reported in September 2020, there may be a decrease, but there is nothing to suggest "net government debt is falling", as claimed by the Prime Minister. And among a sea of economic journalists reporting in the mainstream media, not one has called him out on this. Not one.

So how far is the government prepared to not just stretch the truth, but push outright lies? The Minister for Energy, Angus Taylor, has consistently made misleading statements about greenhouse gas emissions, more recently claiming the Liberal government has achieved a 1.1 billion tonne turnaround since 2013, a claim repeated by the Prime Minister and other Liberal ministers, including former Environment Minister, Melissa Price and Defence Minister, Linda Reynolds. Emissions will have actually risen by 540 million tonnes by 2020, and have increased by 4.3 per cent. Despite this, Taylor continues to say the Liberal–National government has reduced emissions.

At least this outrageous fabrication has been challenged by journalists on a consistent basis but even though there are agreed facts of rising emissions published by many experts in the field, and even agreed to by the government's own figures, Taylor keeps claiming emissions are going down.

When lying isn't enough: the next step

When the obvious lies and misinterpretations of political leaders remain unchallenged, there's a great incentive to continue to ply this trade. Just like criminal cartels in those countries ruled by corruption, a lack of sanction coupled with the protection offered by a compliant media means corrupted politicians are encouraged to persist with their egregious behaviour.

But the spoken lie has limitations, and if there are limits to the political impact these can have, what is the next step? If public trust in politicians is so low and so debauched, and there are virtually no checks on parliamentary behaviour, there would have to be a great incentive to fabricate and present official documents as fact. Which is the point we arrived at last week.

In a classic case of wanting to win every single political point while losing sight of the bigger picture—and a case of winning a political point, even if there wasn't a point to win—Taylor unleashed a political attack upon the Lord Mayor of Sydney, Clover Moore, sending a letter complaining about the increased carbon emissions produced by the City of Sydney Council. He also provided an extract from the Council's Annual Report, detailing $15.9 million of spending on air travel by Councillors.

And not satisfied with just a letter to the Lord Mayor of Sydney, Taylor conveniently distributed this letter and associated documents to the *Daily Telegraph*, which duly published an article on 30 September about Taylor's attack, as well as excerpts from the Annual Report.

The problem for Taylor is the figures in the Annual Report he provided to the media and used as the basis for his attack on Clover Moore were fabricated—it is unclear at this stage who was responsible, but the forged document more than likely originated from Taylor's office—the actual figures of Councillor's travel were $5,934, nowhere near the $15.9 million claimed by Taylor.

The City of Sydney Council declared a climate change emergency in June 2019, and Clover Moore informed the Environment Minister, Sussan Ley, of this decision in August. It's unclear why Taylor, as Minister for Energy, would need to be involved, but he was there, and followed up with his attack in September.

There is also a history of antagonism between the Liberal Party and Clover Moore—the NSW Liberal government created special legislation to force Moore out of state politics in 2012 (she was concurrently a member of the NSW Parliament and Lord Mayor of Sydney since 2004) and even though Moore is not aligned with the Labor Party, the Liberal's obsession with Moore borders on a pathological psychosis.

But Taylor's antics have taken politics to a new extreme. He not only lied about the figures, but used figures from a forged document—he claimed he downloaded the figures directly from the Annual Report contained on the City of Sydney Council website, even though the Council has provided metadata from its website indicating there has only ever been the one version of their Annual Report—and that version contradicts the figures provided by Taylor.

A new low in politics and the media

There is now a new phenomenon in federal politics, where not only do ministers tell unsubstantiated lies, but they present fabricated documents to support their lies. There should be consequences for this behaviour but in that place where there should be sanction and punitive measures, there is a void.

The government now knows how far it can push boundaries. And it also knows it can depend on most of the mainstream media to provide cover and continue to sow the seed of doubt in the public mind. These obvious lies and fabrications continue to be protected by the mainstream media, with few exceptions.

Within days of the self-centred and misguided 'Your Right To Know' campaign implemented by eighteen media organisations and representative groups, we had two senior members of the mainstream media setting up the protective shields around the government.

Network Ten's political editor and contributing editor to *The Australian*, Peter van Onselen, asserted: "I understand [the] frustration ... but when politicians tell falsehoods they can't automatically be deemed liars".

Political editor with News.com.au, Malcolm Farr, in response to a statement put out by Taylor, claimed "he has admitted [a] mistake but not explained it but I think [it's] pretty clear on this occasion we go for stuff-up."

Now, let's take a deep breath and assess these two statements.

"When politicians tell falsehoods they can't automatically be deemed liars."

What could they deemed to be instead? Truth-tellers telling falsehoods in the public interest? Honest brokers attempting to protecting noble ideals for the greater good? No, in this case, Taylor is not acting in the public interest, and is just a seedy corrupt politician with a white face and good looks, using a forged document to attack his political opponents.

"Pretty clear on this occasion we go for stuff-up."

Pretty clear? On what basis? And where is the substantial evidence to support the claims put forward by the Minister that he downloaded the documents from the City of Sydney Council website? There isn't any. Where did his version of the document originate from?

More than likely, this is a case where a Liberal staffer amended the figures from the City of Sydney Annual Report, provided the figures to the Minister who knowingly used the figures to attack Clover Moore, a distant political opponent of little relevance to the federal government.

This is corrupt political behaviour, and while it should be a criminal offence everywhere, at least it exists as a criminal offence in NSW, which is where this fabricated document was prepared and presented.

But what we will see over the next few weeks is most of the mainstream media closing ranks behind this Liberal–National government, reporting as if nothing has happened and protect the Minister.

And in the case where the media does ask the right questions and gets closer to the truth of the matter, an insignificant staffer will be scapegoated—provided with a short overseas holiday and a new job elsewhere in a few months' time. And the corrupt behaviour of Taylor's will continue unchecked.

So much for the claim of News Corp journalist Annika Smethurst during the 'Your Right To Know' campaign: "Essentially, we have journalists to keep the government in line to check on them. If we want a free democracy, we really need journalists to be able to tell the public what's going on." A check on government? A check on power? I really don't think so.

It's a facile claim coming from a News Corp journalist whose publications essentially obfuscate the truth and attack the opponents of the Liberal–National Party; the Labor Party. Even when confronted with a serious case of a politician telling bare-faced lies and using doctored material to support their lies, they downplay the evidence, cover up, and create new issues to move onto, hoping the public will simply forget.

With the words of 'your right to know' still ringing in the ears of the public, the mainstream media had a scandal on its hands and instead of giving true meaning and support to 'keeping the government in line to check on them', they squibbed and reverted to form, showing how hollow their 'Your Right to Know' campaign really was.

Business as usual.

Politics and the media are in a poor shape at the moment. I've said this many times before and, like so many people, I don't know what can be done about it. There isn't a shortage of ideas to rectify this or positive solutions on offer—there are many excellent ideas contained in *Reforming Our Democracy*, a joint report prepared by the University of Melbourne, newDemocracy Foundation and the Susan McKinnon Foundation—but the lack of political will to implement these good ideas is the problem.

The political system will never change while we have political leadership provided by a prime minister of the calibre of Scott Morrison, or a political system containing ministers as compromised and corrupt as Angus Taylor. And it's unlikely a future Labor government will be prepared to concede the advantages offered by the current political system, or renovate a Constitution that is well out of date and unsuited to contemporary Australia.

In his speech to Parliament last week, the Manager of Opposition Business, Tony Burke, made this salient point: "Outside of this Chamber, people live in the world of facts. If their wages aren't moving, false claims here won't change the fact that their wages aren't moving. If the climate is changing, denial in here won't change the fact that the climate is changing. If we are not starting with agreed and obvious facts, the relevance of this Chamber only declines."

Forged documents are not new to politics—in the last days of the Labor government during the 1996 election campaign, Treasurer Ralph Willis, received forged documents claiming the Liberal Party was planning "significant reductions to Commonwealth programs" if they were elected, and tried to make political mileage out of them. We never found out who prepared the forgeries, although there were allegations current Liberal Party Senator, Scott Ryan, was the likely author. The media was quickly informed the documents were actually forged and the issue weighed down an already-failing Labor campaign.

But the behaviour of Angus Taylor is something quite different and leads politics into a darker zone.

The electorate understands politicians tell lies and stretch the truth, but manipulating official documents is something beyond the normal scope of politics. This is a new low in Australian politics, and Taylor remaining as Minister and as a Member of Parliament is a constant reminder of this newly-acquired nadir and a rapidly declining political system.

*

Forged democracy, Labor reviews itself, and climate change politics fired up

13 November 2019

Eddy Jokovich + David Lewis / Podcast

In this episode, we looked at the fine art of lying and misinformation in politics; assessed the Labor Party 2019 election review and discussed whether it would be enough to guide the party back into office; and the politics of climate change, yet again: who can we blame for the New South Wales bushfires? And David Lewis appears as an amateur lycanthrope.

Eddy Jokovich: We've reached a new low in Australian politics, where simply stretching the truth isn't enough for some politicians and next step has been taken where official documents have been manipulated and presented as fact. The Minister for Energy, Angus Taylor, attacked a political opponent, the Lord Mayor of Sydney Council, Clover Moore, over vast amounts of spending on air flights and travel, accusing her of contributing massive amounts of greenhouse emissions in the process. The problem: Taylor used figures from a forged and fabricated document, and we still don't know who committed the forgery, although this incident is under investigation by NSW Police. We've heard a great deal in recent years about "fake news" and how we now exist in the post-fact era, but ministers using forgeries to attack their political opponents? We've reached a new low, and politics is entering uncharted territory.

David Lewis: It wasn't so long ago where a minister definitely would have resigned over such behaviour, and some in the media picked up very quickly that this was another version of the "Utegate affair", where Malcolm Turnbull used fabricated material provided by a public servant, Godwin Grech, to attack Prime Minister Kevin Rudd in 2009. Suggesting Taylor's actions are just like "Utegate", however, is the most generous option. We don't know how Taylor was involved in the forgery, but he was certainly involved somehow. He claimed the Sydney Council uploaded the document he used to attack Clover Moore, then took that document down, and uploaded the correct document, which seems like a far-fetched excuse. It's possible Taylor was directly involved in the forging but it's more than likely one of his staff members, and they would have been the ones to present the forged document to him. Whether he was told it was a forgery, or whether it was provided to him as a genuine document, the main point is that Taylor didn't check. This is highly unusual but it seems like there could be another Grech-like player somewhere in this incident.

EJ: Ministers are very busy people, and it's impossible to believe Taylor would have actually sat down in front of his computer, imported the document into Photoshop and then started amending the figures so he could started talking about this document in Parliament and then send the document off to the New Limited newspapers—the figures and his document were published in *The Daily Telegraph* in September. That's not to say he didn't make the alterations himself—we can never be sure—but, certainly, one of his staffers or someone else in his office would have. It's a question of whether Taylor knew the figures were unrealistic and knew whether they had been forged or not. He claimed the City of Sydney Council had spent $15.9 million air travel in the recent financial year: that's a phenomenal amount. That's virtually every employee from the Sydney Council traveling by plane to Perth and back, every single day of the year; it's incredibly unrealistic. And surely a minister using those kinds of figures to attack a political opponent would have double-checked those figures before standing up in Parliament and making those accusations, as well as tipping off the media about it.

DL: Taylor did give an apology, which was more of the 'I-was-sorry-I-was-caught-and-shouldn't-have-been-caught' type of apology, rather than saying he regretted the incident and had it completely wrong. But he also may have made the apology because he was at risk of being sued: his actions and comments were quite defamatory. The $15.9 million Taylor referred to is an outrageous amount of money for travel. The City of Sydney Council has ten councillors, and that would equate to $1.6 million per councillor for travel expenses, and most councillors don't need to travel very much. Occasionally, there are flights to sister cities in other countries, overseas and interstate conferences: these can be justified, and are often justifiable. But you would expect a minister to understand this, assess figures that might have been provided to him, and think: 'hang on, that can't be right, let's confirm this before we run with this'. But, then again, he's a man under fire and he's a desperate man. And desperation often causes questionable decisions.

EJ: This type of political behaviour does follow on from Donald Trump in the United States and Boris Johnson in the United Kingdom, where they state deliberate mistruths, outright lies or complete rubbish. These leaders also realise very few people in the media will actually call them out on these outright lies, and if they ever do, it's far too late: the lie has travelled far and wide before the truth actually catches up. The Liberal–National government is replicating this behaviour. Morrison, for most of the time, will deny evidence placed in front of him, or just make material up and claim any questioning of him is all in the 'Canberra bubble'. Angus Taylor; we've got evidence about his misdemeanours and fabrication of material, particularly on greenhouse emissions. Barnaby Joyce; he's another member of this government making up material. Another example: there's a new Liberal MP willing to roll along—Katie Allen—he replaced Kelly O'Dwyer in the Victoria seat of Higgins. She claimed greenhouse emissions have fallen in Australia since 2005 even though every key indicator produced by government reports and supported by a wide range of scientific research, has shown greenhouse emissions have increased dramatically since that time. Yet, here we have a Member of Parliament appearing in the media and promoting a complete fabrication. Politicians fabricating information; knowingly publishing false information; and not suffering any repercussions when they do this. Where can we go from this point?

DL: There's a few factors at play here: Australia needs massive media reform because it's the media that should be holding politicians to account, and they're currently not doing that effectively. The media itself needs to be held accountable, of course, but if a politician of whichever stripe—Liberal, Labor, Nationals, Greens, independent—tells a lie, or tells an untruth, or misspeaks or says something that's not right, they should be called out for it. For sure, politicians can say the wrong things accidentally; the wrong word comes out under pressure: they might say 'yes', when they were meant to say 'no'. Sentences are diverted halfway through a media conference, changing the complete meaning of that sentence—politicians do receive a great deal of training in media management and public speaking, but we're all human and everyone makes mistakes. But the reason Taylor has avoided much of the pressure so far—and this issue is far from finished—is because the media haven't run hard enough on the issue. The reason why Joyce escaped scrutiny over his many issues in the past is also because the media didn't hold him to account. For Scott Morrison, it's the same reason: he avoids much scrutiny because the media doesn't hold him to account either. The other important factor is the current formation of the 'right' is not playing by the established rules of politics, and it shows just how fragile the system is: if politicians stop playing by the rules, the system falls apart. It used to be the case that if a minister engaged in wrong-doing, they would need to resign, and this always needs to be the consequence if the public is to have trust in the political system. But the system doesn't work anymore: it has always been a system based on everybody's good will and the examples of Boris Johnson, Scott Morrison and Donald Trump in their respective countries—people lacking in good will—have shown these political systems are actually very fragile.

EJ: According to a survey produced by the Social Research Institute, trust in politics has diminished severely in recent years. Only 41 per cent of citizens are satisfied with the workings of democracy in Australia and that number is down from 86 per cent in a similar survey produced in 2007. And that figure has especially fallen sharply since 2013, when it was at 72 per cent: that's a dramatic decrease in the levels of trust politics in Australia. Without casting too many aspersions, that severe downfall of trust in the political system since 2013 seems to coincide with the six years of the Liberal government, and there seems to be a relationship between these two factors.

DL: It's probably cumulative across different governments. There was the needless instability of the prime ministership of Kevin Rudd and then of Julia Gillard, where both leaders were undermined continually by the media, but particular industries such as mining, and by the Labor Party itself. I'm not suggesting that before this time was a golden age of politics in which there wasn't undermining and sniping, but something happened around 2007, and it's wise to consider all of the factors.

EJ: There's a wide range of factors involved in the decrease of public trust in Australia democracy. There's a distrust of the role of the media and its inability to put a check on political power. There's also a greater role in the use of social media over that time. There's the personalities that have been involved in politics: we could look at someone like Kevin Rudd, who didn't have any factional support within the Labor Party—that's not his fault—but not having that factional support within his own party gave rise to instability and that led to his downfall, among other factors. And then, there's Tony Abbott: his influence in the downfall of public trust in Australian politics can never be underestimated.

DL: There was the global financial crisis at that time, there were challenges in most economies around world. Today, we're seeing protests and instability all around the world: Chile has had riots; instability in Lebanon, Syria, Bolivia. And then there's Brexit. In ten years time, it will be interesting to look back and assess this period with more distance and assess all the factors.

Definitely, the global financial crisis had much to do with it: in 2008, Australia pulled through the GFC virtually unscathed. But the rest of the world didn't and that's probably the root of change and upheaval in other parts of the world.

EJ: There has been some discussion about how trust in politics can be improved: enacting 'truth in politics' legislation, similar to 'truth in advertising', although truth-in-advertising is more of a code of conduct process regulated by the industry itself, which means that it's close to being useless, so it's not quite clear how 'truth in politics' could operate. And, certainly, a government that is the main beneficiary of these low levels of public trust in the political system is not going to want to change the existing system in a hurry. Another area of improvement is funding and donations reform: the public is cynical about the large donations coming in from banking, mining and energy resource companies. But looking out over the political horizon, political reform is nowhere on the agenda, and it's very unlikely to happen in the short-term future.

*

Where the Labor Party went wrong at the 2019 election

EJ: In May 2019, Labor lost an election they were largely expected to win and, after a six-month analysis managed by Jay Wetherall and Craig Emerson, they've released a 92-page report outlining where they went wrong, and what they can do to improve their chances at the next federal election, due at some point before 2022. These types of reviews are rarely made public, but this review is quite a comprehensive document: it looks at policy issues, candidate selection, digital campaign techniques, grassroots involvement of the rank-and-file membership, and election day tactics. But the biggest factors they've nominated are: a weak campaign strategy; the inability to adapt to changing political circumstances; and an unpopular leader. These types of reviews are especially difficult for political parties—the Liberal Party went through a similar process when they lost their version of the 'unloseable' election in 1993 but they managed to get themselves together for a landslide victory in 1996. Is there enough in this review for the Labor Party to lead themselves back into office at the next election or do they need to look for something different?

DL: The Labor Party ran a decent campaign: it wasn't a great campaign—and I'm on record as saying that previously—but it wasn't a bad campaign and, in fact, it was a better campaign than the Liberal Party, in the sense that there weren't as many gaffes. There wasn't any Labor figure saying anything horribly embarrassing, but there were four or five Liberal Party MPs who did and, to be fair, were called out for it by the media. Winning elections is hard from opposition, but that's true for both sides of politics. Labor had sound policies but, of course, they could have been better. In some ways, their asylum seeker policy seems more to be pandering to voters they're never likely to sway, rather than implementing sensible, solvable and usable outcomes. During the campaign, Labor was easily distracted on technical details, such as their franking credits policy, and we pointed this out at the time. It was a distraction that was not going to win them any points and people didn't understand what the policy was. Ultimately, it was a policy the Liberal Party could easily exploit and then direct it towards every older person, whether they were in possession of shares that could earn them a franking credit or not. For many people, Labor's policy was seen as an attack on their grandparents, or on their own parents, and the cost of the policy at present is not such large a amount of money, in terms of the overall Budget, and especially in consideration of so many areas they could have attacked the government on.

EJ: The current franking credits refund is an unfair policy: it is a system which costs a great deal of money and also cost Labor a great deal of political skin too. But to put the cost of the system into context, it's a Budget item of around $5 billion per year—that's a massive amount of money—but that's less than 1 per cent of overall government spending of around $500 billion per year. There is the issue of adaptability within a political campaign, and being able to manage an issue that seems to be developing or ongoing. With Labor's franking credits policy: it wasn't a policy developed or introduced just a few weeks before the election campaign commenced—it was a policy Labor took to the 2016 election as well, so there was definitely enough time to look at the ongoing political ramifications. There's always the benefit of hindsight, but whether it's a fair or unfair policy is irrelevant: it was a policy that caused Shorten and the Labor Party significant political damage. The Labor Party did run a good, solid campaign, but a good campaign is a campaign that wins the election, and Labor didn't win the election. There are many other campaign factors that went on beneath the surface: the digital campaigns on Facebook, Twitter, Instagram. These are the new frontiers still being developed for political purposes, and in this campaign, there was a role reversal: Labor performed very well in the digital field in the 2016 election but, this time around, the Liberal Party outperformed, and that's one key area where Labor was left far behind.

DL: Looking at the results of the 2019 election: how the results were skewed in the previous US election through social media and deliberate manipulation of voting, and how the results were skewed in Britain in the 2016 Brexit referendum, we'd have to consider whether there was interference of the voting through Facebook, Twitter and Instagram. It's a question of whether Australia is a large enough country for outfits such as like Cambridge Analytica to be interested in, or for someone like Russian President Vladimir Putin. Steve Bannon was in Australia before the election, visiting a range of right-wing think-tanks, which suggests there might have been some questionable behaviour with targeted online advertising, internet bots and trolling.

EJ: Players such as Steve Bannon are guns for hire, so if there's a gig for them in Australia, or New Zealand, or anywhere else in the world, and if there's enough money for them to act as an advisor, or to share knowledge about how to implement a fake news campaign or propaganda strategy, they certainly will be there.

DL: It's probably not worthwhile for the Labor Party to chase down this issue of interference through social media because, essentially, it's too difficult to prove, and it doesn't actually get to the main election loss issues. That issue of the unpopularity of Shorten—an issue which featured very heavily in the first draft of the review report, but they then wound it back—probably gets back to Shorten's involvement in the political execution of two prime ministers—Kevin Rudd and Julia Gillard. Shorten wasn't the only player involved at that time, but it was his factional movements in the end that brought both of those prime ministers down. And the electorate still had that issue in their mind, or at least they were reminded of that history constantly by the media. It's often said that the electorate has a short memory but, for some matters, they have very long memories, and that was a part of the thinking that got into people's head, that the electorate couldn't trust Bill Shorten.

EJ: There's a wide range of overt and subconscious factors that come into play. The mainstream media did keep reminding the electorate for most of the past five-and-a-half years, that Shorten is unpopular, and that's something reflected in opinion polls. But conversely, if Shorten was consistently framed as 'unpopular' by the media and by opinion pollsters, the leadership within the Labor Party should have attempted to alleviate this issue—it's hard to know what they could have actually done; whether it was a matter of growing rock-star sideburns onto Shorten's face; providing him with a rock-star sunglasses appearance, or better fitting suits. Former Liberal Party leader John Howard had quite a large public image problem in the early 1990s but he fixed up his teeth, he did the makeover to make himself more electable: it seems superficial but that's what politicians do. The Labor Party did have an issue with Shorten's electability—whether this is fair or unfair is not the issue—but they knew about it, and for some time, but failed to address it. How unpopular was Shorten as Labor leader? In the lead up to the last federal election, his disapproval rating was 51 per cent but Morrison's was 45 per cent, and that's not too far behind. But no one in the mainstream media ever asked: 'why is Scott Morrison so unpopular?; it was always a question only asked of Shorten. It was definitely an issue that was egged-on by the media. And perhaps the Labor Party assumed it was an issue they could skim over because they had been riding high in the two-party preferred polls for three years, and these were the polls that mattered. And perhaps they reminded themselves of Tony Abbott, who was also an unpopular leader in opposition, but still managed to win the 2013 election with a landslide victory.

DL: Labor's quest for attaining government always seems to work best with inspiring, charismatic and unconventional leaders: Gough Whitlam, Paul Keating, Bob Hawke and Kevin Rudd—who had a strange kind of charisma: he didn't have that 'fill-the-room' charisma of a leader such as Whitlam or Keating, but he could certainly draw a crowd to him. Julia Gillard also had a special presence about her. Other Labor leaders who didn't quite make it: Kim Beazley, intelligent and capable, well-liked by his peers and colleagues but couldn't grasp the imagination of the public. Simon Crean: one of the unsung Labor heroes because he reformed the party during his time as Opposition leader between 2001–2003, a process which probably cost him a chance of running for prime minister. But, to be sure, he was a numbers man, and not a very exciting person, compared to how Paul Keating could electrify a room or work his way through media interviews with journalists, particularly once he veered into a topic he really wanted to talk about. Bob Hawke almost had a 100 per cent commitment from the half of the electorate people who liked him but, conversely, totally hated by the other side of politics. I've held off criticising current Labor leader Anthony Albanese because he hasn't done anything terribly wrong so far: he has disappointed a lot of followers who expected more of the 'fighting Tories' approach to leadership but he has taken over, essentially, a broken party, and Labor insiders keep saying he's playing the long game. The pressures of leadership can change people.

EJ: The review document does offer a blueprint for what the Labor Party needs to do if it wants to have a better chance of winning the next election. Political parties that lose an election, especially one they were strongly expecting to win, have to develop winning formulas. But it does need to be pointed out that most long-term governments that have managed to pull off surprise election victories—such as the Liberal government in 2019—that particular term of government ends up being quite poor, and the party usually loses office at the next election. To support this theory, there are three elections from the past thirty years that we can look at: the 1993 federal election, which Labor won against the odds—they were thrashed at the subsequent election in 1996; the Conservatives in the 1992 British election had a similar result—a long-term government winning against the odds, but losing in a landslide to Tony Blair's Labour Party in 1997. At the state level in Australia, the West Australian Labor Party had a surprise election victory in 1989 but they were soundly defeated by the Liberal Party in 1993—these are just three examples. In 1993, the Liberal Party did lose their version of the 'unloseable' election—the party went through much turmoil after that: John Hewson resigned from the leadership in 1994; Alexander Downer became Liberal leader for eighteen months, resigning to make way for John Howard, who became the leader in 1995 and the led the party back into office in 1996. There could be similarities here for Anthony Albanese—just because a political event happened in the past, it doesn't mean it will repeat itself in the future—but history is against long-term governments that achieve the surprise victory, and it usually ends up being their last term in office.

DL: The historian in me looks at events such as the 1961 election, which Labor should have won during a severe credit squeeze and the Liberals managed to scrape back in. We could also look at the 1954 and 1969 elections, both lost by Labor, but for a wide range of factors and luck played a part in the Liberals winning those elections. I don't think we'll ever have twenty years of the one government again, such as twenty-three years of continuous conservative government between 1949–1972.

EJ: There was a large schism between overall expectations and the final result in the 2019 election and it's easy for the Labor Party to look towards the future and wonder: 'how is this going to change?' There was an expectation after the 2004 election that John Howard was going to remain in government until he was eighty-five and beyond. That didn't happen. He lost the next election to Kevin Rudd. There's always a perception that issues are not playing out very well for a political party and it's sometimes difficult to see how events can change. There is much pressure currently on Anthony Albanese, and it's mainly coming from the left of the Labor Party. Statistically in the opinion polls—and there's not so much that can be read into the opinion polls because of their disastrous inaccuracy during the 2019 election, but also the fact there haven't been many that have appeared recently—Albanese is not performing poorly. The Labor Party and the Liberal–National Party are currently locked on 50:50 in the two-party preferred voting pattern, and it has to be pointed out it's still 2019: the next election isn't due until 2022, so there's still a long way to go.

DL: We might be looking at an early election towards the end of 2020, if not before, and it may be forced upon by independent MPs. Scott Morrison only has a one-seat majority in Parliament, and there's a multitude of issues that could force by-elections, such as the Chinese influence on Gladys Liu in the Liberal-held seat of Chisholm. It only takes one by-election, and a by-election loss for the government and, suddenly, everything has changed. And this change could come on very quickly.

*

Climate change and the political fallout from massive bushfires

EJ: Climate change didn't end up being the greatest moral challenge of our time, as former Prime Minister Kevin Rudd claimed in 2007, but it has become the greatest political challenge of our time. Globally, climate change issues have divided along political lines: conservatives either deny human-induced climate change is occurring and want business to continue as usual, in more ways than one, or think there's not much that can be done to mitigate climate change, so why bother. The progressive side of politics wants immediate action and a quick transition into renewable energy and more sustainable environments, based on the overwhelming scientific knowledge in its favour. The only area where the science might be wrong is that severe climate change might be happening sooner than originally expected: we've witnessed unseasonal fires in California and eastern Australia, and there have been many severe bushfires in the north coast region of New South Wales. The NSW Government has made large Budget cuts to fire services in New South Wales, and nationally, Scott Morrison has refused to meet with former fire chiefs for seven months—they wanted to discuss their concerns about extreme fire conditions, and Morrison refused to meet them because their concerns related to climate change issues. It really is time for conservative governments in Australia to stop playing politics with climate change issues, and start taking extreme weather events seriously.

DL: These are the worst bushfires Australia has had for a very long time. I remember the 1994 bushfires and it was like Dante's *Inferno*. I was driving out of Sydney for a family event and couldn't get out of the city: every road going out of the city was blocked and cut off. Of course, that was a highly minimal problem compared to the people who were losing houses and the people who died, but trying to find alternate routes to get through to the Hunter Valley—the road to Lithgow was closed off, going down through Wollongong and back up—it was impossible and there was just no way out of Sydney. These fires look like they could be worse than those in 1994 but there were those claiming climate change has nothing to do with it: they point to the 1925 and 1954 fires, or other incidents to support their claims, but bushfires are happening more frequently in Australia, and occurring within a larger window of time. Bushfire season used to be in January, the hottest part of the year in Australia, and then it stretched slowly into December: now, it's only the beginning of November and we've already passed the point of 'catastrophic'.

EJ: We've also seen bushfires in south-east Queensland in September, in addition to these bushfires in November. In these areas, bushfires are occurring outside the normal peak bushfire periods: bushfires are not meant to occur in early September and they're not meant to occur in early November. And it's not even summer yet.

DL: And all we're getting from those in power are cuts of $78 million in the New South Wales Government Budget to fire services, and in the context of overall Budgets, these are small amounts of money—it's 1 per cent of the franking credits refunds we discussed earlier. NSW Premier Gladys Berejiklian's "honestly, not today" response and wanting to avoid being 'political' when a journalist asked about the link between climate change and bushfires shows a lack of competence. There are Members of Parliament still denying the climate change is happening and still denying anthropogenic influences, not just outliers such as One Nation's Malcolm Roberts, who has form on this, but there's a Liberal Party backbencher, Gerard Rennick, claiming the Bureau of Meteorology is a part of a huge international conspiracy and is falsifying data to "perpetuate global warming hysteria".

EJ: It's always time to be a political and Liberal and National leaders have been quick to say: 'today's not the day to talk about climate change and politicise the bushfires'. But it's clearly an attempt to close down debate, avoid political responsibility and it's these leaders who have actually been politicising the bushfires themselves. The Deputy Prime Minister, Michael McCormack accused those making the link with climate change as "raving lunatics and pure, enlightened and woke capital city greenies". If that's not politicising the bushfires, I'm not sure what is. There's also the New South Wales National Party leader, John Barilaro: he has blamed Greens' policies for these bushfires and called them "a bloody disgrace". And these conservatives have also gone for that old cliché of attacking their opponents as chardonnay-drinking-latte-sipping-inner-city types. When exactly is the time to discuss the link between bushfires and climate change policies? This political closing down of debate is a similar process engaged by the National Rifle Association in the United States: whenever there's a major shooting or a tragic event over there, the NRA sends out a box of 'thoughts and prayers' to the victims' families and say 'now is not the time to discuss this issue', and the issue of gun control never ends up being discussed again. And that's the Liberal and National political strategy, whether it's at the state level or federal: they are quick to dismiss any relationship between climate change and bushfires, they simply say: 'well, we don't want to talk about this, today's not the day'. When will they find the time to talk about climate change issues, and when will they find the time to talk about the relationship between climate change and bushfires? They have been in office for a long time, and they've never managed to find the time to talk about climate change issues before: when will that time arrive?

DL: The Liberals and the Nationals are desperate: they know they are in the wrong. People have already died in these bushfires and I'm sure these political leaders do care about this. But discussions about climate change have to be held now, as well as action to reduce the effects of climate change. When Michael McCormack claimed climate change was really just an issue for inner-city Greens, that's been disputed by one of the councils in his own electorate of Riverina, with the Wagga Wagga City Council recently declaring a climate change emergency. I haven't specifically checked the map, but I'm very certain Wagga Wagga is nowhere near those inner-city suburbs of Saint Kilda, Newtown or Paddington: it's probably closer to a six or seven-hour drive away. In Barnaby Joyce's electorate of New England, the Glen Innes council has also declared a climate change emergency.

EJ: While the National Party MPs are ready to humiliate those people that may think differently to them and live far away, and when they've run out of ideas, they're also quick to attack people in their own regions: they've started going for the personal attacks as well. The Mayor of Glen Innes, a small regional town on the Northern Tablelands, is Carol Sparks. She has been a volunteer for the NSW Rural Fire Service for twenty years; she's a nurse and a midwife; she's a great community person, and she also lost her home in the fires. But that didn't seem to be enough for the conservative forces in the Australia: as soon as they discovered Sparks is also a Greens councillor on the Severn Shire Council of Glen Innes, they started to attack her for publicly making that link between bushfires and climate change as well. It's a case in point for the conservatives: they'll want to hear the stories about bushfire tragedies and exploit these for media opportunities, but as soon as a victim identifies as a Greens councillor, or starts making that link between climate change and bushfires, they'll do their best to tear them down.

DL: And this idea pushed forward that these bushfires were caused by Greens policies—it's laughable. There has never been a Greens government in Australia, certainly not in an outright position of government.

EJ: There was a coalition between the Greens and the Labor Party and the Liberals at various times in Tasmania, and that was some time ago—there is a different political system in that state, the Hare–Clark system of proportional representation. Federally, there was a formal coalition between Labor and the Australian Greens between 2010–2013, but it's difficult to see that as a real coalition, as the Greens only had one Member of Parliament in the House of Representatives. But you're absolutely right: I can't remember the Greens producing a prime minister; or the state Greens or territory Greens producing a premier or a chief minister. It's clearly on the record and it has just never happened, so for people such Barnaby Joyce, McCormack or Barilaro to claim the severe bushfires are a result of Greens policies is completely incorrect, and that's what the real bloody disgrace is.

DL: There have been several local councils controlled by Greens, or with headed by a Greens mayor, such as Carol Sparks in Glen Innes. But thanks to the policies of the federal, local and state governments, local councils have a much reduced responsibility in terms of fire management—even if a rural seat somewhere in Victoria tried to implement Greens' policies, most of them would have been overridden by state and federal policies. So we are seeing this cognitive dissonance with MPs in federal and state governments wanting the electorate to believe something different to what is actually happening on the ground. And, of course, apportioning blame to others is never going to be in short supply.

EJ: In 2015, when Malcolm Turnbull became prime minister, he said his government would be agile, nimble and flexible to change. The problem with a government led by Scott Morrison is that he is inflexible, he is not for changing: he's not agile or nimble, especially when it comes to climate change issues. Even when there are severe bushfires and there are severe climate change issues that need to be addressed, it's an area that he just does not want to venture into. And it's not just Morrison, it's across the broad range of ministers within the Coalition. There's Angus Taylor: just doesn't want to talk about climate change. There's David Littleproud, Minister for Water Resources: just doesn't want to talk climate change either. Many experts in the field of climate change and bushfire management are fobbed off by this government, and they're not being listened to. Climate change at the present time doesn't seem to be moral issue and, based on what we've seen recently from this government, it's not an economic issue for them and it's certainly not an environmental issue. It's seen a political issue for this government that needs to be managed, stakeholders and vested interests need to be satisfied, and then apportioning blame to other people and not taking any responsibilities themselves. Australia is falling way behind the rest of the world on climate change management; greenhouse emissions are rising dramatically, and it's very difficult to see how any of this will change under a conservative government.

DL: There is much evidence to support the idea that Taylor and Littleproud don't want to discuss climate change issues because it might lead to uneasy questions about their multitude of business dealings. This is a government that doesn't really understand the difference between business dealings, private dealings and government dealings. They employ consultants or engage private businesses and then cover up the dealings by claiming the excuse of 'commercial-in-confidence'. Open democracies can't function properly with these types of arrangements: all government tenders need to be public and fees paid by government need to be reported. There might be some areas where a tenderer may be disadvantaged by releasing costs to the public—these situations would be very limited—or they don't want details released about a particular product they're using within their government work, because the patent hasn't come through yet. But it seems that in this case, the government is trying to avoid all scrutiny because it's not a very long path to go through, from bushfires, onto missing and non-existent water deals worth millions, and through to money funnelled through to the Cayman Islands. These are situations that should lead to resignations, possibly criminal charges, and possibly jail.

*

Music in this episode
I'm Not Like Everybody Else, Jimmy and The Boys
A Whisper, Coldplay

The burning world of climate change denial

18 November 2019

Eddy Jokovich

In 1969, a Union Oil drilling platform ten kilometres off the coast of Santa Barbara, a small tourist town in California, had a drilling hole blow-out and, over the next ten days, eight million litres of oil sludge spilled into the ocean, most of it landing on nearby beaches.

At the time, it was the largest environmental oil spillage in the United States, only surpassed by subsequent Exxon Valdez spills in 1989 and Deepwater Horizon in 2010. The spillage had a significant impact on the local wildlife, killing over 3,500 seabirds and other marine animals, and creating ongoing hazards for the citizens of Santa Barbara over the next decade.

Newly-elected US President, Richard Nixon, not noted for any environmental credentials, and barely mentioning the environment during the 1968 election campaign, saw enough of a political opportunity in the spillage to claim: "preserving the beauty and the natural resources are so important to any kind of society that we want for the future. I don't think we have paid enough attention to this. We are going to do a better job than we have done in the past."

Nixon used the Santa Barbara oil spill as leverage to push forward an agenda to reduce pollution, an agenda which gave rise to the US Environmental Protection Agency.

While it's stretching a long bow to suggest Nixon was an environmentalist—he was, after all, simply following the electorate's heightened concern about quality of air and water pollution—he did show right-of-centre politics can engage with environmental concerns, even if Republican Presidents since Nixon—Ronald Reagan, George H. Bush, George W. Bush and now Donald Trump—have repealed much environmental legislation since that time, as well as deregulating the EPA.

Former British Prime Minister, Margaret Thatcher, had a brief dalliance with environmental issues in the late 1980s, when she outlined the effects of global warming, acid rain and pollution, to the Royal Society in 1988 and, in a 1989 address to the United Nations, stressed the importance of international legislation to manage and limit the world's greenhouse emissions.

Although Thatcher never acted upon any environmental legislation in the UK, and her brief appearance in the field of environmental politics had more to do with the rising Green vote across Europe—14.9 per cent of the vote in the 1989 UK European Parliament election—it was, nevertheless, another instance of conservative political leaders engaging with environmental issues, even if they were only looking for political opportunities or mouthing platitudes without an intention of addressing the serious climate issues confronting them. But at least Thatcher made an attempt.

Australia's Prime Minister, Scott Morrison, doesn't even offer the semblance of concerning himself with climate change. He is, after all, the one who brought in a large piece of coal into the House of Representatives, a symbol of his climate change denialism and emphasising the point that he is firmly in the ledger of the minerals and petroleum industries, the largest donors to the federal Liberal Party. And to support these industries, Morrison will stretch and fabricate every piece of data to claim Australia is achieving all of its targeted climate goals, even if these claims are far from the truth.

In September, Morrison addressed the United Nations and attacked global critics of his government's lack of action on climate change, claiming Australia had "overachieved on its 2020 Kyoto protocol targets" and would reduce "greenhouse gas emissions to 28 per cent below 2005 levels by 2030". These are clearly fabrications, as every key indicator shows Australia will not reach its 2020 Kyoto targets, and is unlikely to reach the 2030 Paris Agreement, unless significant policy changes are made.

This LNP government is not for turning

Climate change is anathema to the contemporary Liberal–National Party, and Morrison is even prepared to junk the environment at the expense of burning communities. While it is true that in the case of emergencies such as bushfires and floods, there is not much for a prime minister to do in practical terms—putting out the fires once they've commenced is a task for state and territory authorities—there is still a great deal the Australian Government can do in implementing long-term solutions to minimise the chance of bushfires occurring and, at the least, implement shorter-term solutions to manage crises when they do occur.

One person who did want to discuss these shorter-term issues is Greg Mullens. Not many people might have heard about Mullens, but he is a highly respected expert in bushfire and natural disaster management strategies and was the Commissioner for Fire & Rescue NSW. He also has a strong international reputation, working with fire regulatory bodies in the US, Canada, France and Spain, and representing Australia on the United Nations International Search & Rescue Advisory Committee.

In April this year, Mullens delivered a letter to the Prime Minister on behalf of twenty-three former fire emergency leaders and the Climate Action Group, requesting a meeting to discuss fire management strategies, such as the purchase of a fleet of larger water-bombers and introducing specialised fire retardants, in the belief—proven to be correct—there was a great danger of imminent and severe fires, and a national approach was required to deal with this danger, if and when it occurred.

For the past seven months since the delivery of that letter, Morrison has refused to meet with Mullens, or any other former fire emergency leaders, and government ministers such as Jason Falinski have claimed the Prime Minister is a "very busy man" and too busy to set aside the time to discuss climate change and fire management issues.

Obviously, the May election would have taken up a great deal of the Prime Minister's time, formulating his new ministry and

creating a pathway towards the next federal election due in 2022. However, these are some of the other events that have clearly taken up Morrison's time:
1. In October, he was the thirteenth man for the Prime Minister's XI in an all-day cricket game against Sri Lanka in Canberra.
2. Early in the same month, Morrison was in Fiji running water for the Australian rugby league team, as well as placing the kicking tee into the ground for one of the team members.
3. A few weeks ago, Morrison attended the Constellation Cup netball game between Australia and New Zealand in Perth, taking selfies and chatting with the public during half-time.
4. In September, Morrison attended the AFL Grand Final, another all-day event.

Some of these events, of course, we'd expect the Prime Minister to attend, but others are overt media opportunities and personal sports fetishes. Prime ministers do devote all of their time to matters of state and some leeway has to be provided, but if there's enough time for a seven-hour game of cricket, or being the water boy in a meaningless two-hour game of rugby in Fiji, surely there would be time to schedule a one-on-one meeting with one of the most pre-eminent members of the fire emergency community.

A prime minister needs to consult with a broad range of people and interests group to develop the best policies and the best solutions in the best interests of the Australian community. Neglecting to meet with the Climate Action Group is a serious oversight and, in the wake of these bushfires—currently burning in every Australian state and territory—this is verging on criminal negligence.

While it could be argued that whether Morrison did or didn't meet with Mullens is immaterial—any substantial outcomes from such a meeting would take many months to formulate the processes, protocols and budgets, and procurement would take up to a year from international providers—there are other decisions made by government that do have a material impact on the ground.

In New South Wales, the Liberal–National government cut the capital expenditure budget of Fire & Rescue NSW by $28 million, and the NSW Rural Fire Service by $50 million in the 2019/20 NSW Budget—a total of $78 million. This compares to the $729 million allocated to the demolition and rebuild of the Sydney Football Stadium at Moore Park, and $810 million for the revamp of the Olympic Park Stadium at Homebush in Sydney's west.

When questioned about the significant cost of rebuilding two sports stadiums in Sydney—taking into account the Olympic Park Stadium is less than twenty years old—NSW Premier Gladys Berejiklian said the state could afford the vast amounts, due to the 'better economic management of the Coalition' over the past eight years. Apparently, the coffers are so overflowing that $1.5 billion for an unwarranted and needless rebuild of two Sydney-centric sports projects can easily be found, but critical fire services need to be cut by $78 million to make ends meet.

Something doesn't quite add up here.

A vexed history

Climate change has been a vexed issue for many governments over many years, and despite the many warnings for at least the past forty years from a wide range of experts, analysts, environmentalists and business leaders, little has been achieved.

The first substantial international report of global warming appeared in 1972. The Club of Rome, formed in 1968 and comprised of former heads of state, United Nations bureaucrats, politicians, government officials, diplomats, scientists, economists and business leaders, released *The Limits To Growth*.

The main premise of this report is economic growth cannot continue indefinitely because of resource depletion over time, and it introduced '*problématique*', the understanding that the issues of environmental deterioration, poverty, endemic ill-health, urban blight and criminality needed to solved collectively, not in isolation, and urgent and quick resolutions had to be made to avoid the collapse of the global system by the year 2050.

There was also an expectation—unrealistic as it turned out—that by the year 2020, the international community would have reached global consensus in introducing a raft of mitigating measures, such as emissions reduction and carbon trading schemes, lead reduction in petrol, and elimination of toxic wastage into water supplies.

The second major report published by the Club of Rome, *The First Global Revolution*, appeared in 1991. Its main concern was that since its first report nineteen years earlier, little had been achieved politically and practically, although it recognised there was a greater awareness of global warming among political leaders in the 1980s.

Again, it forewarned that action on global warming and reducing carbon into the atmosphere was imperative and the world had a thirty-year time limit to commence meaningful action, even though it also considered that by 2020, it could be too late to halt irreversible damage to the environment and the world community.

It also pointed out the world community would need to manage the effects of this irreversible global warning and increases in catastrophic weather events such as floods, extreme temperature shifts and hazardous unseasonal fires.

In Australia, climate change and global warming has transitioned from an environmental issue; through to a 'moral' issue in 2007, according to former Prime Minister Kevin Rudd; and now, forty-seven years after the first warnings issued by the Club of Rome, it has morphed in a political issue played by conservative politicians, satisfied to reap the rewards of divisive debate and a divided community, while the rest of the country burns.

Leaders fiddle, the world burns

Ever since he became a Member of Parliament in 2007, Scott Morrison has never shown any intention in implementing climate-based solutions or any interest in global warming.

While Morrison might be the ultimate marketing man, he displays the ultimate in political cowardice. At the height of the bushfires, he virtually disappeared from the public arena for three days, finally appearing at Sydney Airport at a Friday-morning corporate event, welcoming a Qantas Dreamliner long-distance flight from London. The fires were still burning, but the media interest had dropped off, and Morrison felt it was safe to appear in public again.

Of course, the Prime Minister disappearing while the fires were raging around the country was a politically sensible act. Brand 'Morrison' is the winning brand and travelling to areas where he was likely to be abused by victims of the bushfires and asked too many uncomfortable questions about climate change, always had the potential to damage his brand.

Appearing at a Qantas airport promotion, where no one was going to ask climate change questions, or enquire about the symbolism of the amount of emissions generated by that long-distance flight—incidentally, about one tonne of CO_2 emissions per passenger—was always going to be the safe option.

At the end of this week, 1.7 million hectares have been burnt across Australia—mainly on the eastern seaboard—476 homes have been lost, and four people have died. As a comparison, the Amazon fires that spread through Brazil, Bolivia, Peru and Paraguay burnt through 900,000 hectares; and the recent fires in California burnt 100,000 hectares.

The responses from the three leaders in these regions have been equally bizarre and dismissive: US President Donald Trump's response to the California fires was to threaten cuts to federal funding and reiterate his belief that there is no link between the fires and climate change. In response to the Amazon fires, Brazilian President Jair Bolsonaro accused environmental groups of starting the fires and refused all international assistance offered from a wide range of countries.

Locally, Scott Morrison has largely retracted himself from the bushfires, aside from the obligatory sending of 'thoughts and prayers' to the victims, the common response of leaders so bereft of ideas, they have little else to offer.

Before Morrison disappeared from the public view for three days, he did ask for the debate to be taken "down a few notches" and claimed that now was not the time to talk about the links between the bushfires and climate change, or to engage in political point-scoring.

Politicising the bushfires, of course, was left to Deputy Prime Minister, Michael McCormack and National MP Barnaby Joyce, who incorrectly laid the blame for the bushfires on Greens policies and inner-city activists: Joyce humiliating himself further by claiming the two people who died near the NSW town of Glenn Innes "most likely" voted for the Greens, and he rightly received the opprobrium from most of the Australian community for even suggesting this as a factor.

Climate change is an issue that will not be disappearing any time soon. And managing the effects that result from a lack of action on climate change—unseasonal and more frequent flood and fire events—is an area that needs to be managed by government effectively.

Morrison cannot simply defer the debate about climate change by claiming 'today is not the day', or just shrugging his shoulders and saying: "I'm going to leave that debate for another day", a statement he made on a recent visit to the drought-stricken region of Quilpie in western Queensland.

The Liberal–National Party has been in office for seventeen of the past twenty-three years, and a succession of prime ministers—John Howard, Tony Abbott, Malcolm Turnbull and now, Scott Morrison—have done little to address climate change issues. Morrison should be wearing the blame of these bushfires like a crown of thorns, and hammered until he provides effective responses to the crisis and takes on responsibility.

Today *is* the day to talk about climate change.

*

Afterword

Pseudo-politics and the year in review

Eddy Jokovich

The 2019 year commenced with a lie; it ended with a lie. The conservative brand of pseudo-politics was enough to deliver an unlikely victory to the Liberal–National Party at the May election: by the end of the year, this method was overwhelmed by climate change issues and a series of intense bushfires engulfing most of Australia; issues that no amount of political marketing and media manipulation could withstand.

This is the best way to summarise the year in politics, where the Prime Minister, Scott Morrison became the Liberal Party hero scrapping his way towards an 'unwinnable election' victory but, just seven months later, was exposed as a shallow and out-of-depth leader flummoxed at the first signs of pressure and showed few skills in being able to manage a bushfire crisis that commenced in early November and continued through to the new year. The climate change crisis that many had been warning about for some time hit Australia hard, and the Prime Minister couldn't provide the answers. Morrison's public mask has never been securely in place, but by year's end, it had slipped completely and the electorate saw the real face of the Prime Minister for the first time: clueless in the face of adversity.

The breaking point of reality

The overarching theme of the year in politics has been the perpetuation of myth, misspeaking and stretching the truth, with reality reaching breaking point. In January 2019, Morrison appeared in a radio interview where he discussed the environmental credentials of his government, announced legislation protecting endangered species had been passed, and how the Liberal–National Party had been responsible for the carriage of this. Of course, no such legislation exists, nor was there any Bill presented to Parliament for debate or discussion: Morrison may have been confused, but it was purely a fabrication.

Political leaders push the boundaries wherever possible but with very little media scrutiny and the absence of any repercussions, they will continue to make up their material in the hope that no one will notice. By the end of the year, simply offering the lie wasn't enough: known facts were disputed and, in some instances, facts were doctored and manipulated.

There are two minor, but salient incidents that best epitomise the problems facing the political system in Australia, both involved the one federal minister.

In December 2019, the Minister for Energy, Angus Taylor, was exposed for claiming in his maiden speech to Parliament in 2013, the feminist author, Naomi Wolf, had "lived down the corridor" and led a faculty "war against Christmas" at the time he commenced his studies at Oxford University in 1991: she had actually left Oxford three years earlier in 1988 and by 1991, was on an international tour promoting her first publication, *The Beauty Myth*. Even when Wolf provided evidence proving she was nowhere near Oxford during 1991, Taylor doubled down, released a statement outlining Wolf's version was 'disputed' and claimed his version was the correct one.

Compared to the multitude of important issues governments need to manage, whether or not a campus event occurred almost thirty years ago is barely significant, but it goes to the heart of a greater problem within politics and public life: truth and interpretations have become highly malleable commodities and we've reached the strange combined world of Sigmund Freud and Alice's Wonderland, where meaning and truth is based on whatever we would like it to be.

If agreed facts and verified evidence are disputed by government ministers, including the Prime Minister, the only direction where politics can proceed is in a downward descent into oblivion and irrelevance. Who will then collect the pieces? Where will public debate and discourse go once the system has been broken?

It was hard to believe how Naomi Wolf could have entered the scene of Australian politics in such a manner—not too many people would have predicted it—but it wasn't Taylor's most egregious act of the year. In September, Taylor used fabricated documents to attack the Lord Mayor of Sydney, Clover Moore, where he claimed the City of Sydney Council spent $15.9 million on air travel, when in fact, it was a small fraction of this amount. Taylor leaked this information to journalists at the *Daily Telegraph*, which they duly published; he also repeating these fabricated claims in Parliament.

This matter was referred to the NSW Police by the Labor Party, after which, Scott Morrison decided to contact the NSW Police Commissioner, Mick Fuller, for 'a discussion' to determine how the investigation into Taylor's actions was proceeding—a clear interference in the course of justice, but seemingly brushed off by the government and friends in the media. These are small samples, but this is a government that misleads the public on everything, whether it be on climate change, greenhouse emissions, the economy, education and health; or even the simple matter of the amounts the City of Sydney Council is spending on air travel: no target is too small for conservatives to apply their brand of pseudo-politics.

If the public was concerned about the direction of political behaviour and the effect on the democratic process, then many of the actions of government in 2019 would be a cause for alarm: the Prime Minister lying about legislation that doesn't exist; a minister who misrepresents another person, but when faced with the facts, contends that it's the other person who has it wrong; the same minister fabricating official documents to attack political opponents; the Prime Minister interfering in a police investigation into one of his own ministers. This collective behaviour is not the practice of a functioning democracy, but these events—each of which could have brought down ministers and governments in the 1960s—barely rate a mention in 2019.

Announcements by government need to be constantly fact checked for their veracity: after two months of bushfires burning in his home state of New South Wales, Morrison claimed the offer of $6,000 to volunteer firefighters was 'the most generous assistance ever offered' but even this was a fabrication: the schemes offered by John Howard in 2001 and by Paul Keating in 1994 were substantially greater.

The $11 million offered by the government for firefighting assistance was made with great fanfare in the media—not that this is a large amount of funding—but it was actually money allocated for fire services in the previous financial year that had not yet been spent: Morrison's offers of assistance contained so many asterisks and conditions in fine print, they were virtually rendered insignificant.

Aside from the lack of generosity in a time of crisis, Morrison sought political advantage: the compensation scheme was made available only to firefighters in New South Wales—a Liberal state— while the Labor-held states of Victoria and Queensland were left out. The Liberal Party even went to the extent of delivering government funding announcements on social media, with notices about how to make financial donations to the Liberal Party.

Trumpism in Australia

The strength of the lie in politics has become more potent, but it's not an issue that appears in isolation in Australia. Unsubstantiated claims made by political leaders have become more audacious, more extreme and more outrageous, and this style of pseudo-politics has become fashionable: Donald Trump in the US; Jair Bolsonaro in Brazil; Viktor Obán in Hungary; Boris Johnson in the UK—all clown princes that provide distractions to amuse the electorate, and clear the pathway for vested interests to pilfer public assets, interfere in the political process, and consolidate their vested positions. And it's now a style that has afflicted Australia.

It's naïve to assume misrepresenting facts and information is a new phenomenon in politics or there was a mystical golden age of democracy prior to this era, but it has reached a point where demagogic leaders understand that with a pliant media, coupled with disinterested and cynical electorates, the creation of parallel worlds means conservative leaders can easily confuse their opponents, and pick and choose the information that provides them with the most electoral benefits.

If politics has just become an extension of the world of infotainment and there's a distrust of verifiable material, then politics is in a deeply parlous and precarious position, and it's difficult to see how it can be retrieved to any semblance of normality, or in a position of public benefit. But reforming the political system is a longer-term project and, if the political will to make substantial changes is there, it will happen, although there is great cynicism as to whether this will ever happen at all. In the immediate future, there are other more pressing and urgent matters that need to be addressed.

At the end of 2019, climate change continued to be a key factor in federal politics, with bushfires still burning in many states and territories around Australia, but especially in New South Wales and Victoria. The severe smoke and haze are still surrounding the city of Sydney—as they have been for several months—and the air quality on some days reached a level twelve times above 'hazardous'. With the more obvious effects of climate change evident to the public in Australia's largest city, it would have been safe to assume a national government would be more inclined to at least give the appearance of starting to take these issues seriously. If anything, and aside from a few muffled voices on the periphery, the current bushfire crisis has pushed conservatives back into their corners, and any meaningful action from the federal government to address climate change seems to be years away.

En vacances

In Morrison's case, he left Australia for a family vacation on 14 December, eleven days before Christmas; bushfires were still ravaging many parts of the country, and it was just a few days before the New South Wales government declared a state of emergency. Most people would not begrudge a politician taking family holidays, but the position of the prime minister isn't a normal day job. His trip was shrouded in secrecy, the announcement that Deputy Prime Minister Michael McCormack would be Acting Prime Minister was made in an unusually low-key manner; the Prime Minister's Office denied the Prime Minister was overseas, and the clandestine nature of his holiday suggested Morrison knew that being away during a time of crisis was politically the wrong act to follow. In addition to this, Morrison directed a media edict to ban reporting on his departure—acceded to by most journalists.

As it turned out, Morrison *was* actually in Hawaii—again, this was denied by his office—and after being found out by some in the media, he announced curtailing his holiday as soon as 'practically possible,' eventually cutting short his inopportune holiday by only one day.

On his return to Australia just before Christmas Day, Morrison's political antenna had yet again deserted him: a continuing absence from the bushfires; publicity opportunities with the Australian cricket team, followed by a game of 'tip'n'run' backyard cricket; and finally, an exclusive evening meal at Kirribilli House, looking onto the contentious New Year's Eve fireworks display in Sydney Harbour. Even the deluded Romanian dictator, Nicolae Ceaușescu, could read the room in 1989 when he tried to make his final speech at the Palace Square, while the riots and revolution were taking place on the streets of Bucharest and Timișoara. Morrison, for the first time in his political career, faced serious pressure, floundered and was exposed as an insubstantial prime minister.

No amount of media management, spin, and manipulation could save Morrison from the well-deserved public anger and vitriol: he had seriously damaged his political credibility and one key issue for the upcoming political year is to see how he can rebuild his status, if at all.

The hardest job in politics

Early in the year, even the most pessimistic Labor shadow minister must have been thinking about the return to government after six long years sitting on the Opposition benches, the most thankless of all positions in politics. The Minister for Home Affairs, Peter Dutton, joked many times in the media and in Parliament how Bill Shorten was "already measuring up the curtains" in the prime minister's office—it was never explained how Shorten would even access the office in the first place—but it was political bonhomie: even Dutton knew the writing was on the wall for the Liberal–National Party, having already cleaned out his office, shredding ministerial documents and selling his Canberra apartment.

But, Labor lost the election. That six-year wait has been extended by at least another three years and, as is usually the case when a highly anticipated victory fails to materialise, the Labor Party spent the time after their election loss shell-shocked, searching for answers to this loss, attempting to learn from the lessons of defeat and work towards a formula that will facilitate a return to government. The new Labor leader, Anthony Albanese, has yet to fully capture the public imagination—perhaps at this stage of the electoral cycle, this issue doesn't matter too much—but the expectations of Albanese from certain parts of the community were high and, so far, he hasn't lived up to their expectations. These are early days and the next federal election is still two years away but time in politics can move at a rapid pace, and many factors will change during this period.

It was telling, however, that during a climate change rally held in Sydney in early November—during the third week of the current wave of bushfires—the biggest hostilities from the crowd of 10,000 people were reserved for Albanese, and the Labor Party. The audience was highly frustrated about inaction on climate change and, with smoke haze producing an eerie red light more in keeping with end-of-world science fiction and many people wearing facemasks, the rally had the feeling of an impending apocalypse. Ironically, this crowd wanted the Labor Party to feel the effects of the apocalypse more than the Liberal–National Party, which has done more to destroy the environment than any other party in Australia's history.

Labor hasn't been in office since 2013 and won't be able to enact any policy change until at least 2022. To see a spectacle where the political party that at least turns up to every election with tangible and viable climate change policies, and has done so since at least 2001, suggests there is some confusion among the left about where the real culprits on climate change inaction are—the Liberal–National Party—or it may be a case where any political leader is fair game, irrespective of which side of the political fence they sit on.

But this also represents greater electoral issues for the Labor Party. The white-hot anger currently directed by the public towards Morrison on inept climate change management will dissipate—surely his political antenna can't continue to malfunction so badly for such a long period of time—and Labor still has to bridge that gap between effective climate change and bushfire management policies, and its relationships with mining and energy unions and workers in the mining states of Queensland and Western Australia: Labor only holds eleven of forty-six seats in those two states, and they will need to make substantial inroads into these areas if they are to win the next federal election.

2020

Australia is facing many issues that need resolution and it's doubtful whether the Liberal–National government has the ability—or the inclination—to resolve any of them. And, with a protective media to support them and continue the downward spiral of civil politics, there's little appetite for change to come from within the existing political system.

The most obvious and most urgent issues are climate change policy and bushfire management: the government has been absent in both of these areas and is determined to continue being absent. It is difficult to imagine a more pressing issue in Australia—one that is already costing the economy; resulted in many deaths; displaced thousands of people and destroyed many communities and habitat—but it's an area the Liberal–National Party is still keen to divide the electorate along political lines, seek political opportunities, and use its relationships with the media to downplay the need for climate change action. Most of Australia is burning: if the conservative side of politics remains stubbornly attached to their ideological pursuits in such a crisis, like limpets glued to a seaside boulder, then it's patently obvious they will never act, either on effective bushfire management policy, or climate change.

The symbiotic relationship between Rupert Murdoch's News Corp, the Institute of Public Affairs, and the Liberal Party, remains as a malignant cancer on Australia's political horizon. Of course, the removal of the Murdoch influence in Australian politics is a generation away, and especially unlikely during a time when the main beneficiaries of this influence—the Liberal–National Party—remain in government.

The political system itself may not be broken, but the people that make up Parliament are—all sides of politics attempt to deliver benefits for their associates and vested interests, rather than the public interest, but there are limits to how far this support reaches.

The electorate wants a better system of politics—whether that be through a federal corruption commission, donations reforms, freedom of information, media freedom, openness about the relationships between political parties and their respective outside interests, and the greatest aspect of all that has been sorely missing for some time: accountability.

The political party that manages to convince the electorate that these are the constructive reforms it will genuinely implement is more likely to be the party forming government at the next election. Until then, 2020 is going to be a year of business as usual, and opportunities to instill public trust in the political system will continue to be lost.

*

Looking at the future from the past

David Lewis

As we put the finishing touches to this book, Australia is engulfed by fire. Unprecedented blazes are destroying property, communities and lives. At this time, we don't know the actual extent, but we know the results are devastating. As has already been mentioned, this federal government, under the prime ministership of Scott Morrison, is perceived to have failed the nation. The criticism of the Prime Minister has not been confined to what is known as 'the left': the Australian Defence Association has been highly critical; NSW senior minister Andrew Constance has been critical; ex-Sky News presenter David Speers has been critical, and there have even been calls for the Morrison to leave public life altogether. Even the feeble Gladys Berejiklian, Premier of New South Wales, has acquitted herself adequately. Premiers Annastacia Palaszczuk in Queensland and Daniel Andrews in Victoria have also provided appropriate leadership. In contrast, many people are asking: what is the Prime Minister doing? He is starting to make the right noises now, but it is seen as too little, too late. He has lost legitimacy, authority and respect.

This is where things get interesting. As a historian,[1] I have taken a longer view. It is safe to say that Morrison is one of the least effective

---

1   I have worked as a professional historian since 1996. I have an honours degree in History, with a major in Political Science from the University of NSW.

prime ministers we have had. It is quite possible he is the worst, but such judgments can be premature. Since Federation in 1901, we have had mostly good prime ministers, even allowing for political differences. It has not been a glowing parade of great men (and one woman), though Australia 'has punched above its weight' on occasion.

A prime minister can be bad for several reasons: personal failings; party politics beyond their control; national or international events beyond their control. Events overtook the hapless James Scullin, prime minister in the late 1920s. In many ways, Scullin inherited the perfect storm of catastrophe. He won the 1929 federal election just as the Great Depression started. With a tanking economy and—not for the first time—a Labor Party split. But unlike the 1917 Labor split, the party shattered into three parts. His Treasurer, J.A. Lyons moved to the right, and ended up becoming prime minister in 1931 for the United Australia Party. A group led by Eddie Ward split the left flank of the Labor Party. Scullin, who was admired by many, lost the 1931 election badly, but became a Labor elder statesman.

In the Labor split of 1917, the long shadow of William Morris Hughes loomed large. Hughes, the 'little digger', is the one whose belligerence appalled the Paris Peace Conference contingent in 1919, after the end of World War I. Hughes returned from this conference as a conquering hero, and held the office for another few years. His stance on conscription was to alienate Catholic voters and much of the working class. He was adopted by the Right, and made leader of the Nationalist Party, an uneasy alliance of the old Liberal Party and ex-Labor MPs. However, his increasingly erratic behaviour, lack of professionalism and deceptive and untrustworthy behaviour built a team of those opposed to him. His Treasurer, Stanley Melbourne Bruce was irritated and a coup took place. Famously, Hughes was able to exact his revenge, using a vote to force Bruce to an election in which Bruce lost his own seat—the first, but not the last time a sitting Australian prime minister would lose his seat. Hughes remained in Parliament until his death in 1952, having joined five different political parties and becoming the leader of four of those. To dyed-in-the-wool Labor supporters, Hughes was and always be considered 'a rat'. And, perhaps, Mark Latham is a modern equivalent.

William 'Billy' McMahon was considered a good Treasurer, but was held in contempt by at least two of his colleagues: Paul Hasluck and Don Chipp, who themselves were at odds politically, wrote that McMahon was untrustworthy, Hasluck even used the word 'contempt'—Chipp was even less flattering. McMahon spent his time undermining Harold Holt and John Gorton, and Robert Menzies, according to Chipp. As prime minister, McMahon was awkward, and ineffectual. Gough Whitlam, Labor's Leader of the Opposition, was a far more effective debater. McMahon's reputation as an economic manager faltered as inflation rose and he ridiculed Whitlam's attempt to recognise the People's Republic Of China, only to be humiliated when US President Richard Nixon and US Secretary of State, Henry Kissinger, visited China, showing McMahon to be behind the times. He lost the 1972 election, though by a smaller margin than was expected. He remained in Parliament somewhat of a laughing stock, and rumours of his personal peccadilloes were not helpful to his reputation.

I've mention these prime ministers because they were unpopular and divisive figures. Billy Hughes, like Tony Abbott, and dare I say it, Paul Keating, relished the fight. But unlike Keating, Hughes never learned when to act with dignity. Like Abbott, he never stopped swinging, and like Abbott, he lost his political ideology and focussed on the pursuit of power. Scullin was, simply, overwhelmed: he received what is known as a 'hospital pass'. The Great Depression hit hard, and Scullin, unlike Kevin Rudd and Wayne Swan in 2008, had too many conflicting ideas. The conservative wing of the Labor Party wanted to pay down the debt and cut expenditure. The radical wing wanted to default on the debt and increase services. The tensions were too much, and the party tore itself apart.

The bushfires of 2019–2020 have shown Scott Morrison to be out of his depth. Unlike the Depression, these bushfires were not unexpected, although perhaps their intensity was. Morrison believes that government shouldn't be involved in anything, except maybe law and order, and hence, he has cut taxes, maintained the franking credits scheme, and resisted moves to reform negative gearing. His belief that a market system can solve anything has failed, quite miserably. The co-ordination the federal government should have implemented was lacking, and Morrison dithered and diverted the blame to wherever else it could be diverted, even on to his own Liberal Party brethren in the New South Wales Government. He faced criticism—totally justified—for not rapidly returning from a beach holiday in Hawaii in mid-December.

There have been many corrupt federal ministers throughout Australia's political history. Ignoring members with citizenship issues like King O'Malley[2] and John Christian Watson,[3] and the extreme outlier of murderer Thomas Ley,[4] we can briefly look at Solomon Rosevear, Speaker of the House—the one who ran an SP bookies' ring from his office in Parliament House, and permitted illegal gambling in the Chamber.

More seriously, the Treasurer to the hapless Scullin, E.G. Theodore was accused of improper dealings with a mine in Queensland. While it seems he was innocent, and he was cleared of impropriety in the Federal Court, the aura of corruption never left him. Stanley Bruce felt that Theodore was a magnificent speaker and a good administrator but he lacked in character. He attracted bad luck, and according to Bruce, those people who didn't deserve good luck, attracted bad luck.

When one looks at contemporary figures such as Barnaby Joyce or Angus Taylor, you can see Bruce's point: Barnaby Joyce, as a political figure, is a soap opera, with a healthy dose of farce. He's had a variety of affairs, and allegedly harassed many women, including prominent ones: Joyce also tried to hide his new partner's pregnancy, by obtaining work for her in other ministerial offices. Just what she was meant to do was never really publicly revealed, but she claimed it was 'only' worth $130,000. The public outrage was palpable, and

---

2   Born in the United States in about 1858, though he claimed he was born in Canada.
3   Born in Chile to a German father and Irish mother in 1868, Watson's father, Johann Tanck, disappeared from the historical record when Watson was an infant. Watson identified as a British subject from New Zealand, as his mother moved there when he was two and married a man named Watson.
4   Ley remains the only federal Member of Parliament to be charged with murder. His political opponent George McDonald was the Labor candidate for the seat of Barton, where Ley was the Nationalist candidate. McDonald alleged Ley had tried to bribe McDonald, who refused. McDonald lost the election, but appealed to the Court of Disputed Returns. On his way to a meeting with NSW Premier Jack Lang, McDonald disappeared. Ley later moved to Britain, where his mistress's lover was murdered. Ley was sentenced to death, but his sentence was later commuted to imprisonments in Broadmoor. Baiba Berzin's entry on Ley in the Australian dictionary of biography is worth reading: http://adb.anu.edu.au/biography/ley-thomas-john-tom-7191

Joyce lost the leadership of the National Party. Joyce later accepted the role of 'Special Envoy for the drought assistance and recovery': constitutionally, it's unclear what this position entails, but he was sent off to 'examine the drought', and paid a total of $275,000, including four staff and an office.

The result of Joyce's work as 'Special Envoy' was a series of long text messages send from his mobile phone, which are apparently classified under 'cabinet confidence'. These types of minor corruptions pale when compared to the corruption of water. Angus Taylor, Minister for Energy, formed a company based in the Cayman Islands, which has sold non-existent water to the government for $79 million. This water malfeasance has dried up the town of Walgett, and cities such as Armidale, Tamworth and Dubbo in regional New South Wales are at critical levels. The dereliction is staggering, and one wonders what Taylor thought his legacy might be after leaving Parliament, let alone someone like Barnaby Joyce.

The point of all this is not to demonstrate that Australia is a hopeless case politically, nor that corruption has always been endemic. We have had some truly great prime ministers and ministers. Although watching the current government, we see incompetence, corruption and a group of people floundering out of their depth, we can also see, in the leadership of some state premiers and emergency service officials, competence, compassion and professionalism. And it has always been like this.

Labor prime ministers John Curtin and Ben Chifley had to deal with difficult factions. Menzies' cabinets were not always loyal to him. Gough Whitlam saw the rules ignored to ensure his removal from power. Scott Morrison has not grown into the role, and unless there is a dramatic change, he will go down as one of the worst prime ministers of the federation.

Yet, I believe the system will somehow correct. Worldwide, people are protesting against systems that are stacked against them: Hong Kong, Chile, the yellow jackets in France; the climate change marches; Lebanon. Ultimately, it seems *vox populi, vox dei*. However, privilege and vested interests do not bend easily to challenges.

2020 will be another interesting year in politics.

*

Music listing

Each New Politics Australia podcast episode contains music breaks in between each featured topic. The full music selection can be found on Spotify at the 'New Politics Podcast' playlist.

Opening song: *Bumper* (remix), The Cannanes
Closing song: *The Only One That Knows*, Ed Kuepper

A Little Less Conversation (remix), Elvis Presley
A Whisper, Coldplay
Bug Powder Dust, Bomb The Bass
Cantaloupe Island, Herbie Hancock
Confessions of a Window Cleaner, Ed Kuepper
Cosby Sweater, Hilltop Hoods
Dayan Cowboy, Boards of Canada
Demise of a Nation, Greg Dombrowski
Dirty Air, Two Door Cinema Club
Dreaming Of Me, Depeche Mode
The Final Countdown (cabaret version), Gunhild Carling
The Hard Road, Hilltop Hoods
The Holy Grail, Hunters and Collectors
I Am Resurrection, Stone Roses
I'm Not Like Everybody Else, Jimmy and The Boys
La Femme d'Argent, Air
Limousine, Jack River
Mad World, Brooklyn Duo
Madam Medusa, UB40
Rise (instrumental), Public Image Limited
Smoke On The Water (bluegrass version), Iron Horse
Stranger In Moscow (remix), Tame Impala
Sugar (instrumental), Robin Schulz
Sweet Refined Things, Jess Ribeiro
Sweetness and Light, Itch-E & Scratch-E
Under The Sea, Digby Jones
Which Side Are You On, B. Dolan
Would I Lie To You, Eurythmics

Index

A

Abbott, Tony 12–13, 18, 23–26, 35, 48, 52–53, 90, 100, 107, 142, 157, 163, 166, 168–169, 172–173, 176, 195–198, 206–208, 218, 243–244, 246, 269, 273, 292, 297, 313, 325
ABC Learning 247
A Current Affair (Nine) 128
Adani mine 90, 172–174, 179–180, 232
Akerman, Piers 10
Albanese, Anthony 176, 185–187, 189, 206–207, 260, 262–264, 297–299, 320
    2013 leadership ballot 207
    disappointment from the left 320
    fighting Tories 262, 297
Ali, Hassan Khalif Shire 72
Al Jazeera 99–102
Alpha–North Development Plan 179–182, 180–183
Aly, Anne 111
Aly, Waleed 86, 90
Amazon fires 312
Andrews, Daniel 323
Anning, Fraser 70, 87, 99, 103–104, 107, 152, 159
    egging 152
Anthony, Larry 223, 247, 248
ANZAC Day 104
Arab Spring 211, 213
Ardern, Jacinda 74, 90
Area 51 Roswell 271
Ashby, James 99–101
asylum seekers 38–39, 41, 43, 56, 59, 70–76, 84, 90, 160, 218–219, 270
Atkinson, Sally Ann 248
Australia–China trade 267–271
Australia Day 17, 21–23
    changing date of 22
    citizenship 22
    first fleet 21
Australian Association for Cultural Freedom 101

Australian Broadcasting Corporation 10, 13, 31, 34, 57, 86, 101, 135, 137, 138, 165, 176, 184, 193, 199, 247–250, 276
    7.30 (TV) 34
Australian Constitution 54, 233
    section 44 challenge 232–235
Australian Council of Social Services 221, 241, 258
Australian Defence Association 323
Australian Democrats 204
Australian Electoral Commission 45, 102, 103, 164, 175, 182–183, 232–233, 243
    electoral law breaches 182
    signage in Mandarin 175
Australian Federal Police 42, 47, 140, 152–153, 159
    Commonwealth Police 159
    raids on offices of AWU 42, 188
    raids on offices of Labor Party 164
Australian Financial Review (newspaper) 119
Australian National Audit Office 249
Australian Securities and Investments Commission 12–13
    funding cutbacks 35
Australian, The (newspaper) 54, 101, 106, 119, 152, 182, 184, 227, 285
Australia–US trade 267

B

Bainimarama, Frank 243
Bandt, Adam 25, 174
banking corruption 32
Banks, Julia 18, 24
Bannon, Steve 86, 295
Barilaro, John 301, 303
Barr, Natalie 225
Barton, Edmund 83, 326
Beamer, Diane 111
Beazley, Kim 146, 175–176, 262–263, 297
    $10 billion black hole 281
Benedet, Gerard 117

329

Berejiklian, Gladys 60–61, 79, 145, 187, 301, 310, 323
  bushfires response 301
Bernardi, Cory 70
Bishop, Julie 19, 47
Bjelke–Petersen, Joh 138
Blakester, Adam 138, 166
Bolsonaro, Jair 75, 312, 317
Bolt, Andrew 52–53, 86, 193, 275
Bongiorno, Paul 27
Bonner, seat of 147
Boothby, seat of 147
border security 38–40, 74, 90, 263
Bowen, Chris 135
Bracks, Steve 168
Brandis, George 50
Brennan, Frank 52
Brexit 56, 125, 253, 292, 295
British Conservative Party 126, 204–205
British Labour Party 126, 189, 298
Brosnan, Paddy 153
Brough, Mal 9, 248
Bruce, Stanley 324–325, 326
Bryce, Quentin 161
Budget 2019 87, 89, 93
  budget surplus 89, 93, 94, 157–158, 222, 255, 281–282
Bungaree 21
Bureau of Meteorology 301
Burke, Tony 135, 287
  speech about the world of facts 287
Burnes, Andrew 41
bushfires 6, 288, 299–304, 308–309, 311–314, 317–320, 325
  1994 NSW fires 300
  myths about Greens policies 303
  NSW Government cutbacks 300, 309–310
  south-east Queensland 300
Bush, George H. 307
Bush, George W. 226–227, 256, 307

C
Caldwell, Arthur 175
California fires 312
Cambridge Analytica 295

Cam, Scott 277–279
  trades ambassador 277–278
  Utopia sketch 278
capital gains tax 57
Capricornia, seat of 111
Captain GetUp 115–117
Carr, Bob 146
Cash, Michaelia 42, 47, 100, 188, 224, 277
Cassidy, Barrie 57
Chifley, Ben 327
child sexual assault 52, 62
Chinese Communist Party 116
Chipp, Don 325
Chisholm, seat of 166, 174, 232–233, 299
Christchurch shootings 69, 77, 83, 86, 90, 272
Christensen, George 13, 33, 120, 121, 185, 217
  time spent in Manila 120, 185
Christmas Island 71, 74, 84, 90
Ciobo, Steve 9, 47
Clean Energy Act (US) 26
Climate Action Group 308–309
climate change 6, 17, 24, 26–30, 110, 119, 158, 179, 189, 216, 278, 284, 288, 299–304, 306–308, 311–314, 316, 318, 320–321, 327
Clinton, Bill 118, 187, 271
Clinton, Hillary 271
Close, Leanne 43
Club of Rome 310–311
  First Global Revolution (publication) 310
  'problématique' 310
  The Limits To Growth (publication) 310
Coalition agreement 136
Commission on Presidential Debates (US) 145
compassionate conservative, the 256–259
Connolly, Will (Egg Boy) 104
Constance, Andrew 323
constitutional recognition for
  Aboriginal & Torres Strait Islander people 150

Cook, Captain James 17, 21–22
    dispute over circumnavigation of
        Australia 21
Cook, seat of 70, 142
Cooper, seat of 111
Corangamite, seat of 111
Cormann, Mathias 14, 32, 39, 41, 48,
    104, 107, 135
    attacks on asylum seekers 39
    denying need for Royal
        Commission 32
    Helloworld holiday 41, 48
corruption 12, 28, 36, 39–43, 45–49,
    99, 110, 121, 130, 140, 148, 172,
    185, 187–188, 201, 203–204, 217,
    245, 250, 283, 321, 326–327
    Labor Party and Chinese
        donations 261
    Liberal Party resignations 261
Costanza, George (*Seinfeld*) 59
Costello, Peter 8, 96
Cottrell, Blair 86
Council of Australian Government
    274
Country Women's Association 151,
    158
Court, Richard 168
Cowan, seat of 111
Cowper, seat of 139
Crean, Simon 176, 205, 297
credit squeeze of 1961 298
Crewther, Chris 102, 111
Crowe, David 196
culture wars 17, 21, 67
Curtin, John 327
cynicism in politics 30, 318

D
Daily Telegraph, The 119, 161, 184, 283,
    289, 316
Daley, Michael 60–61, 80, 81, 90, 98,
    145, 164, 187
    xenophobic comments 80
Dampier, William 22
Danby, Michael 111
Dastyari, Sam 234–235
Davos economic forum 198
Dawson, seat of 120–121, 147, 185
Deakin, Alfred 48, 54
death taxes 183

Deepwater Horizon oil spill 306
de Garis, David 42
Depression, The Great 98, 324–325
Dickson, seat of 18, 112, 120, 166
Direct Action 29
Divine, Miranda 86
Dixon, Steve 99–101
Downer, Alexander 103, 298
Downer, Georgina 45, 103
    novelty cheque during campaign
        45, 103
Dunkley, seat of 111
Dutton, Peter 18, 39, 56, 59, 69, 72,
    80, 83, 100, 107, 116, 120, 166, 168,
    201, 248, 319
    attacks on asylum seekers 39

E
Eastern Australia Agriculture 121,
    131, 135, 140
    registered in Cayman Islands
        121, 131, 135–137, 304, 327
economic management myth 281
Ellis, John 68
Emerson, Craig 293
energy policy 26, 29, 238
Entch, Warren 13, 33
Environmental Protection Agency (US)
    306
Epstein, Jeffrey 269
Essential opinion poll 133
Exxon Valdez oil spill 306

F
Falinski, Jason 308
Farage, Nigel 56, 75
Farrer, seat of 139, 187
Farr, Malcolm 285
Ferguson, Sarah 86
Fifield, Mitch 135
Financial Times (newspaper) 126
Fisher, Archbishop Anthony 52
Fischer, Tim 139
Flinders, Matthew 21
Flinders, seat of 24
Flynn, seat of 112
Forde, seat of 111

Forrest, Andrew 223, 246–247, 249–250, 268
   Creating Parity report 247
   Fortescue Metals Group 246
Four Corners (ABC)
   'How to Sell a Massacre' 100
   report into banking sector 13, 31
Fox News 118
France, Ali 120
franking credits 17, 19–21, 25, 44, 97, 113, 167, 172, 177–178, 194, 221, 241, 277, 294, 300, 325
Fraser, Malcolm 48, 70, 83, 87, 99, 103–104, 107, 152, 159, 185, 201
French Revolution 211
Frydenberg, Josh 11–12, 14–16, 24, 26, 30–31, 33–35, 43, 56–57, 95–96, 100, 135, 166, 177, 219, 226, 232–233, 242, 252–255, 282
   as Minister for Environment 35
   denying need for Royal Commission 14
   Hungarian and Israeli citizenship 233
   meeting with Great Barrier Reef Foundation 43
   "sea of tranquility" reference to Brexit 253
Fuller, Mick 316

G

G20 meeting 198
Gaetz, Matt 217
Gallop, Geoff 168
Gardner, Georgie 33
Giles, Adam 86
Gillard, Julia
   abuse by media 9, 273, 292
   anti-carbon tax rally placards 9
   carbon pricing 26
   egg thrown at 152, 158
   government 'narrative' 274
   international visit 198
   minority government 195
   public misogyny 10
   Royal Commission into institutional child sex abuse 55
   sandwich thrown 10
Gilmore, seat of 17, 23–24, 111, 112
   Indigenous population 24

global financial crisis 110, 190, 252, 292–293
   Australia avoids recession 252
Goebbels, Joseph 59
Goldstein, seat of 19
GoodStart 248
Gorbachev, Mikhail 212
Gorton, John 325
Governor–General 87, 107, 161
Great Barrier Reef 2050 Partnership Program (Senate Report) 43
Great Barrier Reef Foundation 43, 47, 49–50, 140
Great Replacement conspiracy theory 217
Grech, Godwin 289
Green, Antony 276
greenhouse emissions 26, 288, 290–291, 304, 307, 316
Greenhouse Gas Inventory Report 57
Greiner, Nick 36, 259
Guardian Australia, The 119, 272, 280

H

Hadley, Ray 53
Hancock, Lang 170, 246, 328
Hanson, Pauline 70, 84–85, 100
Hartcher, Peter 113
Harvey, Gerry 245
Hasluck, seat of 112, 325
Hawke, Bob 36, 54, 83, 127–128, 132, 142, 152, 159, 194, 196–197, 201, 297
Hayek, F.A. 150, 256
Hayne, Kenneth 14, 16, 30
Heffernan, Bill 10
Helloworld 41–42, 45, 47–49, 140
Henderson, Gerard 52, 111
Henderson, Sarah 111
Henry, Ken 15
Hewson, John 88, 109, 127–130, 152–153, 159, 298
   egg thrown at 153
   Fightback! package 109, 127–128, 130, 168, 177, 189
   GST interview 128
Heysel Stadium disaster 215
Higgins, seat of 8, 50, 290
Hildebrand, Joe 52

Hockey, Joe 41, 48, 96, 188, 194, 255
   austerity Budget 2014 255
Holt, Amber 151, 153, 158, 160
Holt, Harold 325
House Standing Committee on the Environment and Energy 238
Houston, Brian 268–270, 275
   Frank Houston (father) 270
   NSW Police investigation 269
   US State Dinner 268–269
Howard, John 10, 29, 32, 36, 52–53, 81, 83, 110, 130, 143, 146, 148, 150, 157, 160, 176, 178, 185, 189–190, 194, 196, 197, 200, 218–219, 223, 227–229, 241, 247, 257–258, 260, 265, 273, 296, 298, 313, 317
   1996 election campaign 189
   Asian immigration restrictions 229
   climate change policy 29
   Incentivation 178
   neoliberalism 36
   non-core promises 241
   rank socialism 32
Hughes, Billy 153, 159, 324–325
   egg thrown at 153
Hughes, seat of 24, 153, 159, 324–325
Hume, seat of 121
Hunt, Greg 24, 73, 100, 199
   Best Minister in The World 199
Husar, Emma 10
Husic, Ed 70

I
immigration detention 43, 49, 140
Independent Commission Against Corruption 36
Indigenous Australians 21–22, 24, 218, 231, 237, 246, 258
   voice to parliament 218
Indi, seat of 110
Indue welfare card 222–224, 245, 247–250, 257–259
Insiders (ABC) 10, 57
Institute of Public Affairs 53, 67, 99, 101, 193, 274, 321
In The Thick of It (TV series) 279
Ipsos polling 45, 107, 147–149

J
Jones, Alan
   abuse of Julia Gillard 9
Joyce, Barnaby 28, 40, 59–60, 89, 99, 121, 132, 136–140, 166, 203–204, 222–223, 248–249, 290–291, 302–303, 312, 326–327
   allegations of corruption 40, 135–136, 140
   interview with Patricia Karvelas 137
   Special Envoy 327

K
Karp, Paul 280
Karvelas, Patricia 132, 137–138
Kassam, Raheem 217
Kearney, Ged 111
Keating, Paul 36, 83, 88, 96, 109, 127–128, 130, 132, 143, 149, 155, 164, 194, 196, 200, 255, 272–273, 297, 317, 325
   flick the switch to vaudeville 149, 155
   recession that Australia had to have 127
   sweetest victory of all 130
Keelty, Mick 140
Keenan, Michael 18, 42, 196
Kelly, Craig 24, 52, 217
Kennett, Jeff 168
Kernot, Cheryl 10
Kidd, Chief Judge Peter 62, 66
Kinnock, Neil 126–127, 130
Kirribilli House 272, 319
Kissinger, Henry 325
Koch brothers 101, 191
Kooyong, seat of 24–25, 166, 232–233
Kruszelnicki, Karl 278
Krygier, Richard 101
Kyoto targets 58, 307

L
Labor Party review 293–298
Labor split of 1917 324
Landry, Michelle 111
Latham, Mark 79–81, 146, 176, 197, 324
Laundy, Craig 112
Leyonhjelm, David 107

Ley, Sussan 139, 187, 217, 284
Ley, Thomas 326
Lindsay, seat of 110
Littleproud, David 121, 304
  business dealings 304–305
Liu, Gladys 175, 232, 299
Longman, seat of 27
Lowy, Frank 181–184
Lyons, Joseph 98, 273, 324

M
Macdonald, Ian 40
MacManus, Rove 160
Macnamara, seat of 111
Macron, Emmanuel 265–269
Major, John 126–127, 205
Malaspina, Sisto 72
Mallee, seat of 139
Mant, Jon 10
Manus Island (PNG) 39, 43, 49, 73–74, 160, 218
Markus, Louise 70
Martin, Fiona 112
Mathieson, Tim 10
Mayo, seat of 45, 103
May, Theresa 205
McCormack, Michael 39, 59–60, 138–139, 301–303, 312, 318
  attacks on asylum seekers 39
  criticism of climate change link 301
McEwan, John 'Blackjack' 139
McGowan, Cathy 110
McKay, Jodi 204
McKellar, Michael 201–205
McMahon, Billy 124, 325
McMahon, Brother Daniel 65
Melbourne Response 62
Menadue, John 281
Menindee Lakes 28
  fish kills 26, 28, 139
Menzies, Robert 48, 152, 159, 178, 218, 252, 282, 325, 327
  deficits during 1960s 282
Midwinter Ball 273
Migration Amendment (Urgent Medical Treatment) Bill 39, 46, 74
Minchin Protocol 200–204

Minerals Council of Australia 181–184, 237–240
  anti-Labor advertising campaign 181–184
Ministerial code of conduct 199–203
Moore, Clover 283–285, 288–289, 316
Moore, John 201
Morgan, Hugh 53
Morris, Jeff (whistleblower) 33
Morrison, Scott
  anti-Muslim sentiment 69–76, 83–87
  attacks on asylum seekers 39
  authority within Liberal Party 195
  bingo halls 154
  bushfires inaction 308–309, 314, 325
  Canberra bubble 143, 196, 290
  Captain Cook commemorations 21
  China–US trade war 266
  climate change denialism 303–305, 307, 311–313
  denying need for banking Royal Commission 11, 13, 32
  drinking alcohol 141
  egging 151–152
  election victory 172, 314
  Hawaii holiday during bushfires 318, 326
  ineffectiveness 324, 327
  installs Warren Mundine 23, 112
  in Washington 265–269
  leadership rules 206
  lump of coal 27–28
  lurch to the right 92
  manipulation of truth 56, 280, 282, 316
  misrepresents Queensland Labor 122
  national integrity commission 203–204
  Paris climate agreement targets 60
  political marketing 95, 187, 219, 257, 263, 278, 309, 311–312, 314, 319
  preselection battle in 2007 70
  prime minister for standards 22

quiet Australians 191
racism 69–76
religious discrimination 196
replaces Malcolm Turnbull 40
scare campaign on unions 33
setting election date 104
shadow cabinet meeting in 2010 84
shearing sheep 221, 240
spouse Jenny Morrison 162
supporting Kelly O'Dwyer 10
support of Cronulla Sharks 228
unfunded empathy 217, 220–221, 225, 240, 241
unpopularity 113, 119, 145, 296
welfare as a good deal for investors 258
who do you trust 190
whose side are you on 216, 218–219, 226, 228
Mother Theresa 256
Mullens, Greg 308, 309
Mundine, Warren 23–24, 112
Murdoch, Lachlan 267–268
Murdoch, Rupert 53, 57, 67, 101, 163, 184, 191, 321
   Catholic church 53
Murray–Darling Basin 26, 28, 187, 203–204
Mussolini, Benito 22

N
national broadband network (NBN) 90, 196, 229
national debt 95
National Disability Insurance Scheme 94–95, 176, 187
National Energy Guarantee 35
national government debt 149, 197
National Integrity Commission 138, 141
Nationalist Party 324
National Press Council 13
National Rifle Association 101, 257, 301
Nauru 39, 43, 56, 73–74, 90, 160, 218
Nelson, Brendan 207, 262
neoliberalism 36
Neville, Paul 248

New England, seat of 138–139, 166, 302
Newman, Campbell 87, 168
News Corporation (Murdoch) 10, 53–54, 57, 161, 163, 165, 175, 184, 196, 268, 286, 321
New South Wales state election 2019 77–81
Newspoll 45, 51–52, 91, 107, 128, 133, 147, 148, 166, 264
Newstart 20, 217, 218, 221–225, 241–242, 248, 249
Nixon, Richard 306, 325
Norman, Greg 268
NSW Greens
   internal divisions 28
NSW Labor Party 40–41, 60, 146, 168, 187, 204
   election loss in 2011 40
nuclear power 26, 230–231, 236–239
   Chernobyl 231, 238
   Fukushima 231, 238
   reviews and feasibility 230–231, 236–237
   Three Mile Island incident 231, 238

O
Obán, Viktor 317
Obeid, Eddie 40–41
O'Brien, Llew 13
O'Doherty, James 122, 123
O'Dwyer, Kelly 8–10, 14, 18, 290
O'Malley, King 326
O'Neill, Tip 167
O'Sullivan, Barry 13
O'Toole, Cathy 111

P
Pacific Islands Forum 243
Packer, James 245
Paladin 43, 47, 49, 140
   contract for immigration detention services 43, 49
Palaszczuk, Anastacia 87, 168, 323

335

Palmer, Clive 118, 132, 134–135, 178–180
    anti-Labor election advertising 178–181
    Minerology 178
    unpaid entitlements 134
Parakeelia 140
Paris targets 58, 308
Peacock, Andrew 176, 262
Pearce, seat of 112, 147
Pell, George 47, 52–55, 62, 66–67
Pentecostal church 70, 160, 268–270
    Horizon church 160
    QAnon 270
Petrie, seat of 112
Phelps, Kerryn 27, 110, 133, 166
Playford, Thomas 236
Plibersek, Tanya 135, 260
Port Arthur shootings 257–260
Porter, Christian 50–51
Pratt, Anthony 267–268
pre-poll voting 156, 276
    two-party preferred vote 276
Price, Melissa 100, 102, 282
    announcing grants before opening date 102
Prince Philip, Duke of Edinburgh 23
Princess Diana 75
privatisation 49, 258
Protocols of the Elders of Zion 271
Putin, Vladimir 135, 295
Pyne, Christopher 19, 47, 199–201

Q

Q&A (ABC) 86, 135, 163
QAnon far-right conspiracy 270–274
    4chan 271
Quadrant magazine 5, 101
Queensland Government 122
Queensland Nickel 134–135
Queensland state election 109
Question Time 37, 38, 218, 219
    Dorothy Dix questions 38, 218, 228
    origins of Question Time 38

R

Racial Discrimination Act 193, 227, 275
    section 18c 193, 275
Radić, Stjepan 37

Reagan, Ronald 227, 256, 259, 307
recession 6, 126, 127, 149, 190, 230, 242, 251–252, 254–255
red-tape repeal day 13
Reforming Our Democracy (report) 286
Reid, seat of 70, 112, 147
Religious Discrimination Bill 192
religious freedom 190–191, 193
Rennick, Gerard 301
Republican Party (US) 26
Reserve Bank of Australia 150, 242, 252, 255
Reynolds, Linda 282
Ridsdale, Gerald 66
Rinehart, Gina 53, 181, 245, 267
Riverina, seat of 302
Roberts, Malcolm 103, 301
Robert, Stuart 44, 187, 217
    excessive internet costs 44
Robodebt 225, 259, 274
Rosevear, Solomon 326
Rothschild, Baron 255
Rove Live! 160
Rowland, Michael 176
Royal Commission into institutional child sexual abuse 55, 66
Royal Commission into Misconduct in the Banking, Superannuation and Financial Services Industry 11–16, 17, 30–36, 110
Royal Commission into Nuclear Fuel Cycle 238
Royal Commission into Trade Unions 106, 164
Rudd, Kevin 26–27, 83, 107, 110, 132, 157, 160, 163, 172, 176, 178–179, 181, 184, 189, 196–197, 205, 208, 258, 264, 289, 292, 296–299, 311, 325
    2007 election campaign 189
    ALP leadership rules 206
    campaign against mining policy 27
    greatest moral challenge of our time 299, 311
    Kevin '07 178
    Utegate 289
Rumsfeld, Donald 94
Ryan, Scott 287

S

Sales, Leigh 34
same-sex marriage 24–25, 193
Santa Barbara oil spill 306
Sattler, Howard 10
Saturday Paper, The 184
Savva, Nikki 195
Schultz, Grant 23–24, 112
Scott, Elfy 280
Scullin, James 324–326
Scullion, Nigel 18
Senate Economics References Committee 13
Seven Media Group 224
Severn Shire Council 302
Shanahan, Dennis 119
Sharkie, Rebekha 45, 103
Shooters Fishers and Farmers Party 78–79, 89
    winning NSW seat of Orange 139
Shorten, Anne 161
Shorten, Bill
    blame for banking sector faults 12
    Budget right of reply 97
    calls for banking Royal Commission 13, 33
    election debates 145
    mother, Anne Shorten 161
    proposal for national integrity commission 45
    resignation 175
    superannuation policy 122
    'The Bill Australia Can't Afford' meme 183–184
    town hall meetings 186
    unpopularity 106, 113, 119, 123, 135, 144, 169, 172, 277, 296–297
Shorten, Chloe 162
SIEV-221 sinking 71
SIEV-X sinking 70
Sinclair, Ian 139
Sinodinos, Arthur 188
    Sydney Water Corporation 188
Sky News 122, 149, 175, 323
Slipper, Peter 45, 200
Smethurst, Annika 286
Smith, Tony 44
Snedden, Billy 262

Social Research Institute 292
    falling trust in politics 292
South China Sea 234
Southern, Lauren 217
Sparks, Carol 302–303
Speers, David 323
Steggall, Zali 24–25, 176
Stewart, Isaac 111
Stewart, Tim 272–274
    @BurnedSpy34 272
    in Kirribilli House 272
Stokes, Kerry 181, 198, 245, 268
Sturt, seat of 147
Sudmalis, Ann 23, 112
Sunrise 134, 218, 224
Superheroes 116–117
Swan, Wayne 13, 112, 147, 176, 190, 199, 252, 325
    Finance Minister of the Year 199
Sydney climate change rally 320
Sydney Morning Herald (newspaper) 113, 162, 175, 184, 196

T

Tampa crisis 84, 115
Taylor, Angus 29, 57–59, 121, 131, 135, 136, 188, 203–204, 217, 229–232, 236, 239, 282–291, 304, 315–316, 326, 327
    business dealings 304–305
    claims about Naomi Wolf 315
    climate change indifference 304–305
    corruption in water buy-back scheme 121–122, 131, 135–137, 140, 327
    declining political standards 287
    fabricated Sydney Council documents 283–285, 288–291
    Insiders appearance 57
    misrepresenting greenhouse emissions 282
    Watergate 203–205
Tehan, Dan 249
Tetlow, Michael 42
Thatcher, Margaret 26, 126, 150, 205, 227, 258, 307
    address to the Royal Society 307
    Thatcherism 36
Theodore, E.G. 326

The Project (Ten) 86, 90–91, 122
Tingle, Laura 119
Today Show (Nine) 33
Topham Guerin 183
Towke, Michael 70, 142
Triguboff, Harry 181, 245
Trump, Donald 56, 75, 125, 198, 205, 265–267, 269, 271, 281, 290–291, 307, 312, 317
    US presidential campaign 125
Turnbull, Malcolm 6, 14, 24, 26, 31–32, 40, 43, 92, 100, 107, 118–119, 124, 133, 136, 142–143, 148, 157, 163, 165, 169, 172, 176, 177, 196, 217, 229, 261, 279, 289, 303, 313
    denying need for banking Royal Commission 14, 31
    end of prime ministership 26
    meeting with Great Barrier Reef Foundation 43

U

Uhlmann, Chris 122
UN Declaration of Human Rights 212
United Australia Party (contemporary) 133–134, 170, 175
    preference deal with LNP 169, 173
United Australia Party (original) 132
US State Dinner 265–269

V

van Manen, Bert 111
van Onselen, Peter 285
Veep (TV series) 279
Victoria state election 2018 27
Von Felten, Enrico 152–153

W

Wagga City Council 302
Ward, Eddie 324
Warringah, seat of 24–25, 166
Watson, John C. 326
Wead, Douglas 256
    The Compassionate Touch 256
Wentworth, seat of 27, 81, 109–110, 133, 166
    by-election in 2018 27

West Australian, The (newspaper) 145, 149, 198
Western Australia state election 1993 88
Wetherall, Jay 168, 293
White Australia policy 85
Whitlam, Gough 83, 178, 197, 297, 325, 327
    It's Time 1972 178
Willesee, Mike 128
Williams, John 13, 33
Willis, Ralph 287
Wilson, Harold 159
Wilson, Tim 19–21, 44, 257
    breaking convention 44
    cousin Geoff Wilson and franking credits 19
    Wilson Asset Management 44
Windsor, Tony 138
Wingerei, Kim 209–214
    Why Democracy Is Broken 209, 211–212, 214
Wolf, Naomi 315–316
Wong, Penny 104, 135
WorkChoices 194, 195
World Bank 271–270

Y

Yates, Oliver 24, 232
Yes, Minister (TV series) 116, 266, 279
Yiannopoulos, Milo 86
Young Liberals 9, 54, 142
Young, Mick 201
    Paddington Bear affair 201
Your Right To Know campaign 284, 286
Yusuf, Irfan 70

www.ingramcontent.com/pod-product-compliance
Lightning Source LLC
Chambersburg PA
CBHW050304010526
44107CB00055B/2099